Britain and the western seaways [by]
E. G. Bowen. [London] Thames and
Hudson [c1972]
196 p. illus. (Ancient peoples and
places, v. 80)
Bibliography: p. 143-147.

1. Europe - Commerce. 2. Gt. Brit. -
Hist., Naval. 3. Gt. Brit. - Hist. - To
1485. I. Bowen, Emrys George, 1900-

*Ancient Peoples and Places*

# BRITAIN AND THE WESTERN SEAWAYS

*General Editor*

DR GLYN DANIEL

## ABOUT THE AUTHOR

*Professor Emeritus E. G. Bowen graduated with first class honours in geography and anthropology from the University College of Wales, Aberystwyth, in 1923. Since then he has held the posts there of Lecturer, Senior Lecturer and Professor of Geography and Anthropology (1946–68). He was awarded a D.Litt. (Wales) in 1970. A Fellow of the Society of Antiquaries, Professor Bowen has won numerous distinctions and awards during a long and distinguished academic career. His special interests have always been in Celtic Archaeology and Historical Geography, particularly in primitive navigation and exploration. His books include* Wales: A Study in Geography and History, *1941;* The Settlements of the Celtic Saints in Wales, *1954;* Wales: A Physical, Historical and Regional Geography *(ed), 1957; and* Saints, Seaways and Settlements in the Celtic Lands, *1969.*

# BRITAIN AND THE WESTERN SEAWAYS

E. G. Bowen



61 PHOTOGRAPHS
17 LINE DRAWINGS
27 MAPS
1 TABLE



T & H
THAMES AND HUDSON

THIS IS VOLUME EIGHTY IN THE SERIES

*Ancient Peoples and Places*

GENERAL EDITOR: DR GLYN DANIEL

*First published 1972*

*Filmset by Keyspools Ltd, Golborne, Lancs and printed in Great Britain by Camelot Press Ltd, Southampton.*
*Not to be imported for sale into the U.S.A.*
ISBN *0 500 02076 0*

# CONTENTS

# *List of Illustrations*

PLATES



FIGURES

# *Preface*

This volume differs from many others in this series in that it does not deal with the civilization of a specific ancient people, such as the Phoenicians or the Etruscans, or even with any specific ancient place, be it Babylon or Wales. The theme is far more general, touching upon a variety of places in Western Europe from Iceland to Spain, and a variety of peoples from the lowly hunters and collectors of the remote Mesolithic to the Breton onion men of today. Nevertheless, there is an underlying unity in the theme based on the age-long tradition of the sea. The sea has always been the natural highway linking island to island and peninsula to peninsula along the Western Fringes of Europe.

In developing this theme a number of important considerations have to be borne in mind. In the first place, history, geography and archaeology are inexorably interwoven in the story. It was the application of the geographical approach to the study of archaeological material that demonstrated, without any possibility of doubt, the spread of early cultures by sea from one territory to another, thereby frequently uniting adjacent coastlands in a common cultural inheritance. So frequently, indeed, is this demonstrated in pre- and proto-historic times, that we have come to regard it today as axiomatic that primitive man found it easier to move by sea than to negotiate mountains and boglands on shore. We do not always appreciate what a real breakthrough in scientific thinking the realization of this fact was, for previous to the days of modern archaeology we were accustomed to take it for granted that the seas divided and the lands united. We were all the more deeply entrenched in this belief by the knowledge that the greatest Empire the Ancient World had ever seen was held together by its network of roads. In the pre-modern era our knowledge of the past depended either on the Bible, or on the works of the Classical authors, or on both, and in neither case did the sea play a prominent part.

A second matter for consideration is that no sooner did the archaeologists realize the importance of the sea-routes in bringing the elements of civilization from the Mediterranean zone into the remoter lands of northern and western Europe than they rushed to grandiose conclusions. Fleure, Forde, Peake, Fox, Childe and many others began to speak of major sea-routes linking the Mediterranean with our western islands and peninsulas. These routes were usually indicated cartographically by enormous sweeping, arrow-headed curves suggesting an unbroken ocean trackway along which, presumably, hundreds, if not thousands, of colonists moved with their southern cultures into the northern mists. Modern technological processes, however, especially the use of Carbon 14 for dating purposes, are seriously challenging this over-simplified picture. Discoveries and practices once thought to be first developed in the Mediterranean Lands can now be given an earlier date in parts of our western margins. It would thus appear that some of the advances in civilization, particularly those associated with certain burial customs, were made independently in many parts of Europe and, therefore, to assume a simple outward spread by either land or sea from the Mediterranean completely misrepresents the most recent scientific evidence. We must be content presumably with smaller and more localized movements of people and cultures, with many of them already practising advanced ideas, independently developed.

There is no doubt that the third factor that has to be borne in mind is, in many ways, a corollary of the second. The implication is clear. Peoples and cultures reaching 'the Atlantic ends of Europe' by sea at any time did so on a small scale. The incoming cultures could in this way be easily absorbed into those already existing. These Western lands have thus been rightly termed 'The Lands of the Continuity of Tradition'. It is impossible, therefore, to draw worthwhile limits to any era in the west—the past always appears to merge unbroken into the present. A realization of this important matter at once enlarges the scope of the material to be dealt with in this book. It ranges from the Epi-Palaeolithic through the Neolithic and Bronze Ages into Iron Age times, and thence unbroken via the Celtic Saints and the Vikings on to the Medieval pilgrims and crusaders, and ultimately onto the seafarers of Nonconformist Wales.

It is clear that attention must, therefore, be given to the sea as a highway; to the method of movement along the seaways; and to the ancient mariners of every age. This formidable task may seem too vast for one volume of the size prescribed for this series. Two attempts, therefore, have been made to assist the reader in encompassing this vast array of material. In the first place, it was decided to focus attention on the British area, and it was for this reason that the book was entitled 'Britain and the Western Seaways'. This does not mean that other areas along the maritime fringe of the Continent have not been adequately dealt with —it simply means that our islands (occupying as they do a central position on the western margins of Europe) have received the greatest attention and, likewise, most of the illustrative material has been drawn from the British scene. It is hoped that in this way we have not presented an unbalanced picture of the part played by other western European territories in the development of the full story of the western sea-routes. The second matter relates to the notes supplied on the plates. Much fuller notes are provided than is usual in other volumes in this series. It was felt that a brief caption alone would be insufficient, as the exact relevance of the picture to the overall theme frequently needed a fairly comprehensive statement to place it in its correct position in the vast array of material under review.

In writing a book of this nature it is obvious that I have profited greatly by the works of others and I trust that the long list of distinguished names appearing in the bibliography is some indication of my indebtedness. I am particularly grateful to Mr Paul Johnstone for allowing me to read the relevant chapters of his book *The Ships of Prehistory* in advance of publication. My text has been enormously improved as a result. In the preparatory stages I found a readiness to help in every possible way from all those whom I approached for photographs and for information. I should especially like to mention Miss E. R. Payne, formerly of the University of Birmingham School of Education; Mr A. J. Bird, Map Curator of the Department of Geography, University College of Wales, Aberystwyth; Mr J. Ll. Jenkins Senior Photographer in the Department of Physics in the same college; and, in particular, Mr Eric Peters and his staff at Messrs Thames and Hudson. My special thanks are due also to Miss M. H. Bigwood for her excellent work in preparing the maps and line-drawings for publication, and to Miss Elsie Bird for her care and efficiency in typing the manuscript.

To Dr C. A. Ralegh Radford, formerly Chief Inspector, Royal Commission on Ancient Monuments (Wales); Professor Melville Richards, Head of the Department of Welsh, University College,

Bangor; Professor J. Caerwyn Williams, Head of the Department of Irish, University College of Wales, Aberystwyth; Professor E. Estyn Evans, formerly Head of the Department of Geography, Queen's University, Belfast, Northern Ireland; Dr D. Q. Bowen of the Department of Geography, University College of Wales, Aberystwyth; Miss L. F. Chitty and Mr A. J. Bird; Dr Nora Chadwick and Dr Kathleen Hughes, Newnham College, Cambridge—I am very greatly indebted for constant encouragement, help and advice on many technical matters. Furthermore, my special thanks are due to Miss E. R. Payne not only for preparing the index, but also for reading the original manuscript and making the most valuable suggestions regarding matters of style and presentation.

Finally, I am most grateful to Dr Glyn Daniel and the publishers for inviting me to write this book. In its preparation I owe a special debt of gratitude to Dr and Mrs Daniel, both of whom read the original text and made the most valuable suggestions for its improvement. Without their constant and inspiring help this work would never have been completed in its present form.

E. G. B.

CHAPTER I

# In the Beginning

The earliest seamen known to us are the Minoans who preceded the Greeks and the Phoenicians in their domination of the Mediterranean. They were the first to sail in 'ocean'-going ships as distinct from the earliest boatmen who rowed on the Nile and the Euphrates. As soon as 'ocean'-going ships became available around 3000 BC, maritime activity and trade in the Aegean increased considerably. Winds and currents were favourable in this tideless sea for long-distance voyages, not only between Crete and the neighbouring islands, but between Crete and Egypt in one direction, and Crete and the Asiatic mainland of Syria and Anatolia in the other. Indeed, there is evidence that through Syria and Anatolia the Minoan seamen were tapping the distant Mesopotamian markets.[1] In later times, the maritime activity of the Phoenicians and the Greeks brought them into contact with the farthest shores of the Mediterranean, frequently uniting its coastlands under a single cultural stimulus as in the heyday of the Greek City States.

However, the emphasis placed in the nineteenth century on classical learning and the history of the great Empires of the Mediterranean world with which it was associated, coupled with the fact that until the dawn of the present century the prehistoric archaeology of early Europe was, as yet, in its infancy, has tended to blind us to the important fact, that maritime enterprise had also been moving men, their goods, and their ideas about the western fringes of Europe, very much in the same way as had happened in the Mediterranean lands. Indeed, it would seem that, in spite of the marked differences in physical geography, there was a close parallel between the maritime activity existing in prehistoric and historic times along the 2,500-mile axis of the Mediterranean from Gibraltar to Syria and that which took place along an axis of almost equal length in Atlantic Europe from Gibraltar to Iceland during the same period. As in the Mediterranean, so on the Atlantic seaboard, there were times—such as, for example, during the 'Megalithic Age', or in the Early Christian period—when the whole length of the coastlands of the Atlantic fringe were united in a common cultural inheritance dependent

| Time, based on C14 dating | Pollen Zones | Blytt & Sernander divisions & climate | Vegetation | Sea Level | Cultural Periods |
|---|---|---|---|---|---|
| | VIII | SUB-ATLANTIC cold and wet oceanic | Oak—Ash Birch—Beech Hornbeam | Minor Fluctuations | Romano-British<br>Iron Age |
| 500 BC | VIIb | SUB-BOREAL warm and dry continental | Ash—Oak—Lime<br>Elm decline | | Bronze Age<br>Neolithic |
| 3000 BC | VIIa | ATLANTIC warm and moist oceanic | Ash—Oak—Elm—Lime | Main Submergence ends | |
| 5500 BC | VI | BOREAL | c. Oak—Elm—Lime<br>b. Oak—Lime<br>a. Elm—Hazel | Subsidence begins | Mesolithic |
| | V | Warmer than before and dry | Hazel—Pine—Birch | Land Bridges submerged<br>Straits of Dover formed in late Boreal | |
| 7600 BC | IV | PRE-BOREAL Sub-Arctic | Birch—Pine | Sea level 100 ft below present | |
| 8300 BC | | | | | |

*Climate, sea-level and natural vegetation in Post-Glacial times*
*The divisions between cultural periods are only approximate. Although shown as being time-parallel, they would not have developed everywhere at the same time. (After D. Q. Bowen.)*

upon intensive maritime activity. Herein lies the story of the western seaways which forms the central theme of this book.

The traveller along the Atlantic coastlands of Europe today is impressed by their fragmented character. Galicia is separated from Brittany by the stormy Bay of Biscay; Brittany from Cornwall by the Channel Approaches; Cornwall from south-west Wales by the Bristol Channel; and south-west Wales from Ireland by the St George's Channel, and from Llŷn and Anglesey by Cardigan Bay. The Isle of Man stands on its own—a focal point in the Irish Sea Basin—while further north, south-western Scotland is separated from northern Ireland by the narrow north Channel with its fast-running currents and difficult navigation. The coast line of western Scotland and the Isles, which lie beyond, seems to be even more fragmented and uninviting, while still further northward lies the 600-mile stretch of open sea that separates Scotland from Iceland and Scandinavia. A closer look at these scattered fragments shows that they have much in common structurally and physically. They are all built up of highly resistant igneous or metamorphic rocks of great variety, giving much-denuded massifs, varying in height from a few hundred to several thousand feet. The harder rocks have everywhere resisted the pounding of the waves and, in consequence, stand out as peninsulas and headlands, while the softer rocks have been much eroded, and form bays and inlets among the headlands. In these sheltered hollows glacial and post-glacial soils have frequently accumulated. They are surprisingly fertile, especially when they contain lime, and they certainly stand out in sharp contrast to the thinner, poorer soils of the uplands themselves. Although the proportion of highland to lowland increases as we go northward in Atlantic Europe, it must not be forgotten that it is the raised beaches with their better soils that line these sea inlets, which, in turn, have given the seafarers throughout the ages an opportunity to find both shelter and a safe foot-hold in these lands of wind-swept uplands and abundant rains.[2]

While we have described the present, it should be remembered that conditions were not like this in the days of early men. With the final melting of the ice sheets about 10,000 years ago, the British Isles emerged, not as separate islands, but as part of the great continental land mass. There were no Straits of Dover and the southern parts of the North Sea were dry land. When relieved of the great weight of the massive ice sheets the land rose gradually in relation to the sea, before the increased volume of water in the oceans (resulting from the melting ice) could have its effect. This upward movement of the land was largely a feature of northern Britain. In many areas the land stood more than 100 feet above its present level, so that large tracts in the northern part of the Irish Sea, for example, were
*Fig. 1* dry land. The Isle of Man was certainly continuous with the land surface that then existed in the eastern part of the Irish Sea between Wales, Cumbria and south-western Scotland. Elsewhere land bridges, more or less unbroken, joined south-western Scotland to north-eastern Ireland. It is, therefore, clear that in immediate post-glacial times, the existence of passages along the western seas, as known in later times, would not have been possible. It was during this period that the beds of peat that now underlie the highest marine and estuarine deposits in Scotland and northern Ireland were laid down. Radiocarbon dates so far available for these peats range from 7700 BC to 6100 BC. It is important to note that

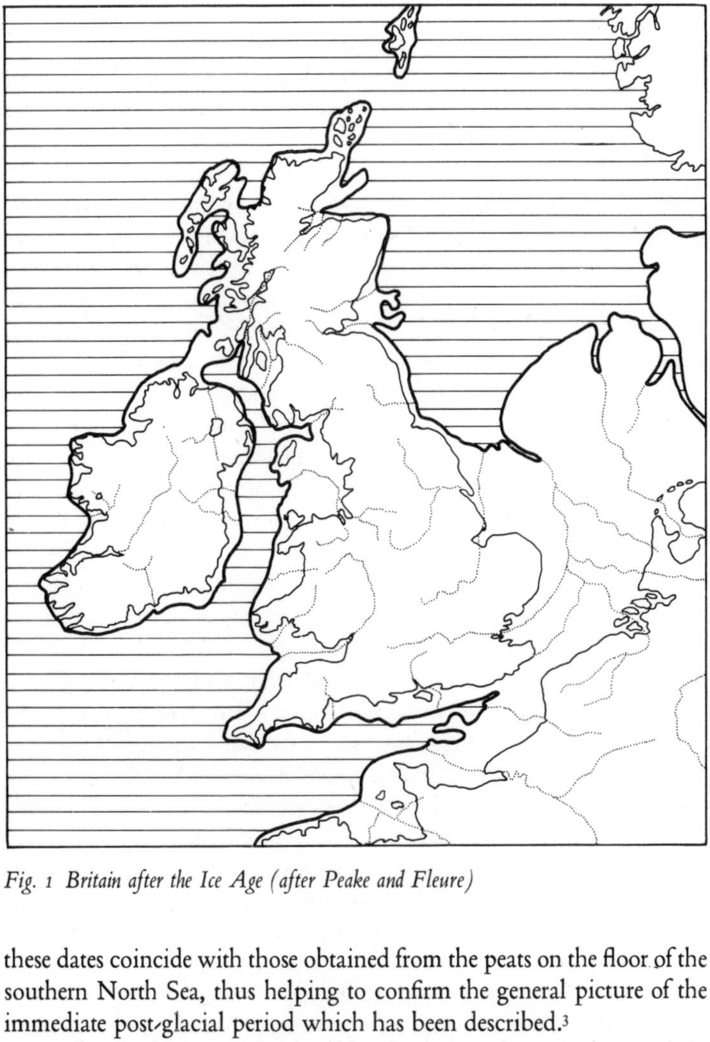

*Fig. 1 Britain after the Ice Age (after Peake and Fleure)*

these dates coincide with those obtained from the peats on the floor of the southern North Sea, thus helping to confirm the general picture of the immediate post-glacial period which has been described.[3]

Conditions began to improve slowly during the Boreal Period (*c.* 7600 BC to 5500 BC). This name is derived from the classical word Boreas (the North Wind) and was used together with the name 'Atlantic' by Blytt and Sernander in their famous climatic divisions of the post-glacial era in north-western Europe.[4] During the Boreal period the climate was dry but still very cold, producing cold steppe-like conditions

*see Table, p. 13*

generally. With the aid of pollen grain analysis, we are now able to reconstruct a fairly accurate picture of the contemporary vegetation. The forests in the Boreal period were mainly composed of hazel and pine, being replaced towards the close of the era by more deciduous trees, as Atlantic conditions approached. Throughout the whole period coastal subsidence was gradually taking place and warm Atlantic waters began to flood our sea-lanes, yet as late as 6400 BC much of the southern North Sea was still land, the sea-level being still 90 feet below its present level. The land connection with the continent was, however, finally broken towards the close of the Boreal period by about 5500 BC, when the Straits of Dover were formed. The sea-lanes were now opened and it is interesting to note that the archaeological and distributional evidence now at our disposal indicates that primitive man seems to have taken full advantage of the sea-routes as soon as they became available. The cave-dwelling hunters of the Old Stone Age, with their massive flint implements, had occupied that part of the continent that was to become Britain only in the warmer interglacial stages, and the presence of Old Stone Age implements near our western margins is rare indeed. The interesting point is that it was during the Mesolithic period (the period between the Old and the New Stone Age) that Man first settled near the Atlantic shores of the continent. Mesolithic settlements can be dated to between 8000 and 3000 BC and, as indicated on the diagram, this was precisely the period when a gradual submergence was taking place along our western shores, and the seaways were literally being opened up for the first time. By 3500 BC a final major rise in sea-level took place initiating not only full Atlantic conditions climatically, and the introduction of ash, oak, elm and lime trees into our forests, but also giving the British Isles something of its present form.[5]

The Mesolithic people, whom we claim as the first known users of the western sea-routes, were primarily fishers, fowlers, hunters and food-gatherers who lived either near to the sea-shore or on the high moorlands, especially where flint was available and the land free from a heavy forest cover. They were particularly dependent on the sea-shore for wild fowl and sea birds, as well as the fish and the molluscs which multiplied greatly as the warm waters of the Atlantic flooded in. We have little evidence of their actual dwellings—they were probably just wind-breaks made of twigs and the branches of trees. All that remains for us today are the sites on which they chipped their tiny flint blades, which they must have hafted in some way to provide a fishing spear or harpoon. The tiny flint blades are, to the casual observer, of all shapes and sizes. Some of them are like the blades used in the Old Stone Age, but smaller in size, others are crescentic in shape, while many are triangular or trapeze-like in form. The archaeologist, however, attempts to classify them quite simply into two groups—the non-geometric forms (which are believed to be the earlier) and the geometric flints. In some places in Atlantic Europe, for instance in north-eastern Ireland, just mounds of chipped flints remain, all unbedded except for the fact that they are associated with post-glacial marine deposits, existing, unfortunately, not in their primary positions. They have been washed up by the sea from the original sites on which they were worked during the final flooding of the Irish Sea in early Atlantic times. The culture which we have described is known generally as the Tardenoisian—a name derived from the type station, Fère-en-Tardenois, Aisne, France, where the culture was first studied in detail.

Plates 1, 3

Plate 4

The map on the following page is an attempt to show the general distribution of this culture in the western parts of the British Isles.[6] Several interesting observations can be made, but, before doing so, it should be pointed out that the map is far from complete, as flints of this and associated cultures are, in fact, very widespread in their distribution, and several sites remain unrecorded. In addition, each site shown on the map should be taken to represent, in most cases, not a single flint-chipping floor, but a closely related group of flint mounds. When allowance is made for all these limitations of the map, it is abundantly clear that the Tardenoisians must have been thoroughly familiar with sea navigation as so many of the sites have a coastal location. The primary cause of this preference for coastal sites was not, of course, the Tardenoisians' interest in sea navigation as such, but the presence of flint pebbles—the raw material of their industry—on the sea-shore. Nevertheless, their boats (skin-boats and dug-outs) must have been used, not only for fishing and collecting, but also for movement from one part of the coast to another. Indeed, we have considerable evidence that an extensive trade must have taken place in certain beach pebbles. We know that grit and siltstone pebbles, roughly ovoid in cross-section, and on an average some seven or eight inches long, are fairly widespread on Tardenoisian sites on the

*Fig. 2*

*Fig. 2 Mesolithic sites along the western seaways*

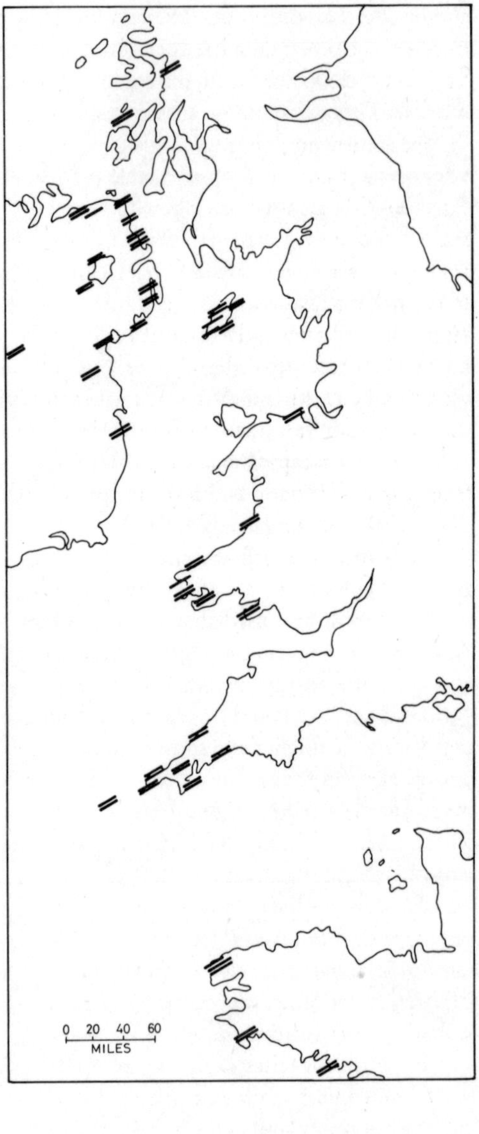

shores of Atlantic Europe. These implements might have served many purposes including their use as hones for sharpening bone points, but the traditional use to which they are said to have been put was as 'limpet-scoops'. They are found on sites in southern France; at places such as Ile Téviec in Brittany; on the Cornish coast; and on several sites in south-west Wales and again much further north in association with the Larnian–Obanian culture. Some sort of trade or transfer of these 'limpet-scoops' must have taken place.[7] In view of their wide coastwise location, from southern France to the Western Isles of Scotland, we may well be looking at the first recorded use of the western seaways, in the economic sense, over considerable distances. The map, in turn, directs special attention to three areas where Tardenoisian settlement seems to have been particularly marked: the Cornish peninsula; north-eastern Ireland and the Isle of Man. It is useful to examine these areas in turn. Plate 2

It is widely accepted that the Tardenoisian culture reached Cornwall from western Brittany and from further south along the Atlantic coast of France where similar sites occur. Here, therefore, may be the beginning of a connection which was to increase in importance in nearly every succeeding period in prehistoric and proto-historic times. We need not be in any way surprised that Cornwall and Brittany were so closely connected at this early period, for although they were separated even then by as great an expanse of sea as they are at present, we must assume that if the Tardenoisians could handle a sea passage as difficult as that between the Scottish mainland and some of the outer Islands, they must have had boats that could cross from Cornwall to Brittany.[8] The Cornish evidence can be carried a stage further. The Tardenoisian sites in the south-west indicate, not only Atlantic connections, but also imports and exports to and from south-eastern England. Herein lies yet another important aspect of the cultural life of the far western peninsulas of Europe at this and later times—elements deriving ultimately from continental cultures tending to survive in these western lands until later epochs. In this way, these lands function both as places of refuge and as stepping-stones of coastal diffusion.

The abundant relics of the Mesolithic Age in north-eastern Ireland may be attributed in the first place to the copious supplies of flint available in the chalk layer preserved beneath the Antrim basalt rocks, and then to the fishermen and food-gatherers who had drifted northwards

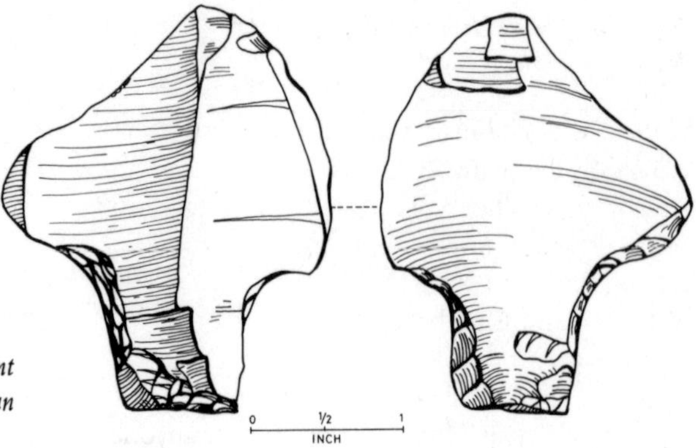


*Fig. 3 A Bann river implement from Glencrutchery, Isle of Man (Manx Museum, Douglas)*

along the sea-routes from south-western France. In addition, we must not overlook the proximity of the Larnian coast to the British mainland, and the consequent use made of the short sea-crossings by some of the settlers. The flint implements are certainly concentrated on the coast of County Antrim and around Strangford Lough in County Down, but this is not exclusively the case, for they are also found in large numbers especially in the valley of the Lower Bann in central Ulster. Here the Tardenoisians developed at a slightly later date a specialized flint-working technique of their own. The Bann River folk in time spread down the east coast southwards into Dublin Bay, eastwards into the Isle of Man, and south-westwards along the rivers and by the lake-sides into Connacht. There is no evidence of Mesolithic settlers in central and southern Ireland.[9]

*Fig. 3*

The Isle of Man provides very interesting evidence, as it has been possible to locate several occupation sites on the island. Some clearly belong to the Tardenoisian culture and others to the Bann River culture of northern Ireland. Grahame Clark maintains that whether the Tardenoisian people reached the Island across dry land (for we are not certain to what extent the flooding of the north-eastern part of the Irish Basin had proceeded by the time of their arrival) or whether they came by sea, it seems fairly certain that they were from the English mainland. On the other hand, the Bann River people unquestionably came from Ireland as the Isle of Man is the only place, outside Ireland, where this type of flint workmanship is found. It is certain, too, that they arrived by sea, for we know that the sea bed between northern Ireland and the Isle of Man is deeply slotted by a submarine trench over 50 fathoms deep. This,

*Fig. 4 Maglemosian tranchet pick from Pencaer ('Castell Pocha'), Pembs, (National Museum of Wales, Cardiff)*

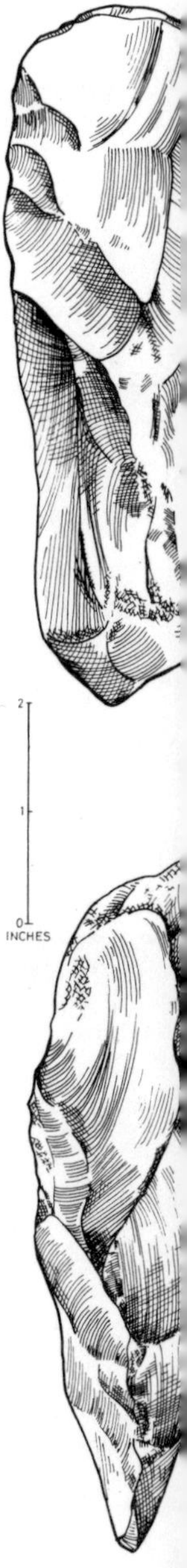


obviously, would mark the course of a deep-water channel that had to be crossed by the Bann River folk on their voyage to Man even at this early stage in the evolution of the present Irish Sea basin.[10] In this context we see the Island beginning to assume its role as a cultural focus, a function for which it was admirably placed, being equidistant between the coasts of Ireland and Cumberland, while a short sea-voyage of some 16 miles separates the north of the island from the coast of south-western Scotland. A slightly longer distance of 44 miles separates its extreme southern point from Anglesey in North Wales. Indeed, anyone who climbs Snaefell, the highest peak in the Island, can see on a clear day England, Scotland, Ireland and Wales in one sweep.

As the 'Atlantic' climatic phase approached, conditions, as we have already noted, gradually became milder and damper, and were accompanied by an increased forest growth. In some parts of Europe, and especially in the southern Baltic lands, the survivors of the Mesolithic people attempted to adapt themselves to these new conditions. This they did fairly successfully, not only by extending their fishing and hunting techniques around the numerous lakes amidst the forests, but by developing larger and stronger implements wherewith to deal with the forest growth. In this way the Maglemosian culture came into being. It is known as Maglemosian after the Great Peat Bog near Mullerup, on the island of Zealand in Denmark where it was first studied. One of its characteristic implements was the 'tranchet' axe. This was really a flake-axe—an elongated block of flint which was chopped at one end by being struck transversely on either side in order to make a sharp cutting edge, producing in the end a much heavier tool, or 'pick', than anything the Tardenoisian people possessed. Maglemosian influences spread beyond the Baltic lands, particularly across the southern North Sea into south-eastern Britain, where several of these 'tranchet' picks have been found.[11] It is interesting to note that one of these implements was dredged up from the sea-bed some years ago by a fishing trawler operating in the southern North Sea. We do not know, of course, whether this implement was lost by some Maglemosian folk proceeding towards Britain on what was then dry land or mud flats, or whether it was lost at sea, as the Maglemosian people certainly had 'dug-out' boats, the remains of which have been found preserved in the Danish peat bogs.

*Fig. 5 A semi-polished stone axe from Graig Lwyd, Caernarvonshire*

The point of interest in the present context is that sometimes even the Tardenoisian sites on the coasts of western Europe have recorded a 'heavy' industry, including 'tranchet' picks and perforated stone hammers of Maglemosian type found together with the ordinary Tardenoisian flints. 'Tranchet picks' occur on Tardenoisian sites in Cornwall, at Burton in south Pembrokeshire, and one has recently been recorded from Solva, near St David's, while another has been found on the Pencaer peninsula, in north Pembrokeshire.[12] They appear again in North Wales and in north-eastern Ireland, particularly on sites along the North Channel coastlands. Such a distribution clearly suggests the possibility of coastal movement, but whether from north or south along the Irish Channel cannot, of course, be decided. We can only assume that the basic elements involved in the 'heavy' industries spread out from the Baltic lands, and on reaching the western shores of Britain were subsequently rediffused by sea. No definite sea-routes were, as yet, in being, but movement by sea from peninsula to peninsula and from island to island is clearly indicated.

The final phase in this story occurs when the inhabitants of the western fringes of Europe began to use their own resources for the manufacture of heavy stone cutting tools to cope with the new environment. This phase, however, could not take place before new influences began to affect Europe towards 3000 BC. By this time, cultural influences from the great civilizations of the riverine lands of the Middle East began to spread throughout the continent. The valleys of the Nile, Tigris and Euphrates had already developed civilizations and, in particular, had learned the arts of cultivation of the soil and the domestication of animals. Very slowly, these new and vital skills began to spread westward, and with them went other fundamental elements of civilization such as the making of pottery and the manufacture of superior tools, first of polished stone and later of metal. These new discoveries were spread, partly by trade and partly by bands of settlers moving in search of new homes. In this chapter, we are concerned mainly with the making of superior tools. Polished stone axes may be looked upon, in many ways, as unquestionably marking the Neolithic Age, yet they are often found on Tardenoisian sites, indicating that Neolithic folk frequently elected to settle on already existing sites.

The art of grinding and polishing stone to produce a better cutting edge was a real advance in attempting to deal with forested lands, while

*Fig. 6 A Neolithic stone axe from Graig Lwyd, Caernarvonshire*

at the same time the new implements could be used as hoes in agriculture. For making the new tools, fine grained, yet tough, igneous and metamorphic rocks, especially greenstones and bluestones were essential. The western peninsulas of Europe contained many exposures of such suitable material and the polished stone axe became, in turn, a veritable commercial asset of the Atlantic coastlands. Quite small exposures of suitable rock are known to have been exploited and several axe factories came into operation. Ceremonial axes of jadeite, diorite and chloromelanite are known to have been traded from Brittany along the Atlantic seaways,[13] while at Sélédin in the commune of Plussulien (Côtes-du-Nord) there is another fine axe-factory which has recently been studied in detail. At least a dozen axe-factories are thought to have existed in Cornwall, while the spotted dolerite of the Prescelly hills in Pembrokeshire, and the rocks of the great Langdale group in Cumberland help to locate other well-known factories in Britain. The most famous factories of all in the British Isles for the production of polished stone axes, judged by their output and the wide distribution of their exports, were those of Rathlin Island, off the coast of Antrim, and the Tievebulliagh factory on the nearby mainland, together with the equally famous Graig Lwyd factory on Penmaenmawr in Caernarvonshire.[14] *Figs 5, 6*
The map on the following page shows the location of the Tievebulliagh *Fig. 7*
and Rathlin Island axe factories and the distribution of the axes made from the local 'bluestone' which outcrops at both sites. It is abundantly clear that their landward hinterland, although locally intensive, was geographically limited. On the other hand, axes were exported far afield into lowland Britain, as well as to such places as Barrow-in-Furness, Dunbartonshire and Dublin Bay (served by the Irish sea-routes) to say nothing of those found on Tory Island, off the coast of Donegal, which is well-nigh in the Atlantic itself. No one can doubt the use of the sea-routes in this context, and if such doubts should arise, the situation is made abundantly clear by the presence of axes of Prescelly stone—the famous bluestone of the inner circle at Stonehenge—in County Antrim. There is only one way in which they could have been traded, and that is by sea. A similar argument could be put forward to explain the presence of Welsh and Westmorland axes in Cornwall.

Finally, it is worth looking at an interesting group of five adzes or polished stone axes made of foreign materials (*i.e.* rock materials not

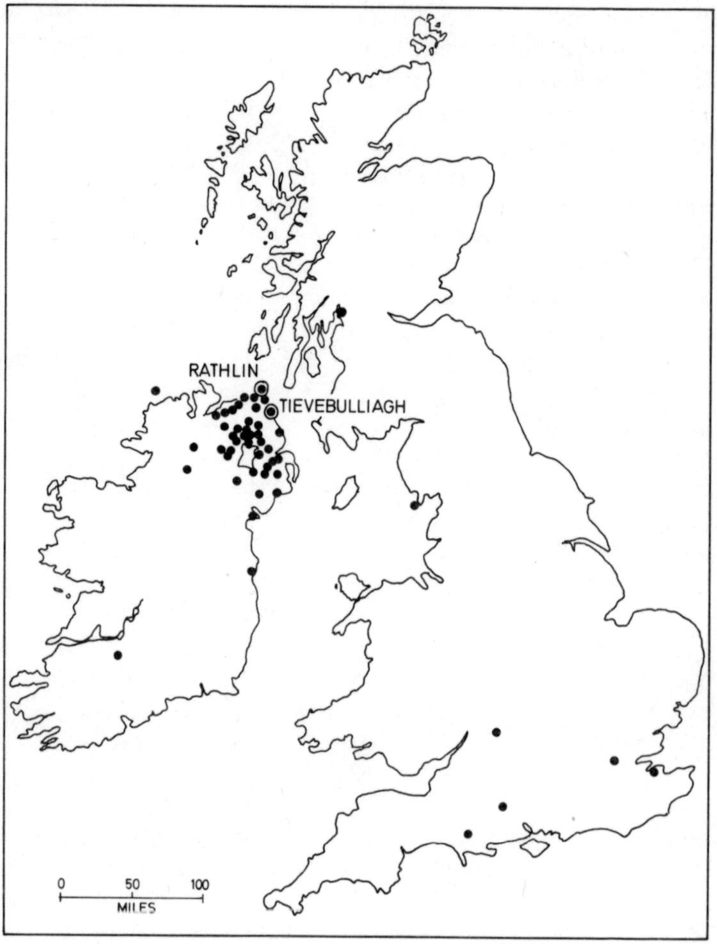


*Fig. 7 Distribution of polished stone axes from north-eastern Ireland (after E. M. Jope)*

found within the area) occurring in Cornwall. They are all variants of the same basic design with an asymmetrical cutting edge. The distribution of the implements is definitely coastal. Three of them come from the extreme tip of the peninsula in the Penwith area, one—a dolerite adze—

from Tuckingmill in the Red River area is of particular interest in that it was reported in 1870 to have been found in a dug-out canoe. This occurrence together with the fact that the adze is a boatbuilder's implement strongly suggests a maritime origin for the adzes as a whole.[15] Whatever the situation may have been, we would appear to have here an interesting piece of evidence suggestive of the widespread use of the seaways and the corresponding westward connections of Cornwall during the Neolithic period.

This chapter has shown that, while no clearly defined western sea-routes can be distinguished in Mesolithic or early Neolithic times, yet there is little doubt that trading from peninsula to peninsula and from coast to coast was already well established. It would appear that it was easier for the Tardenoisians and their successors to move by sea than it was for them to move through the swampy, heavily forested countryside inland. They appear to have taken advantage of the western sea-routes almost as soon as they were opened, and they certainly blazed a trail that was taken up later by the Megalithic folk, who initiated the first Golden Age of the western seaways.

CHAPTER II

# *Neolithic Argonauts*

The revolutionary changes which accompanied the diffusion of food production and distinguish the Neolithic Age from the ages of savagery that had gone before have been discussed in the previous chapter. Until recently it was thought that the art of cultivating the soil and the ability to domesticate animals were not introduced into north-western Europe until toward the end of the third millennium BC, but now radiocarbon dating places their introduction into the British area before the millennium opens.[1] The Neolithic Age thus gains considerably in length and importance. It is well-known that throughout this period immigrants reached Britain along three major routes: across the southern North Sea from the north European Plain; across the newly formed Straits of Dover from northern France; and from Atlantic Europe by way of the western sea-routes. We have already suggested that the last-named route was used as soon as the physical conditions permitted, and there is much to be said for the view that it was along these western sea-routes that the elements of civilization first reached the far distant fringes of the continent.

As the Neolithic Age progressed, it would appear that more and more colonists used the sea-routes. Some may have been looking for pockets of fertile land wherein to practise the new arts of cultivation and animal husbandry; others may have been seeking precious minerals among the ancient rocks of the western peninsulas and islands. Prospectors and merchant adventurers there undoubtedly were, and among the most spectacular features of the field archaeology of Atlantic Europe are the remains of their massive collective burial chambers, built for the most part of enormous upright stones set alongside one another above ground and covered by corbelled vaulting, and the whole structure frequently buried beneath a massive cairn or earthen barrow. Whether all these ancient tombs were covered over in this way we do not know, but it is very likely that in many cases where the great stones are now standing uncovered the original cairn or barrow has been completely removed with the passage of time or, even more likely, by attempts to pillage these graves for the treasure they might contain. In any case, covered or un-

Plates 5, 8, 9

covered, these massive sepulchres have attracted the attention of peoples of subsequent ages, not the least of whom include first the antiquaries and then the archaeologists of recent times. The enormous size of the stones employed in the building of these tombs fully justifies the adjective 'megalithic' (great stone) now generally used by archaeologists to describe these most spectacular survivals of Neolithic culture.

There is no evidence in most regions to indicate that the first building of megalithic tombs coincided with the beginnings of farming, still less with the coming of metallurgy. In Brittany, southern England, Wales and Ireland and still more in north Germany and Denmark where these tombs are found, the earliest farming settlements (often closely associated and intermingled with those of the aboriginal hunting and fishing folk of the Mesolithic) appear older than the collective tombs; yet megalithic tombs must be classified as Neolithic in the sense that the earliest burials in them were never accompanied by any metal goods, or by articles shaped with metal tools. Indeed, it has been suggested that the megalithic builders quickly integrated with the earlier mixed hunting, fishing and farming folk with whom they came into contact, and, indeed, learnt much from them. The earlier farming communities among whom the megalithic folk would appear to have settled may well have supplied them with food, especially fresh fish, as well as with flint and stone axes. It is important, however, for us to remember that in the present context we are concerned, not so much with attempting to reproduce a full picture of megalithic culture, as with examining more the distribution of the various types of megalithic tombs in western Europe, and to concern ourselves with the possible origins of the various groups, and the extent to which the western seaways were involved in general cultural diffusion at this time.

The megalithic monuments of western Europe have been studied scientifically by archaeologists for over a hundred years and many types of work have been undertaken including excavation, the detailed measurement of the monuments concerned, and, particularly, the classification of the lay-out or plan presented by the various tombs. This led to a variety of theories and concepts. It will not be our concern to enumerate these in any detail, but merely to note that during the thirties of the present century (based largely on the work of Childe and Daniel) a fundamental division of western European megaliths into two groups grad- Plates 5, 6 ually emerged.[2] The two major groups were the passage graves and the gallery graves. The passage grave consists of a circular stone chamber, where the burials took place, entered by a lengthy stone-lined passageway. The gallery grave, on the other hand, as its name implies, shows no such distinction between passage and chamber. Based on this fundamental distinction Childe built up a vast diffusionist model to explain the origin of British megalithic and non-megalithic long barrows. He sought the origin of the collective burial tombs of western Europe in the rock-cut tombs of the eastern Mediterranean—the idea being carried westward to Sardinia, the Balearic Islands and Iberia, and there translated into artificial chambers built of huge stone uprights with capstones to represent the rock-cut tomb of the eastern Mediterranean. Archaeologists, including Fleure, Forde, and Daniel, were deeply influenced by this diffusionist model and traced the spread of the passage graves from Almeria in south-eastern Spain to south-western Portugal and on to the Biscayan coast of France from the Gironde estuary to southern Finistère. Thence the passage-grave tomb-builders spread into the Irish Sea Basin and onto the Irish coast and ultimately northwards by way of the North Channel to the Western Isles of Scotland and around to the Moray Firth. Writers like Fleure, Forde and Fox, then carried the megalith builders across the North Sea into Germany, Denmark and Sweden.[3] In similar manner, it was argued that the gallery graves of Sardinia, Corsica and the Balearics were diffused into the Pyrenean area and into southern France generally. From these areas they passed into western and northern France and especially into the neighbourhood of the Loire estuary, and then into Brittany and the Paris Basin. The Severn-Cotswold group of megaliths in Britain were derived from the lower Loire region and other spreads carried the idea into the Irish Sea province and onto the shores of Ireland itself. Further diffusion carried this type of megalith into Arran, Bute and the Clyde region of south-western Scotland. Daniel summarized the diffusionist model in a paper published in 1941[4] which attracted much attention, and which scholars at that time thought had said everything that it was possible to say about the origin and spread of European megaliths for many generations to come.

This, however, was not to be. As has already been pointed out the coming of radiocarbon dating and the enormous expansion in our knowledge derived from expertly conducted excavations has so greatly increased the length of the Neolithic Age that we are presented with a complex overlapping of cultures in the early Neolithic before the megaliths were built. A recent writer has spoken of 'the palimpsest that is Europe's third and even fourth millennium BC prehistory'[5] (a palimpsest being the word used for an ancient parchment that has been written over by many hands, in many directions, and in many styles). This ever-increasing vista of the enlarged Neolithic in western Europe has in turn caused us seriously to question the over-simplified diffusionist model of megalithic origins in the west, so skilfully and authoritatively disseminated by Gordon Childe and other well-known archaeologists in the nineteen-thirties.

In the first place, Renfrew in his recent studies of the Neolithic and Early Bronze Age cultures of the Cyclades and their external relations and his work on Colonialism and Megalithismus[6] has made a very good case for no east-west Mediterranean contacts at this period, as opposed to the more traditional views of Blance who spoke of Early Bronze Age *colonists* in Iberia. This means that we can no longer look to the eastern Mediterranean for the origin of the Iberian and western Mediterranean megaliths—so the diffusionist model is shaken to its very foundations. Equally important in its implications is the final report on the excavations at Fussell's Lodge long barrow in Wiltshire, with a radiocarbon date of 3230 ± 150 BC, by Paul Ashbee.[7] These excavations revealed a long barrow built entirely of earth and timber, with a narrow entrance at one end. In reviewing his results, Ashbee suggests that the wide distribution of monuments of formal trapezoid plan possibly points to an earlier tradition of a long communal grave burial underlying the complex pattern of cultures characteristic of Europe in the third and even fourth millennium BC. What does this tradition imply and what is its significance?

It implies that the non-megalithic long barrow had an antecedent which was, perhaps, ultimately a long house with its ridge pole and posts—the houses of the dead being a copy of the houses of the living. The significance of this tradition is that the next step was to copy the non-megalithic long barrow in stone—what Daniel has called the lithicization of non-megalithic traditions, much in the same way as the wooden henge monuments were translated into megalithic henge monuments like Avebury and Stonehenge.[8] This means that after a century of research it

*Fig. 8 A gallery grave from Kergonfals, Morbihan (after René Galles)*

now appears that the European megaliths did not have a common origin, but came into existence independently in different places, possibly in Malta, Portugal, Brittany, western Britain, Ireland and Denmark. No longer can we look to the eastern Mediterranean, or to the supposed Aegean colonies in Spain and Portugal for the origin of our northern megaliths. We must abandon at the same time the idea that our megalithic tombs in north-western Europe resulted from two 'colonizations', one of gallery graves and the other of passage graves emanating from southern Europe.[9]

Further study must be based on those regions where we suspect that the great stone monuments developed independently from non-megalithic antecedents. Recent work in Denmark has been most rewarding in this respect—solving the age-long controversy as to whether the Baltic megaliths arrived by way of northern Scotland and the Orkneys, or by way of the recently opened English Channel, or even came overland by way of the Paris Basin. At Konens Høj in Jutland, a non-megalithic long grave, constructed with a paved floor and a wooden superstructure carried on two gables of massive timber has recently been revealed by careful excavation. The grave itself has been excavated in a Neolithic settlement with a radiocarbon dating of $3310 \pm 100$ BC, one of the earliest Neolithic dates in Denmark. The tomb yielded a radiocarbon date of $2900 \pm 100$ BC. Here then is clear evidence of the existence of a non-megalithic long tomb in the Baltic lands, possibly one of many, from which the Baltic megalithic tombs must have developed *in situ*. Likewise, it is argued that the *allées courvertes* of Brittany, like Lesconil and Poullan, together with those of the Loire and the Paris Basin are direct translations into stone of the wooden ridged tombs of the Konens Høj type, which are thought to have been very prevalent in northern France from the Pas de Calais to Brittany. Similarly the non-megalithic tradition of mortuary houses gave rise to the chambered long barrows of southern France and perhaps those of the Balearics[10] and southern Italy[11] as well. Daniel has seen in these southern megaliths the results of the changes in style that had taken place independently in northern Europe. 'This is all the work', he says, 'of Northmen not Southmen.'[12]

We can now turn to the British area where it is claimed that exactly the same process has been at work. It now looks as if a tradition of the long grave may lie behind the non-megalithic long barrows of Wessex and

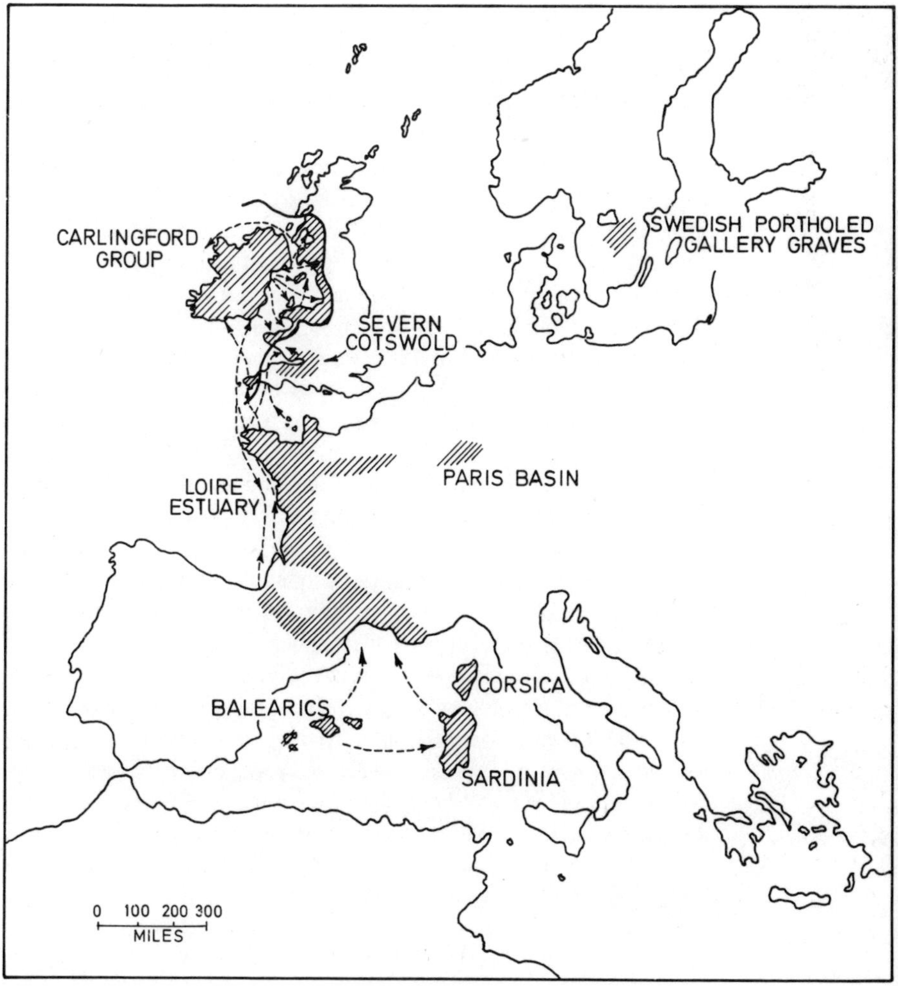


*Fig. 9 Megalithic gallery graves in western Europe (after Daniel, with modifications)*

Sussex and that the most likely explanation of the origin of the megalithic long barrows of the Severn–Cotswold group may be the turning into stone of these antecedents. In exactly the same way the Clyde–Carlingfor group of megaliths may stem back to the non-megalithic long barrows of Lincolnshire, Yorkshire and Scotland.

*Fig. 10 A Lusitanian passage grave from Pavia, Portugal (after V. Correia)*

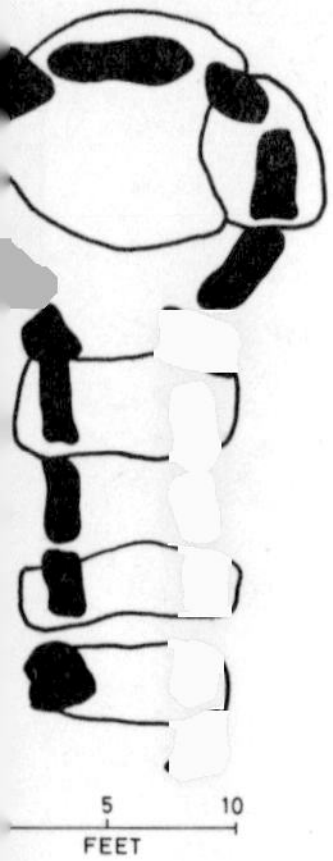


*Fig. 9*

It is a matter of greater interest to us in our present thesis that in spite of the independent origin we are claiming for the various regional groups of megalithic monuments, there were at an early date several secondary diffusions by way of the sea-routes. The Clyde–Carlingford group must have sent off several offshoots to the Galloway and Solway area. The well-known Manx megalith Cashtal yn Ard belongs to this series, as do the monuments of the southern Peak district. Gallery graves occur in Anglesey, Caernarvonshire, Denbighshire and Merioneth in north-west Wales, and again in north Pembrokeshire and west Carmarthenshire, as well as in the Penwith area of Cornwall and in Devon and Dorset. It is obvious that such a distribution pattern can only reflect the intense activity that must have characterized the Irish Sea Province at this time.

Plate 5

So far, we have concentrated our attention on the megalithic and non-megalithic long-barrows and their antecedents. We must now turn to consider the megalithic passage graves ending in circular chambers. Basically the same kind of argument can be advanced concerning their origin and diffusion. Contrary to older beliefs the first chamber and passage graves do not appear in Iberia, either in Almeria or in south-western Portugal, but in Brittany. Radiocarbon dating has shown that it is Brittany itself which provides, at the moment, the earliest dated megalithic chamber with passages, and it can be argued on the analogy of the long barrows, that the Breton chamber and passage tombs were a funerary version in stone of the earlier well-known prehistoric round house—the sort that survived in Skara Brae. These houses must have been built originally of timber and turf. Since radiocarbon dating shows that the earliest megaliths in Brittany go back to the fifth millennium BC, while those of Los Millares are nearer 3000 BC and some of the British passage graves nearer 4000 than 3500 BC, it is possible that they could have first evolved in Brittany and voyaged both up and down the seaways—northwards to the Orkneys and southwards to Iberia. This does not preclude the view that the Alcala–Ile Longue type of chamber and passage grave originated independently in Brittany and that the Pavia–Kercado type originated similarly in southern Portugal, as well as independently in Denmark. The use of the seaways is clearly involved. To the north, the

*Fig. 12*

passage graves of the valley of the Boyne cannot be overlooked. Here again is a case for independent origin worthy of examination, as the

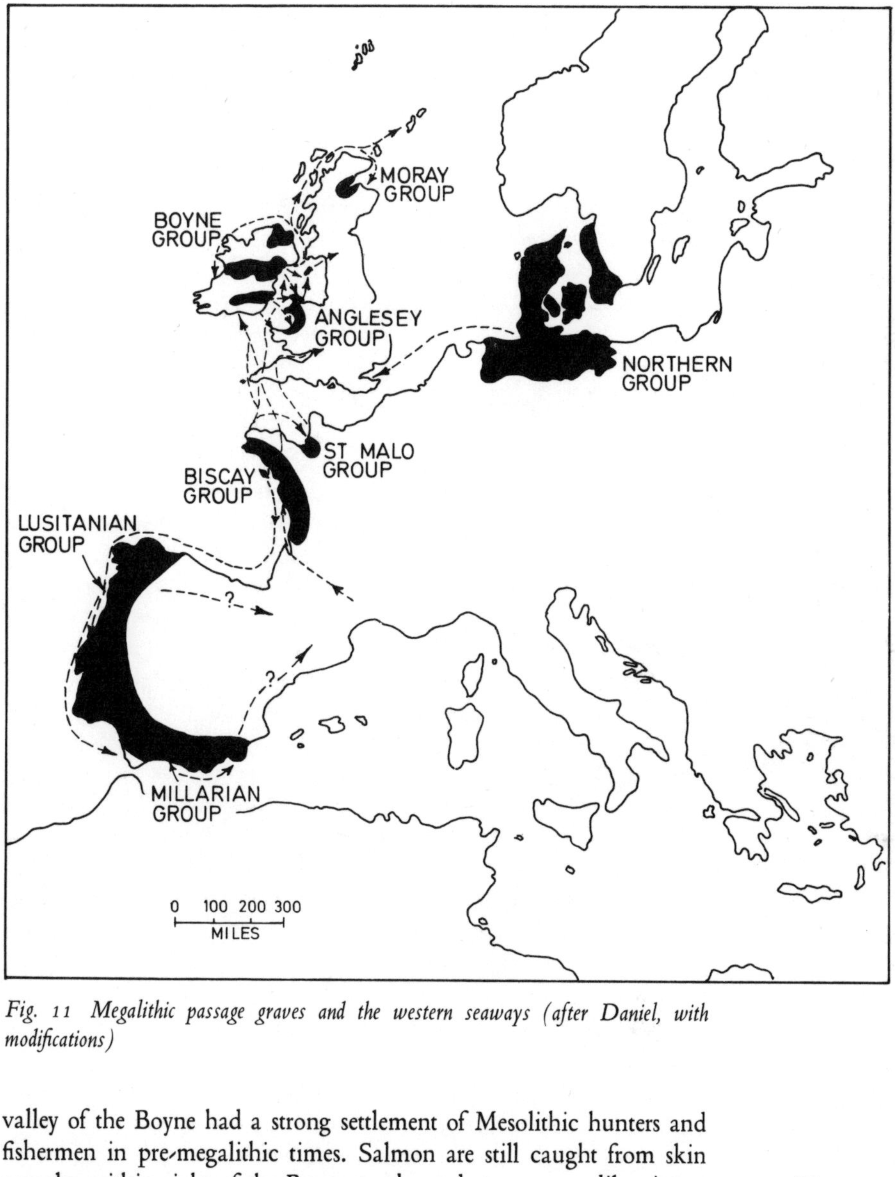


*Fig. 11 Megalithic passage graves and the western seaways (after Daniel, with modifications)*

valley of the Boyne had a strong settlement of Mesolithic hunters and fishermen in pre-megalithic times. Salmon are still caught from skin coracles within sight of the Boyne tombs and one can readily picture gangs of primitive fisher-folk carrying millions of pebbles up from the Plate 32

Boyne terraces to help build the tombs on the heights above.[13] The Boyne culture spread throughout a wide hinterland in Ireland, being mostly characteristic of the northern half of the central lowlands. Traces of this pattern of tomb building can be followed along the shores of the Western Isles and thence around the extreme north of Scotland to the Moray Firth, where there is a well marked concentration of this type of chamber-with-passage tomb. The megaliths of this area might indeed be shown to have had an independent origin when more is known of their archaeological antecedents based on the primitive round house.

*Fig. 11*

As in the case of the gallery graves, diffusion along the shorter sea-routes must have occurred. The megalithic passage graves of the Channel Islands must have originated in this way. Likewise, the passage graves in south-western Cornwall and the Scilly Isles mark a secondary off-shoot (*via* a short sea-crossing) of the primary focus in Brittany. Another branch route impinged on south-eastern Ireland from Brittany direct, for late passage graves of a special type are found in county Waterford forming what is locally termed the Tramore culture. Sea movements in the opposite direction are possibly represented by the presence of Passage graves of the Boyne type in the Scilly Isles, on the Land's End peninsula, in western Pembrokeshire and again in Anglesey and the Llŷn peninsula. It is just possible that the Boyne culture might have extended to the Isle of Man where the Ballaterson monument in Maughold appears to be of this type. Further examples of this culture on the Scottish mainland and islands help to complete the picture. When we recall what was said earlier about the people who built long barrows and think of their movements on the sea as contemporary with those who built passage and chamber tombs around the shores of the Irish Sea Province, we are able to appreciate the significance of Childe's famous remark that in megalithic times 'the grey waters of the Irish Sea were as bright with Neolithic argonauts as the Western Pacific is today'.[14]

Plate 7

We must turn to Ireland once more to examine yet another type of megalithic monument. Few would dispute the fact that the megalithic 'court cairns' of Ireland are unquestionably a native development derived, no doubt, much in the same way as the other types we have discussed, from non-megalithic antecedents. The 'court cairns' are a special type of gallery grave, segmented as in the Severn–Cotswold type, but also provided with a semicircular forecourt made of upright stones. This type

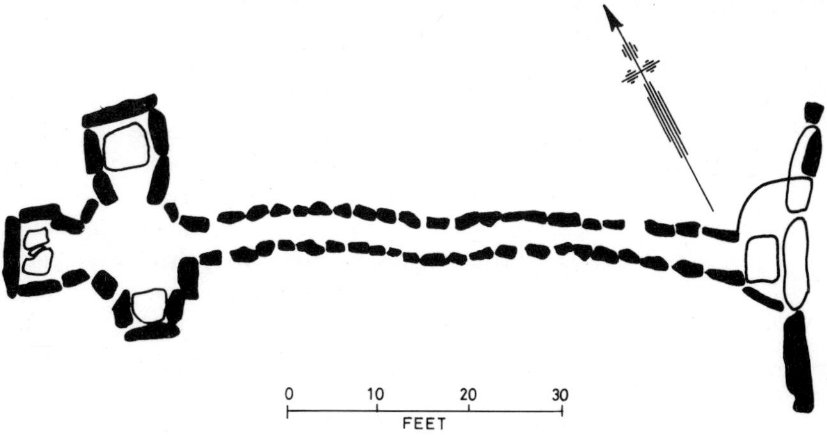


*Fig. 12 New Grange, Co. Meath, Ireland (after Daniel)*

of monument extends in a general north-east to south-west direction across northern Ireland to counties Donegal, Sligo and Mayo, where the most elaborate of these 'court cairns' are found. Sometimes they take the form of double-horned cairns and have the appearance in plan of a lobster with its claws. The significant feature of their distribution pattern is the fact that, during recent years, an ever-increasing number of these 'court cairns' of all types have come to light in the Sligo–Mayo–Donegal region of north-western Ireland. In fact, this area now appears to be the focus of their distribution. Professor de Valera (who first suggested the name 'court cairn' for this type of megalith) has seized upon this newly emerging distribution pattern to suggest that the 'court cairns' of western *Fig. 13*

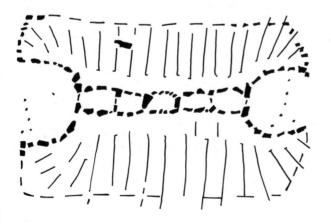


*Fig. 13 Dual court gallery grave, Cohaw, northern Ireland (after E. E. Evans)*

Ireland are sea-borne in origin and that the 'horned cairns' of eastern Ireland in the neighbourhood of Carlingford Lough, developed from those of the Sligo–Mayo–Donegal area and not the other way round as had previously been argued.[15] It would appear to be more in keeping with modern ideas if we concluded that the development of the 'court cairn' megalith in western Ireland was just another example of the independent regional developments in western Europe already discussed elsewhere. The spread to the eastern coastlands would then be another offshoot of the local culture, very much in the same way as the sea-routes carried such offshoots to areas bordering the estuary of the Clyde in Scotland. It is significant for our general thesis that in the most recent maps attempting to show the distribution of megalithic monuments in the British Isles, Professor Estyn Evans has marked the entire region from western Ireland away to the Clyde estuary as the province of the 'Connacht–Carlingford–Clyde' culture. This certainly presupposes the use of the outer oceanic seaway, and there is slight evidence to suggest that the Mesolithic folk of the Larnian–Obanian culture had some affinities with the remote Azilian sites of south-western France, and that the oceanic sea-route might even at this earlier time have been involved. That it was so involved in later times is certainly beyond doubt: we have but to recall the semi-legendary tales of St Brendan (see page 90).

*Fig. 14*

The feats of navigation and seamanship performed by these intrepid voyagers verges on the incredible. What ships had they at their disposal that were capable of negotiating the waves, the tide races, the whirlpools and the cross-currents of the open ocean? We can be quite certain that these feats of navigation could never have been accomplished in dug-out canoes: only skin-boats would have been capable of attempting such tasks. We come to this conclusion for several reasons, judging the qualities of these boats by comparison with their present-day equivalents —the sea-going curraghs of western Ireland. If we forget the modern calico and flannel used as a covering and a few brass nails used in their construction today, and revert to the primitive conditions, we find that we are dealing with a similar vessel built of wickerwork sides and ribs and covered with cow-hide sewn together, whose seams were sealed with pitch. The primitive craft would be about twenty-five feet long, and possibly six feet wide, and could carry nine or ten persons. The Irish seamen today consider two cows and twenty-one sheep as a good load to

Plate 31

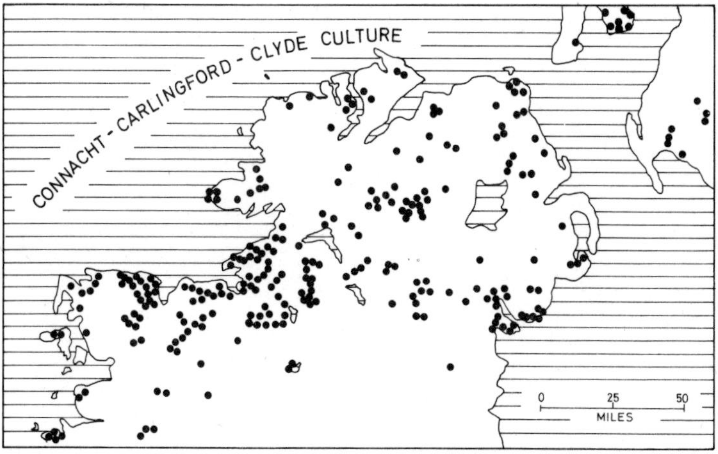


*Fig. 14 Distribution of megalithic monuments of the 'horned cairn' type (after De Valera and E. E. Evans)*

take to sea, so that if the curraghs of the megalithic age were anything like their modern equivalents (as most authorities believe they were), then the pioneers of British agriculture (whom we think arrived in Britain before our megaliths were built) could easily have brought their stock over in this way.

These skin-boats have a fine curved sheer and long lifting bows which enable them to rise and ride over almost any sea. With a good following wind it has been estimated that they can accomplish as much as ninety miles in a day. We do not know whether the earliest curraghs carried sails or not, but some later versions of them certainly did so. The primitive navigators who sailed in these skin-boats knew of the extraordinary liveliness and vigour with which they rise to, and surmount the waves. This was not their only advantage. Frequently, when these craft were being carried under stormy conditions at the mercy of the wind and tide, they would be forced to land in narrow sandy coves or, indeed, wherever opportunity allowed. The fact that the skin-boat could be so easily beached and dragged up beyond the tide-line and required no moorings, as a wooden ship does, was an inestimable boon to these early western European navigators.[16]

A second reason why we confidently believe that it was in skin-boats of this type that the megalithic voyagers undertook their sea journeys is that we possess a reasonably unbroken record of their history that takes us back to megalithic days and beyond. It is almost certain, for example, that the Mesolithic peoples of the Western Isles and Ireland used skin-boats since the separation of Ireland from England entailed considerable sea crossings from an early date. If we by-pass the megalithic period as such for a moment we find direct Bronze Age evidence of the skin-boat in the famous bowl from Caergwrle in Flintshire. Most archaeologists agree that this is a model of a boat of the British Bronze Age. Its V-shaped section suggests a skin-boat much more strongly than a dug-out, which by definition has the rounded section dictated by the original tree trunk. The bowl has representations not only of sea-waves, but also of the wicker framework normally involved in the construction of skin boats. More interesting still are the 'oculi', or boat's eyes, painted in the conventional manner, and found on boats in very many areas along the Atlantic fringe of Europe. T. C. Lethbridge has shown the links between the saveiros of Portugal and the curraghs of Ireland in the way in which their oars are attached to the boat.[17] The saveiros are still conspicuous for their 'oculi'. All this strongly suggests the survival of a Bronze Age contact between western Britain and Iberia—a link by no means unrelated to our general theme.

Plate 33 The sequence is continued in the Iron Age by the Broighter boat from Ireland which can be dated roughly to the second century BC. It is a wonderful specimen being modelled all in gold. It also has a mast of gold, proving conclusively that this type of boat was fitted with sails.

Next we hear of the Roman author Rufus Festus Avienus who gives us a detailed account of the Britons who disdained to make their boats of pine and fir, but used skins sewn together and in this way braved the ocean on a hide. Avienus tells us that the sailors to whom he refers were the seamen of the Oestryminides, a cape in western Brittany famous in early literature as being along the sea-route taken by British merchants engaged in the Cornish tin trade in their voyages from St Michael's Mount in Cornwall around to Corbilo at the mouth of the Loire.[18] Some experts think that Avienus himself was basing his account on a much earlier Greek manuscript that might well reach as far back as the sixth century BC.

We now come to the famous carving on the Bantry pillar, situated on a hill-top overlooking Bantry Bay in Kerry in south-western Ireland. The boat depicted on the column is unquestionably a curragh and Dr Françoise Henry has been able to date the carvings to the eighth century AD. We have here, therefore, a drawing contemporary with the Age of the Saints—the kind of vessel in which St Brendan himself must have sailed. The modern Irish curragh is a direct descendant of the Bantry boat whose subsequent lineage may be traced through the drawing made by Captain Phillips for Samuel Pepys in 1670 of a 'portable vessel of wicker commonly used by the wild Irish'.[19]

Our third reason for postulating the use of the skin-boat in megalithic times is based on the most direct evidence of all, that is the representation of carvings of skin-boats on the megaliths themselves. The shape and form of the boats carved on the Mané Lud megaliths of the Morbihan in Brittany clearly indicate long skin-boats of the curragh class. If this is accepted, they can surely take their place in the suggested sequence outlined above and so add final proof to the argument here presented.

We must, however, be careful not to overemphasize the importance of skin-boats on the western seaways in early times. Significant as they were, they were not the exclusive means of early water transport in pre- and proto-historic times. There was the smaller version of the curragh—the coracle—which survives in parts of Britain and Ireland to the present day and there was also the dug-out boat and later the wooden ship.

Dug-out canoes have been studied in great detail by Fox, based on an example recovered from the shores of Llangorse lake in Breconshire.[20] Other scholars have studied the evolution of the wooden ship in western waters: in 1962 the discovery of a sunken vessel beneath the shadow of Blackfriars Bridge on the Thames prompted Peter Marsden to point out how closely it resembled Caesar's description of the ships of the Veneti. Both were made of oak, had flat bottoms, high bows and sterns, massive cross-beams fastened with nails and were heavily built.[21] The present day *meia luas* of Portugal are built in almost the same way; so, too, is the French *toue*.[22] These likenesses seem too striking for mere coincidence. They would seem to suggest that there existed a tradition of shipbuilding on the Atlantic seaboard of Europe which owed nothing to the Romans, the Byzantines, or the medieval shipbuilders, but appears to have carried on the more primitive flat-bottomed, semi-skeleton type of construction which, in turn, may reach back to the dug-out tradition. In summary, therefore, it can be said that on the seas of western Britain and Ireland in prehistoric times the skin-boat and the simple dug-out dominated the scene, as indeed, they continued to do until the later Middle Ages, while in eastern Britain and along the shores of France and Iberia a continental flat-bottomed design—with raised bow and stern, semi-skeleton form of construction; transverse bars placed through cleats left in the solid when the planks were adzed; and, in the beginning, constructed with sewn planks—introduced variations and developments on the dug-out that in time transformed it from being a river barge into a fully fledged sea-going craft. With the passage of time, as we have seen, the skin-boat survived in the stormier and remoter lands of the north-west.[23]

Before leaving the problems of early navigation along the shores of western Europe, reference must be made to matters that probably reduced the hazards to some degree. One is the clear, long-distance visibility which frequently occurs in these otherwise cloudy and mist-shrouded lands. The most favourable conditions occur after rainstorms, when the ensuing 'cold front' brings cold, clear, northerly air to replace the damp, foggy, misty, rainy weather so characteristic of the depressions that pass into the continent from the open Atlantic. The resulting visibility can be quite outstanding; for example, distant views of England, Scotland, Ireland and Wales are often possible from the summit of Snaefell in the Isle of Man, while the summit of Holyhead Mountain in Anglesey offers excellent views further south. While it is likely that early navigators would use the Menai Straits in their passage northwards through the Irish Sea, this does not imply that they did not set foot on the island; the numerous megalithic tombs in Anglesey are clear evidence to the contrary. If these men climbed Holyhead mountain on a clear day they would see the whole of the northern basin of the Irish Sea ringed around with
*Fig. 15* uplands—the Wicklow hills, the mountains of Mourne, Snaefell in Man and the Fells of the Lake District in the distance. These would appear to them as 'islands' or 'mountains rising out of the sea'. They would inevitably set sail towards such beacons and there can be no doubt that much primitive navigation was done in this way.

Another way of reducing the hazards of primitive navigation was the widespread practice of utilizing transpeninsular routes and thereby

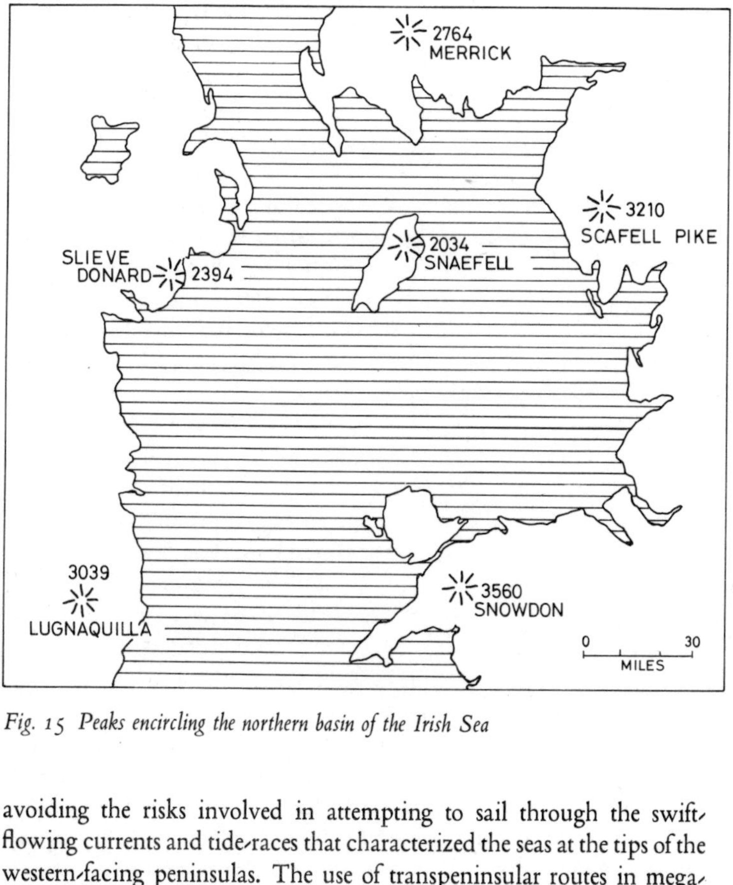


*Fig. 15 Peaks encircling the northern basin of the Irish Sea*

avoiding the risks involved in attempting to sail through the swift-flowing currents and tide-races that characterized the seas at the tips of the western-facing peninsulas. The use of transpeninsular routes in megalithic times is clearly shown by the distribution of tombs in Cornwall, south-west Wales, north-west Wales and the Galloway peninsula. They occur along isthmus roads that were used by voyagers who had landed on one side of the peninsula and crossed over to the other before re-embarking to continue their journey. Their curraghs were either carried or hauled across the peninsula by the seafarers themselves.

In retrospect, there can be little doubt that the first effective exploration of the western seaways was the achievement of the 'Megalithic Age'. It would appear that these primitive navigators, traders and prospectors were united by a powerful religious cult. We have no knowledge of the details of its magic or ritual except that it was clearly associated with the cult of the dead.[24] The enormous stone tombs erected for collective burial have remained prominent features of the landscape of these western lands throughout the ages. Their presence has haunted men's minds for centuries, and around these sepulchres have gathered many superstitious customs, most of which (as if reminiscent of the Neolithic Age itself) are associated with attempts to influence the forces of Nature and induce fertility in crops, beasts and man. Such beliefs have survived in the countryside into our own day, and there is much evidence that Christianity itself had to compromise with the aftermath of this powerful cult, as we have many instances in Britain, Cornwall, Brittany and elsewhere of deliberate attempts to Christianize these monuments in some way or another.[25] 'The Western Façade of Europe' in the 'Megalithic Age' not only witnessed great activity on the seas off its shores but, in addition, has retained, in a very special way, long-standing memories of this Golden Age.

CHAPTER III

# *Copper, Gold and Tin*

The increment in wealth and activity that characterized the lands bordering the sea-routes in megalithic times lasted well into the Bronze Age when gold, copper and tin were added to hard stones as commercial assets of the Atlantic fringe. In particular, the gold-bearing gravels of the valleys among the Wicklow Hills in south-eastern Ireland, together with the adjacent deposits of copper, should be noted. There was copper to be obtained in Cork and Kerry as well as in Anglesey on the British side of the Irish Sea, while tin-streaming in Cornwall, Brittany and north-western Spain was of great renown. There can be little doubt that the megalithic folk, or those among them who were prospectors, had already discovered the great mineralogical resources of the Atlantic margins before the end of the third millennium BC. Yet, as we have seen, the builders of the great tombs were not the people who developed these resources, nor indeed were they the first to introduce metal implements into the western lands. It would appear that the use of metal reached the Irish Sea area from the Near East by two channels. One was the invasion of the south-eastern parts of our islands by the Beaker Folk who, about 1800 BC, came to eastern Britain from the Lower Rhineland. They buried their dead in small round barrows with no chambers and often placed in the grave a distinctive type of pot, called a beaker, which probably contained a food-offering for the departed. The people derive Plate 16 their archaeological name from this distinctive type of pottery. When they invaded eastern England, they brought with them a type of little riveted dagger, together with some flat axes of copper or poor bronze, which had lately been developed in central Europe. Their flint daggers found in lowland Britain are copies of these copper ones. Further westward in Britain, however, the central European dagger is found again among Beaker immigrants, reproduced first of all in copper, and then in bronze. It has been shown that in these western parts of the country, the demand by the Beaker Folk for this type of dagger was being met by Irish metal merchants, so that, as Fox remarks, 'the Bronze Age in Britain came not from the south or the east, but from the west'.[1] The implications of this statement are clear. It is obvious that, in addition to the early metal

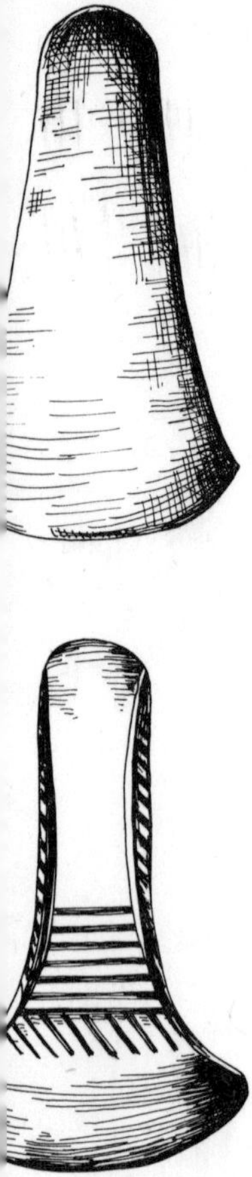

*Fig. 16 A flat celt and a cast flanged axe of the Early Bronze Age (National Museum of Wales, Cardiff)*

implements introduced by the Beaker Folk, ideas of primitive metallurgy had also been spread along the Atlantic seaways, from Spain into Brittany, and thence on to Ireland, where the manufacture of metal implements soon became strongly established. Since Ireland produced at this early stage not only copper but bronze axes and daggers, it is clear that the prime trade secret—of adding a little tin to the copper to make the alloy—must also have been disseminated along the seaways. This is all the more obvious since Ireland has virtually no tin deposits of her own, and must have relied at an early date on those of Cornwall, Brittany and north-western Spain. In any case, once the process of alloying copper and tin to make bronze was firmly established in places as far apart as these, the European Bronze Age may be said to have begun.

We do not know exactly how these basic ores were obtained. There could obviously not have been any deep mining. Surface workings could have been of two types—burrowing into an exposed rock face in pursuit of the lodes or, more likely, the method known as streaming. We have abundant instances in Cornwall of tin-stone being washed out of a hillside outcrop, with a stream of detritus flowing down the slope and spreading out fanwise on the valley floor beneath. Tin pebbles could be dug out of this stream by primitive 'picks', presumably of antler bone. The black tin pebbles or pieces of tin-stone would then be broken up and smelted on an open rock surface to obtain the ore. A similar procedure must have been adopted to obtain gold and copper ores. A recent excavation at Treviskey in Cornwall revealed a hoard of cassiterite tin on the occupation floor of a hut which could be dated by the associated pottery to the Late Bronze Age. These little black pebbles, presumably from a stream working, are the first direct evidence we possess that Cornish tin was worked before the Roman occupation.[2]

It is now time to return to the Early Bronze Age. One of the most distinctive weapons of this period was the flat bronze axe with a fairly wide blade. Later, the blades were widened still further, and the edges beaten up into flanges to make the hafting more secure. Ireland became one of the most important centres in Northern Europe for the manufacture of these implements. The general distribution of flat and hammer-
*Figs 16, 17* flanged axes of Irish type in the British Isles is shown on the map on the opposite page. One of the outstanding features of the distribution pattern

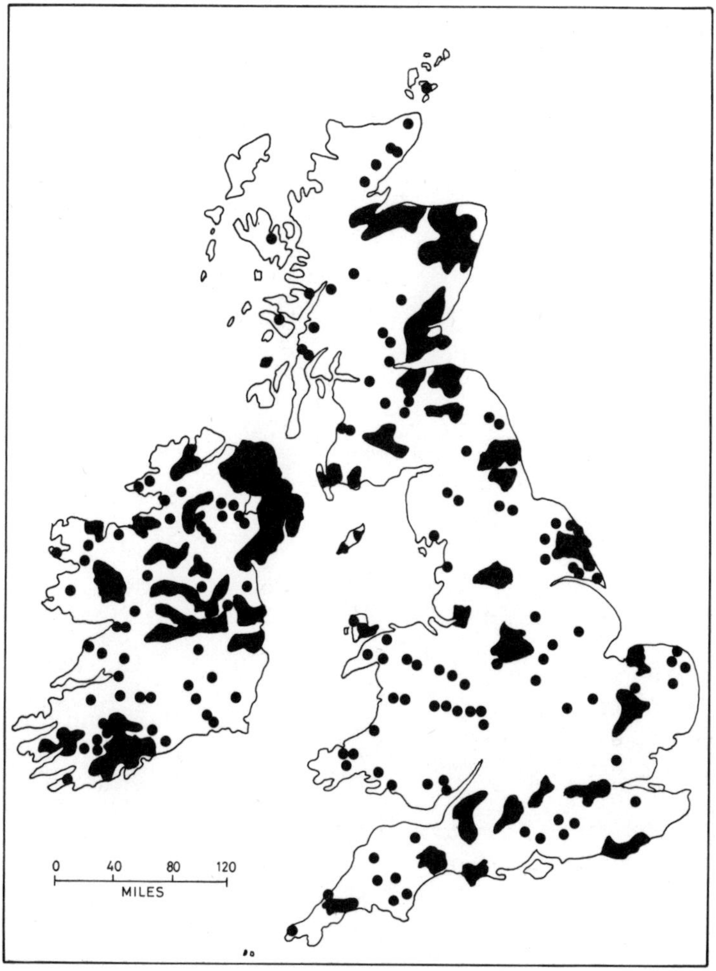


*Fig. 17 Combined distribution of flat and hammer-flanged axes of the Early Bronze Age. Areas of solid black indicate relatively heavy concentrations (after L. F. Chitty)*

is the concentration of these finds in north-eastern Ireland, especially in counties Antrim and Down. We remember that it was precisely in this area that the products of the polished stone axe 'factories' of Rathlin Island and Tievebulliagh were most densely distributed. It may well be that this

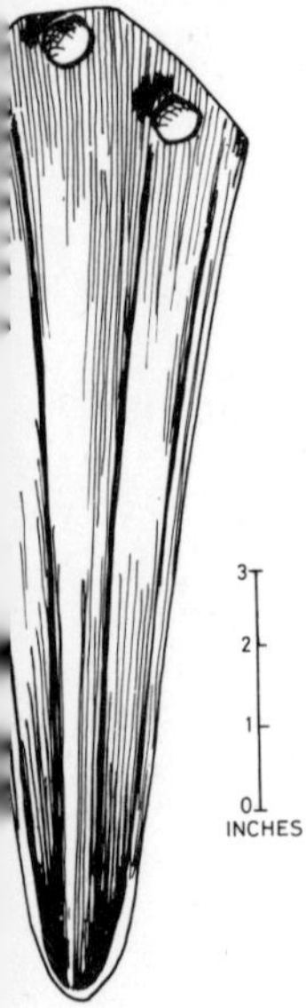


*Fig. 18 A halberd blade of the Early Bronze Age (National Museum of Wales)*

area had acquired, over a long period, an interest and skill in the making and handling of weapons and tools, and that this skill was handed on from generation to generation, so that the descendants of the Neolithic axe-makers adapted themselves easily to working in metal. We must, however, be careful not to press the matter too far, for no 'workshops' associated with the sites of Neolithic axe-factories developed in Europe in the Early Bronze Age. It would appear that at this time, with the possible exception of the Eastern Mediterranean, no single tribal group or individual chieftain would normally have been rich enough to support a resident smith, and keep him regularly supplied with bronze. Thus, for the most part, bronze tools and weapons would have been both distributed and worked by itinerant smiths who must have ranged over considerable areas making weapons and ornaments for their local patrons.[3] Nevertheless, the map indicates that there must have been considerable activity in north-eastern Ireland. At the same time, by virtue of its geographical position alongside the major sea-route, it was exceptionally well placed as a base for itinerant smiths and the dissemination of their products. We note the use made of the short crossings to the Galloway peninsula and the Firth of Clyde. The smiths must have crossed Scotland from the west coast by well-defined tracks to eastern ports near Aberdeen and on the Tay estuary, whence axes and other weapons crossed the North Sea to Scandinavia and the Baltic lands. It would appear that the local manufacture of Early Bronze Age weapons persisted for a long period in the lowlands of Eastern Scotland, for it is known that several moulds for casting the axes have been found in the area. The Isle of Man naturally received its share of implements, while the Ribble and Aire gaps carried axes to eastern Yorkshire from whence further contacts with Scandinavia and the Baltic countries were made. Further south, the sea-route between Dublin and North Wales is clearly implied. It passed thence by way of the Severn valley towards Gloucester and the Thames. Many hold the view that this was the chief southern route to France at this time. The map shows traces of other crossings of the Irish Sea, for instance, into the Dyfi estuary in Cardigan Bay, and thence across mid-Wales to the Severn. Further south still, we can detect the south-west Wales transpeninsular route, and movement along the south Wales coastal plain to southern England. Finally, there was direct contact between Ireland and south-west Cornwall.

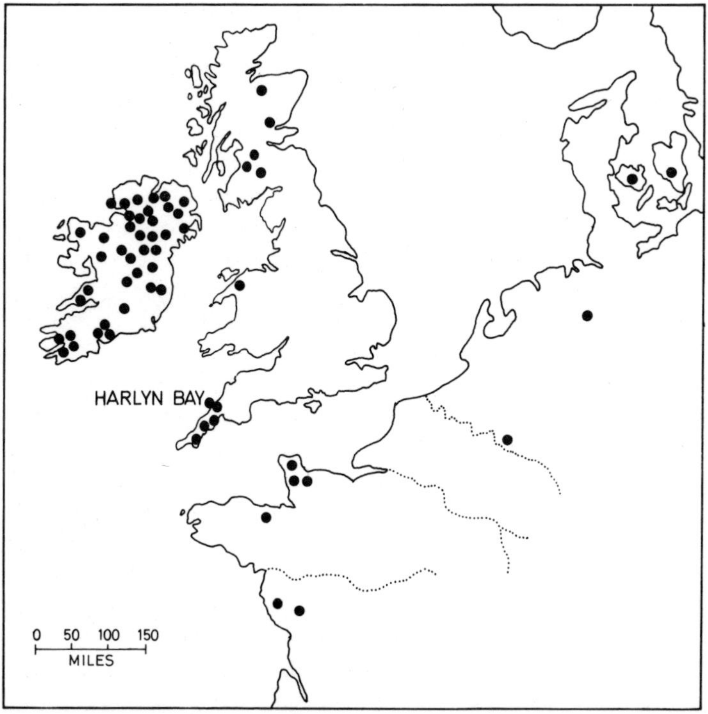


*Fig. 19 Distribution of Irish gold lunulae of the Early Bronze Age (after Coffey and Fox)*

Incidentally, three flat axes found together at Trenovissick in St Blazey parish in Cornwall are lavishly, though somewhat crudely, decorated with an arrangement of roughly incised lines—a type of decoration known to be very fashionable in Ireland at this time.[4] Many other flat axes in Britain show this same type of decoration.

Another Irish implement of the Early Bronze Age was the halberd, where the blade was hafted at right-angles to a long handle. The distribution of the halberd in Britain reveals similar, but numerically fewer, points of entry. Nevertheless, the main sea-routes are clearly marked and it is well-known that these weapons were also widely spread in Northern Europe. *Fig. 18*

Two other features characterized the Early Bronze Age. The first was a considerable improvement in the production of daggers, as the first small

ineffectual type developed into a longer and stronger weapon. Secondly, gold ornaments appeared and spread widely by way of the sea-routes. The interesting feature is that most gold ornaments found throughout the
Plates 11-14 Atlantic seaboard, and even far into the mainland of Europe, are of Irish gold. For example, at Harlyn Bay in Cornwall, there have been found in association with one another a typical flat axe of this period, and two large gold crescents. The latter were decorated in much the same way as the three flat axes from Trenovissick and are unquestionably of Irish origin. They are made like all other crescents of the period of very thin gold, and are apparently breastplates such as would have been worn by a high dignitary on a ceremonial occasion. These gold lunulae were first mapped by G. Coffey before the First World War, and although several additions have been made to his map since that time, the over-all picture
*Fig. 19* remains unchanged.[5] We note a vast concentration in Ireland, and then a fanning out into Scotland, North Wales, Cornwall, and the North Sea and English Channel margins of the continent from Denmark to Brittany, with a slight concentration in the Cotentin peninsula of Normandy.[6] No lunulae have been found in lowland Britain, and the suggestion is unmistakable that the western seaways with their Scottish–North Sea and English Channel links are once more in operation.

Meanwhile, other great centres producing bronze implements were appearing all over Europe. The famous Aunjetitz (Únětice) centre in Bohemia was an early example. Others arose in Saxo-Thuringia, Hungary, northern Italy, south-eastern Spain and south Russia, and a little later in the Rhône valley, and in north Germany. The routes of the merchant-smiths who supplied this European market with bronze can
Plate 19 be traced by the 'hoards', or the lost travelling-bags of the itinerant smiths. The contents of the hoards show that they dealt not only in bronze ware,
Plates 15, 17, 18 but also in gold, jet, amber, and other luxuries. They might also have traded in salt and other substances which, of course, have left no trace behind them. Amber, in particular, was very highly valued and is found in many hoards. The most important deposits of this fossil resin are in Jutland and east Prussia; since the people of the Baltic lands began to barter amber for the metal wares, there are very clearly marked amber routes across central Europe from the Elbe to the Danube and the Adriatic. In this way these routes linked the people of Northern Europe with the advanced civilizations of Greece and Minoan Crete.

As the northern lands grew in prosperity, the old-established centres in the Western Mediterranean tended to become eclipsed, and their trade to die away. All this profoundly influenced the Atlantic seaways and there followed a period of temporary decline in their activities.

This Middle Bronze Age Period, as it is known to archaeologists, certainly saw further advances in metallurgy and the fashioning of weapons. The evolution of the looped spear-head and the rapier are examples of this technological advance in Western Europe, but throughout, there was very little inspiration from the great civilizations of the Eastern Mediterranean. Indeed, some authorities would argue that not only did we have at this time a slackening of trade and activity along the sea-routes but that an actual reversal of tradeflow occurred. They would point to the evolution of the cast-flanged axe and its distribution in the British area to prove their argument. The intense activity in the manufacture in Ireland of bronze tools for export steadily declined, while in Central Europe the Bronze Age culture in the Aunjetitz region produced the well-known broad-bladed axe with cast flanges, much more effective as a weapon than the earlier hammered-up Irish types. The British trade with the continent, already mentioned, familiarized our craftsmen with the new weapon, and with the art of bronze-founding. Large numbers of cast-flanged axes were produced in lowland Britain and actually exported westwards to Ireland. This axe, therefore, represents the first indication in Britain of the change in the European economic situation, which temporarily limited activities along the western sea-routes.[8]

The changing situation did not appear to have affected the trade in gold objects quite to the same extent. Ireland still had its gold in the Wicklow Hills, in Kerry and in Cork. New fashions certainly appeared and the fashionable ornament now was the torque made of long twisted ribbons of solid gold. It was traded across the Irish Sea to the British mainland, utilizing mainly the Mersey–Dee entries, with an ultimate concentration of gold objects in eastern and southern England. From these areas, the torques spread across the Narrow Seas to the coasts of northern France which lay opposite the British shores. As far as Britain in relation to Europe was concerned, this was clearly overland and not maritime commerce.

The period that saw the close of the second and the beginning of the last millennium BC ushers in what is known technically as the Late

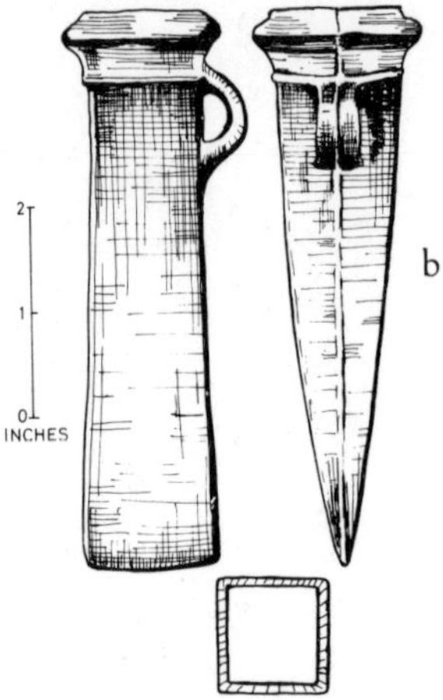


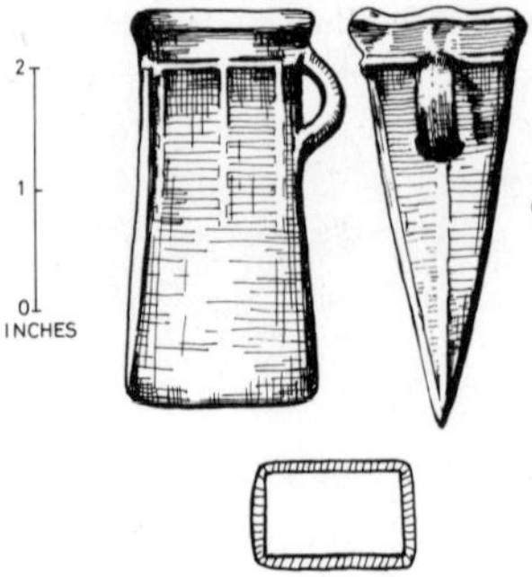


Bronze Age. For south-eastern Britain, it was a period of invasion and turmoil. Warlike bands from the Continent landed in Britain at intervals throughout the period, which lasted in south-eastern Britain down to 450 BC. These disturbances broke up the peaceful economic conditions that had existed throughout the Middle Bronze Age. Consequently, in the new era we find trade and commerce reverting once more to the western seaways. The invasions brought with them a host of new metal objects from the Continent. They included, in particular, new swords with double-edged blades, such as the leaf-shaped sword and the carp's-tongue sword, whose very names help to explain their form.[9] There were new bronze spear-heads also, as well as the new axe-head with a socket at one end for the insertion of the handle and a little loop through which the axe could be further secured to the handle by a cord. Another type of weapon evolved in Central Europe and entering Britain at this time was the bronze winged axe. This implement seems to have evolved by the hammering back of the flanges over the main body of the axe in such a way as to give the impression of a creature with its wings folded back almost at rest. This device facilitated hafting. The over-all impression of the Late Bronze Age is, therefore, not only one of invasion and turmoil, but one in which new weapons and new utensils (such as bronze buckets and cauldrons) made the bronze-founding industry more intensive and extensive than ever before. This great increase in activity is reflected in the fact that a great many bronze weapons are found together in what are described as 'founders' hoards'; these contain, besides whole bronzes,

*Figs 20–22 Late Bronze Age metalwork: bronze swords from the Thames, a, leaf-shaped and e, carp's-tongue; socketed axes, b, of Breton and c, of Welsh type; d, winged axe. b, c and d from the National Museum of Wales, Cardiff*

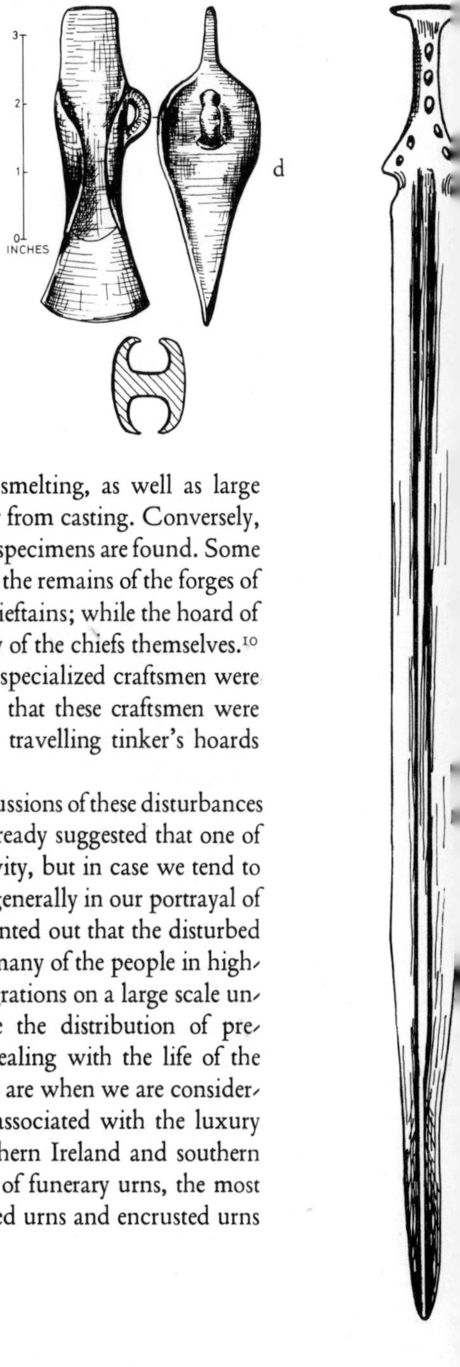


many fragments, obviously collected for re-smelting, as well as large pieces of metal and other waste pieces left over from casting. Conversely, there are other hoards in which almost perfect specimens are found. Some scholars think the 'founder's hoard' represents the remains of the forges of the smiths who accompanied the invading chieftains; while the hoard of unused specimens may be part of the armoury of the chiefs themselves.[10] At all events, the whole picture suggests that specialized craftsmen were now attached to individual war leaders and that these craftsmen were more numerous than the finds of the earlier travelling tinker's hoards would suggest.

It is time now to examine some of the repercussions of these disturbances on the distant western seaboard. We have already suggested that one of the chief results was a revival of trading activity, but in case we tend to over-emphasize trade and economic activity generally in our portrayal of the use made of the seaways, it should be pointed out that the disturbed conditions in south-eastern England caused many of the people in highland Britain to become restless, and mass migrations on a large scale undoubtedly took place. When we examine the distribution of prehistoric pottery, we are more likely to be dealing with the life of the ordinary people and their settlements than we are when we are considering the distribution of weapons or articles associated with the luxury trade. The Late Bronze Age people of northern Ireland and southern Scotland seem to have evolved special types of funerary urns, the most characteristic of which are known as cordoned urns and encrusted urns

respectively.[11] These names attempt to describe the type of urn used, one cylindrical with an added cordon or band decoration, and the other decorated before firing with additional clay rosettes and bands to give almost a pie-crust effect. It is the distribution of these urns, shown on the
*Fig. 23* map on the opposite page, that is our immediate concern, as it provides some indication of the movement of peoples. The use of the western seaways, other than by merchants or tradesmen, is clearly demonstrated. From the northern concentrations we note the presence of these folk in the Isle of Man and, by using the Mersey–Dee entries, their settlements in the English Peak district. Special attention may be given to the grouping of these burial urns along the shores of the Menai Straits, a short sea-cut which ancient mariners found very convenient. We find the urns again on the Cardigan Bay coast and more particularly across the transpeninsular route in south-west Wales, from north Pembrokeshire to south-west Carmarthenshire. Finally, there are indications of movement along the South Wales coastal plain, and by the short Severn crossing into Somerset. An isolated example is found on the coast of east Kent, in the forefront of the invasion zone! What, we may ask, made this solitary western exile travel so far from home? This digression has shown beyond all reasonable doubt that the ordinary folk moved as much by sea in the western lands in early times as did the gold, copper and tin merchants.

The re-establishment of trade along the western seaways at this time is clearly demonstrated by the study of the distribution of the double-looped palstave. In addition to the great activity which characterized Central Europe in the Late Bronze Age, we know that new centres of bronze-working arose in the Western Mediterranean from 1400 BC onwards. These centres were especially important in northern Italy, Sicily and Sardinia. Copper was in each case available locally, but the tin was brought from Galicia. These Galician industrialists, in turn, began making bronze weapons of their own, based to some extent on
*Fig. 24* British models. The double-looped palstave was one of their creations,
*Fig. 25* and the map shows the unmistakable concentration of find-sites in northern Portugal and north-western Spain. Some of these palstaves were traded back, not only to Sardinia, but to south-western France and northern Brittany, with some reaching the valley of the Seine, the Low Countries and even southern Sweden. Gordon Childe, commenting on the map as a whole, makes special reference to Britain. 'It reveals,' he

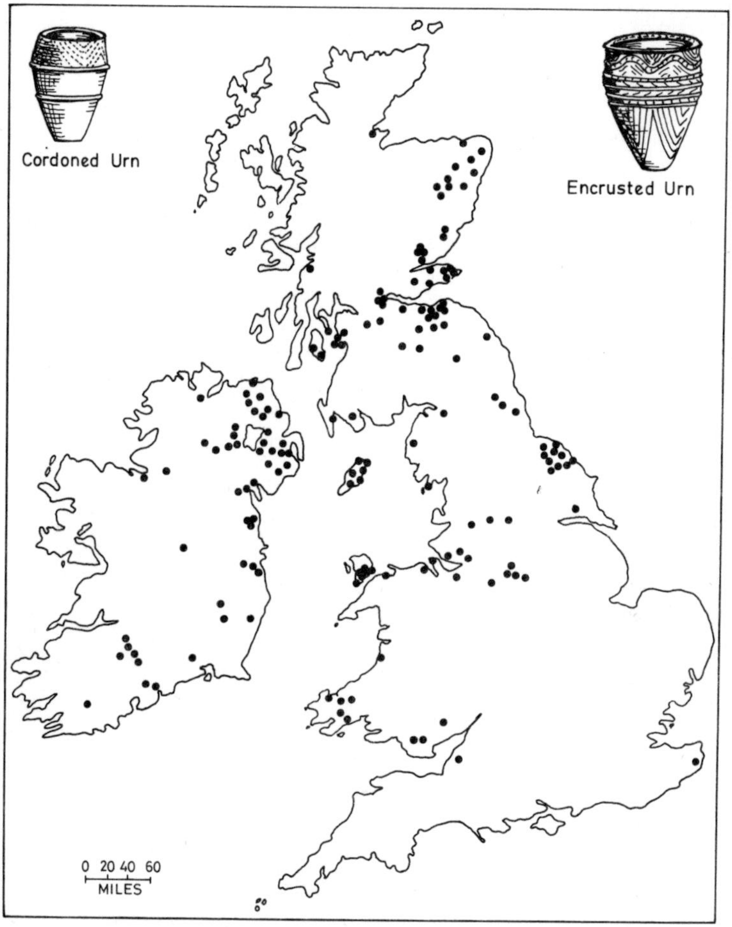


*Fig. 23 Distribution of both cordoned and encrusted urns of the Late Bronze Age (based on L. F. Chitty)*

says, 'not only the centre of dispersion, but leaves little doubt that the British examples were the result of direct overseas trade with the Peninsula.'[12] It is well worth noting for future reference the chief landfalls in the British Isles. These are the Wessex coastlands, the Cornish peninsula and the hinterland of Cobh Harbour in southern Ireland.

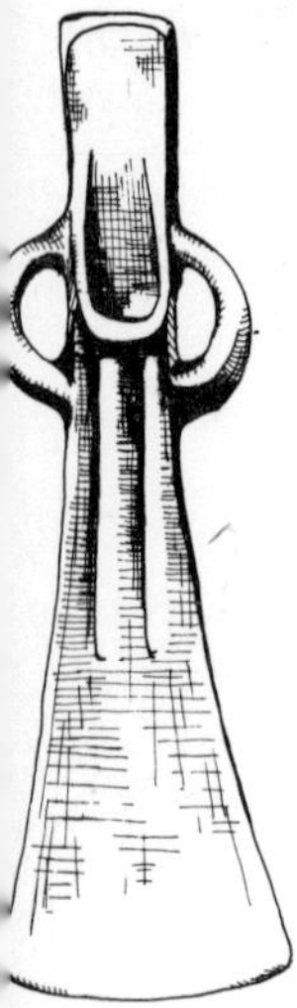

*Fig. 24 Double-looped palstave, Late Bronze Age (National Museum of Wales)*

It was not only bronze palstaves that were carried along the sea-routes, but bronze cauldrons and shields; almost certainly of Irish workmanship. Most of these are found in Britain and indicate once more the use of the shorter crossings over the Irish Sea. Reverting to the major route itself, we can instance two interesting bronze hoards at either end of the seaway. A hoard from Huelva harbour in north-west Spain (said to be associated with a sunken merchant ship) contained spears cast in the British Isles, brooches from Sicily and many 'Western European swords and ornaments'. At the other end of the seaway, a hoard belonging to this period, found on the island of Lewis in the Outer Hebrides, contained many Irish bronze implements, beads of Irish gold, some Baltic amber, a piece of Mediterranean glass and a broken bronze cup of Central European workmanship.[13] Here is the western seaway in action, and presumably by this same route British spear-heads and objects of Irish gold reached the Baltic lands. The occurrence of Late Bronze Age ornaments and weapons of Irish manufacture in the Orkney and Shetland islands is an additional confirmation that the seaways had reverted to full activity.

Another feature of the intensive manufacturing activity which characterized this age was the development of several local schools of bronze-working. The alloy was now so cheap and plentiful and the smiths so numerous that many of them had to settle down to produce everyday tools and weapons for local consumption. The smith became more closely associated with local tribal groups, and goods were made to suit the divergent tastes of customers. We can in this way easily identify three schools of metallurgy specializing in the production of socketed axes. There was, first of all, the Yorkshire school producing a socketed axe with a sub-rectangular socket and three ribs cast on the face. Then

*Fig. 21c*

there was a south-east Wales school producing an axe with a heavy cornice-like moulding around the mouth and again with three ribs, but rather more closely set than the Yorkshire ones, and even sometimes converging. Across the English Channel was the Breton school whose

*Fig. 21b*

axes were square in cross-section and had no surface decoration. Such local variants cluster around their centres of origin, though stray specimens were traded far and wide along the seaways. Yorkshire axes spread through the Pennine gaps into the Irish Sea province; one is found in the Isle of Man, another in north-eastern Ireland and yet another in the Galloway peninsula, a clear indication of the fact that the seaways had

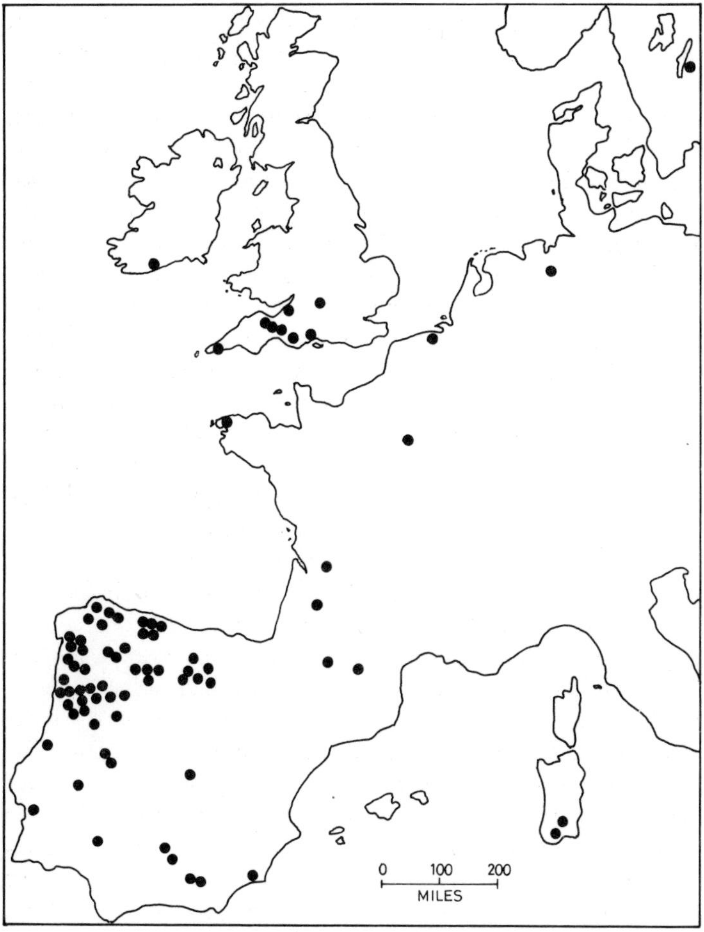


*Fig. 25 Distribution of double-looped palstaves of the Late Bronze Age (after V. G. Childe)*

been used. The Breton axes show traders frequenting the ports along the whole of the south coast of Britain. They appear in at least three hoards in south-western Cornwall, and they occur again in the Gower peninsula and along the South Wales coastal plain near Bridgend. Likewise, the distribution of scattered finds of socketed axes of the south-east Wales

*Fig. 26* school is very indicative of trade along the seaways. One is found in the Teifi valley in Cardiganshire, another in the Dee valley in North Wales, while the occurrence of several specimens around the coasts of Somerset, Devon and Cornwall indicates the use of the numerous little harbours in south-western Britain at this time. Outlying finds are recorded from places as far removed from one another as East Anglia and the Channel Islands.[14] We shall find that it is worth while noting these landfalls for future reference, as they become especially illuminating when we seek comparisons with later movements along the seaways.

As was to be expected, the trade in gold objects greatly increased during the Late Bronze Age. Gold objects are found well scattered over Irish soil, but the greatest concentration in Britain was now no longer in the Wessex country, but in the extreme south-east, indicating possibly an extension of the western seaways by a movement up-Channel. A similar movement is clearly indicated in the distribution of the double-looped palstave. Even more marked is the presence of a vastly greater number of objects of Irish gold in eastern Scotland, the Clyde province, Galloway, Anglesey, south-west Wales and Cornwall, indicating unmistakably the return of trade to the western seaways. The most fashionable gold objects of this period were heavy bracelets and large golden loops with expanded trumpet-like ends. A very interesting group of six large bracelets has been found in a treasure near Morvah in western Cornwall. Three of the bracelets have trumpet-like ends and are clearly Irish. One of them has an engraved geometric pattern like that found on the earlier Irish gold crescents, while the remaining three bracelets in this find, even if not made in Ireland, are most likely to be of Irish gold.[15]

Plates 11-14

As the late Bronze Age draws to its close or, better stated, as the Early Iron Age cultures begin to spread by land and sea into Atlantic Europe, we naturally hear less and less of gold and copper as commercial assets of the Atlantic fringe, but somehow or another a persistent romantic flavour remained attached to the Cornish tin trade. For the people of the Mediterranean lands, Cornish tin stood out as the one product around which the trade of Ancient Britain revolved. Its fame was known to the literate Greek trading communities from the fourth century BC onwards, while references to it, of varying quality, survive in Greek and Latin texts. The written references themselves are extremely vague; for example, the source of the tin supplies was said to be the Cassiterides, but, in fact,

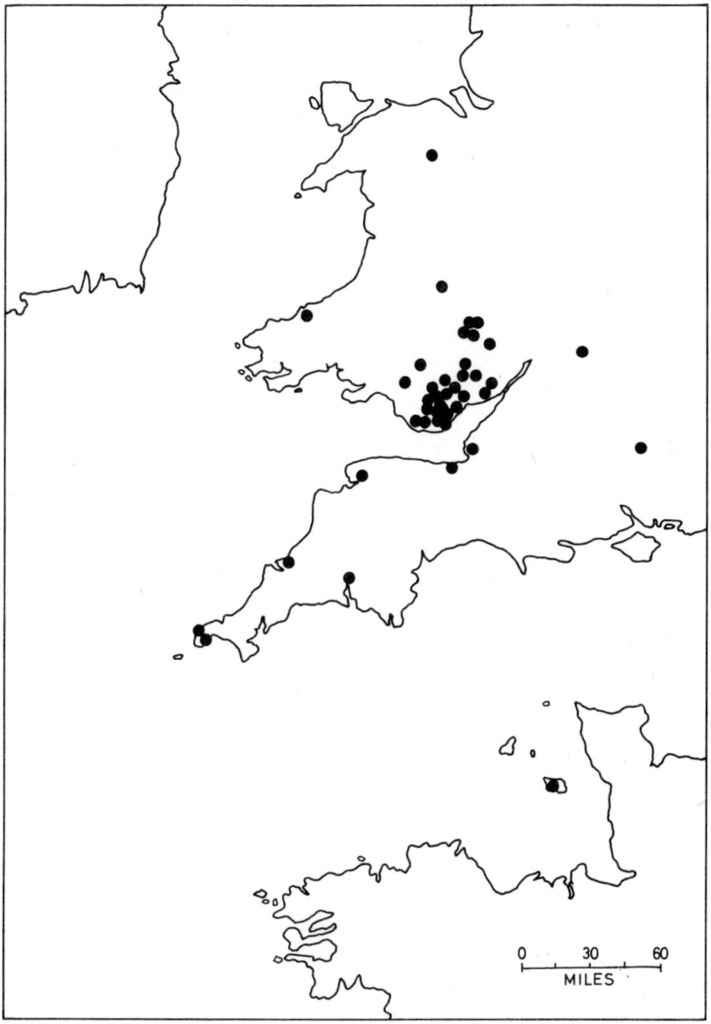


*Fig. 26 Distribution of Late Bronze Age socketed axes of Welsh type (after Fox, Hyde and Chitty)*

this was no more than a name vaguely applied to the Atlantic tin lands before they became part of the Roman Empire. The references in Strabo and Avienus to Phoenician, Carthaginian and Tartessian ships engaged in the trade almost certainly refer to voyages made to north-west Spain or

Brittany, but hardly going as far as Cornwall. The really outstanding period in the final phase of the Cornish tin trade began after the Carthaginians in the sixth century BC blockaded the Straits of Gibraltar preventing Greek ships from passing through. One of the results was that the Greek merchants at Massilia and elsewhere attempted to short-circuit the Gibraltar route by establishing a land route across southern France to the estuary of the Gironde and thence *via* Corbilo, at the mouth of the Loire, to Brittany and beyond. The famous Greek geographer and traveller Pytheas managed to break through the Carthaginian blockade and certainly came as far north as Cornwall, mentioning Belerion (the name Ptolemy used later for Land's End). Unfortunately, Pytheas's work is lost, but it has frequently formed the basis of the writings of later authors such as Timaeus, Posidonius, Pliny and Diodorus. Most scholars now think that Diodorus's account (whatever its precise origins may have been) seems to put all that the Ancient knew about the tin trade into its true perspective, and represents a most valuable and detailed account of the last phases of the prehistoric tin trade using the western seaways. Diodorus's account is as follows:[16]

> The inhabitants of that part of Britain which is called Belerion are very fond of strangers, and, from their intercourse with foreign merchants, are civilized in their manner of life. They prepare the tin, working very carefully the earth in which it is produced. The ground is rocky, but it contains earthy veins, the produce of which is ground down, smelted and purified. They beat the metal into masses shaped like astragali, and carry it to a certain island lying off Britain called Ictis. During the ebb of the tide the intervening space is left dry, and they carry over into this island the tin in abundance in their wagons. Now there is a peculiar phenomenon connected with the neighbouring islands, I mean those that lie between Europe and Britain, for at the flood-tide the intervening passage is overflowed, and they seem like islands, but a large space is left dry at the ebb, and they seem to be like peninsulas. Here then the merchants buy the tin from the natives and carry it over to Gaul, and after travelling over land for about thirty days, they finally bring their loads on horses to the mouth of the Rhône.

A number of comments can be made on this passage. In the first place, Belerion is clearly Land's End, as has already been mentioned. Ictis is

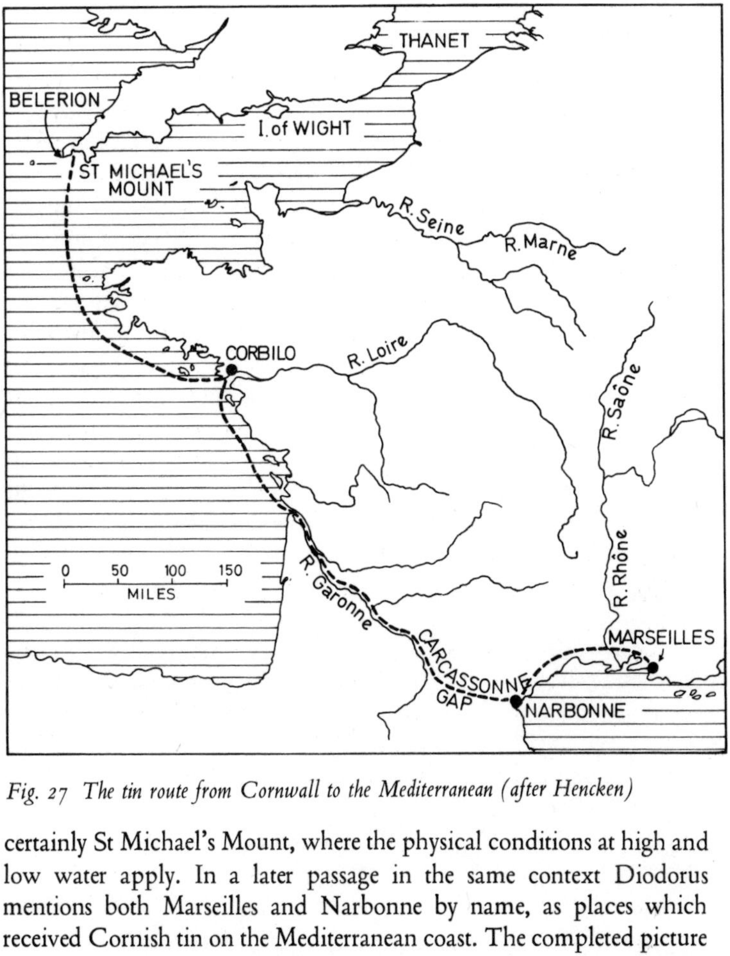


*Fig. 27 The tin route from Cornwall to the Mediterranean (after Hencken)*

certainly St Michael's Mount, where the physical conditions at high and low water apply. In a later passage in the same context Diodorus mentions both Marseilles and Narbonne by name, as places which received Cornish tin on the Mediterranean coast. The completed picture of this important section of the Atlantic sea-route (traversed partly by land and partly by sea) would, according to Hencken,[17] be as follows: leaving St Michael's Mount, it passed by way of the Oestrymnides—the small islands off the Breton coast, which themselves were probably engaged in exporting Breton tin, and are mentioned by Avienus as being visited by Tartessian traders—to Corbilo. The merchants would then either begin their landward crossing from this port or re-embark for

Plate 20

*Fig. 27*

the Garonne estuary, and begin the landward journey from there, moving by way of the Carcassonne gap to Marseilles and the mouth of the Rhône.

There is no doubt, however, that the importance of this route began to decline with the discovery of Spanish tin by the Romans early in the last century BC; nevertheless, the passage quoted gives ample proof of a flourishing tin trade from Cornwall to the Mediterranean from the fourth to the first centuries BC, which was of sufficient importance to interest the Mediterranean world. It is in some ways ironic that it was a contemporary of Diodorus, Julius Caesar, who was the last classical author to mention tin as a product of Britain, for it is to him more than to any other man that we must ascribe the final destruction of the Cornish tin trade. Caesar's own reference to tin as a British product is well-nigh valueless. He merely says that it came from the interior. His contacts with Britain were, however, confined to the south-east and his knowledge of the west was probably non-existent. By his conquest of the Veneti—the powerful seafaring people who inhabited southern Brittany—he dealt a fatal blow to the tin trade. He himself says that the Veneti were accustomed to sail to Britain in high-prowed, oaken ships with leather sails. The Veneti almost certainly brought Cornish tin to Corbilo, and it is worth recalling that after his conquest of this tribe, and the destruction of the entire Armorican fleet, and possibly of Corbilo itself, in 56 BC, no more is heard of the British tin trade from classical sources. Nevertheless, the routes along which it travelled were to become prominent again in later times; in circumstances very different from those described in this chapter.

CHAPTER IV

# *An Escape to the North*

With the expansion of Roman power northward in Europe during the last century BC, considerable apprehension prevailed in the lands abutting on the western sea-routes. Things came to a head with Caesar's rough handling of the Veneti and his subsequent raids across the Channel into south-eastern Britain. There is no doubt that a great deal must have been heard in south-west Britain concerning the disaster that had overtaken the Veneti in 56 BC, as the contacts between both territories were very close. Strabo relates that the Veneti 'had an emporium in Britain' before the Roman aggression,[1] and there is considerable archaeological evidence to show that Venetic influences were strong in western Cornwall before 56 BC. It was only natural, therefore, that those who managed to escape destruction at Caesar's hands fled to Cornwall and the south-west peninsula, spreading alarm and despondency wherever they went. Indeed, it may well be that the marsh villages of north Somerset—such as Meare and Glastonbury—were already well known to the Veneti as trading centres, for sea-traders liked to be cut off from landward interference when conducting their business, and the marsh villages readily provided such protection. With the influx of Venetic refugees it may be said that the south-west peninsula, during the second half of the first century BC, experienced a maritime Iron Age culture that was both commercial and warlike, as witnessed in the Cornish castles and the Somerset lake-side dwellings.

Other pressures from a different source were also beginning to be felt in south-west England about this time. In 75 BC powerful Belgic peoples had entered south-eastern Britain from Gaul. Their culture is known to archaeologists as Iron Age C.[2] They spread their influence quickly over the territory south-east of a line from the Wash to Southampton Water and they soon pushed westward as conquerors among the Iron Age B peoples of the south-west. A powerful tribe with advanced technological equipment, known as the Dobuni, had settled in the Cotswold region and Iron Age C influences were being felt, not only in Somerset and Dorset, but also among the hill-fort dwellers overlooking the South Wales coast north of the Severn.

In 55 BC came the startling news that Caesar himself had landed in Britain, and his raids in the south-east were soon followed by the arrival of refugee chieftains and their followers from the war zone, who added to the general confusion in the south-west. Although Caesar's raids were not followed up immediately by a full-scale conquest, such a sequel must have seemed inevitable, and, indeed, actually materialized in the Claudian invasion of AD 43. The interval between 55 BC and AD 43, therefore, in south-western Britain may have been one of population pressure and unrest, so that many of these south-western people decided to seek new homes and new lands to settle on by escaping northwards by way of the sea-routes.

Our archaeological knowledge of the Wessex area and the south-west generally at this time is not as yet sufficiently precise to permit us to say exactly which groups left the area—we do not know their tribal names nor in detail the localities from which they came. On the other hand, our knowledge is sufficiently advanced to show that they appear to have settled peacefully in the north accompanied by their wives and families. Circumstantial evidence points to one very interesting archaeological aspect of this movement in that one of the most spectacular of Scottish proto-historic remains—the massive stone-built broch towers—emerged at about the same time as the arrival of these refugees in the north. Much has been written about the origin of the Scottish brochs, but it is only within recent years that it has been shown that they developed their characteristic features in the Western Isles of Scotland, especially on Skye and Tiree.[3] It would appear that, however much the brochs owe culturally to the Iron Age B round houses, such as those found at Little Woodbury in Wiltshire, Maiden Castle in Dorset, Castle Dore in Cornwall, Caerau in Caernarvonshire, they certainly developed their characteristic form in the Hebridean area from local antecedents, such as the D-shaped and promontory semi-brochs, towards the middle of the first century BC. This date is supported by the radiocarbon date of 115 $\pm$ 105 BC for charcoal from the rubble of the foundation platform of the Dun Ardtreck broch on Skye. Recent excavations at the Vaul broch on Tiree show that the primary broch level can be dated AD 5 $\pm$ 90, clearly indicating that the broch itself was built early in the mid-first century BC. Below the primary broch floor are the remains of several earlier habitation levels and a full stratigraphical sequence can be worked out. Roots from

Plates 23–6

*Fig. 28*

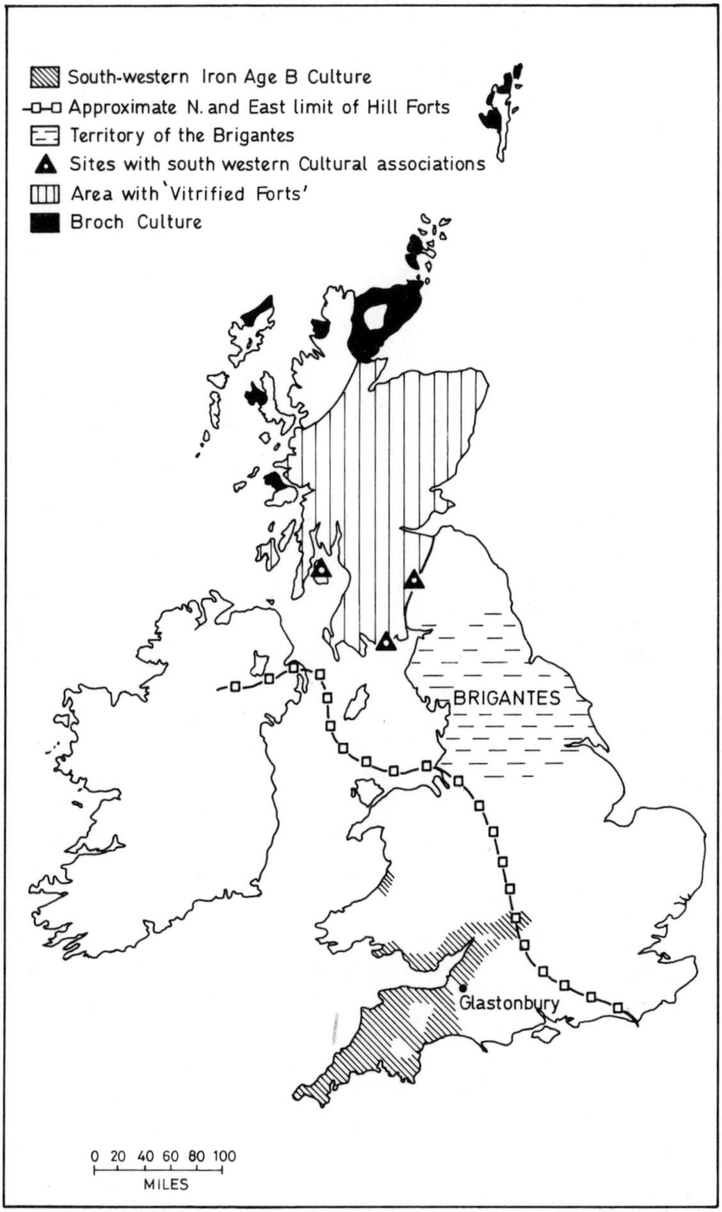


*Fig. 28 Distributi of Broch and associated cultures in the first century AD (after V. G. Childe)*

the old ground surface on which lay the earliest midden under the broch were dated 470±110 BC, while a sample of charred barley from a similar low level gave a radiocarbon dating of 517±90 BC. Near-by also was found a double-cordoned everted-rim pottery sherd which certainly can be dated to the sixth or fifth century BC. As Euan MacKie argues, since this everted-rim pottery with internal fluting on the rim would appear to have an ancestry in the Late Bronze Age Urnfield and Early Iron Age Hallstatt cultures of the Continent, there is the possibility of a direct movement of people of French Urnfield origin to Atlantic Scotland, perhaps as early as the seventh century BC.[4] Whatever view we take of this evidence, it does appear to indicate quite clearly that our mid-first century BC refugees from south-western Britain were by no means the first people to have made extensive voyages from their homeland by way of the western sea-routes to these far northern islands and coastlands of western Britain.

From the area of characterization on Skye and Tiree, the broch culture spread into the Outer Hebrides and hence to the Orkneys and Shetlands, while on the mainland the Abernethy population living north of the Dornoch Firth in Sutherland adopted brochs on a large scale. Some were later built around the Firths of Forth and Tay, near to the northern frontier of Roman rule.

With the political and military situation in the south being what it was, it is to be expected that the exodus of refugees from the south-west developed into a long continuing process. For example, we know that the broch-dwellers in the Scapa Flow area of the Orkneys received additional settlers from the south early in the first century AD. We can prove this by the sudden appearance there of a new pottery style, which can be matched directly with that in use at the time in the Somerset lake-dwellings. In a well-known passage in the writings of the Roman historian Orosius, we are told of Claudius's annexation of Britain, which was followed almost immediately afterwards by the submission of the Orkney Islands, occupying 'the outermost position in the Ocean', to the power of Imperial Rome.[5] According to Gordon Childe, it was most probably the recent arrivals in Scapa Flow who sent the message of Orcadian submission which is believed to have reached Claudius on his annexation of Britain. This would explain Orosius's reference.[6] So sophisticated an action would also be in keeping with the advanced cultural development in the south-west, implying that there were now

*Fig. 29 Plan of Dun Fiadhairt broch, Skye (after Lindsay Scott)*

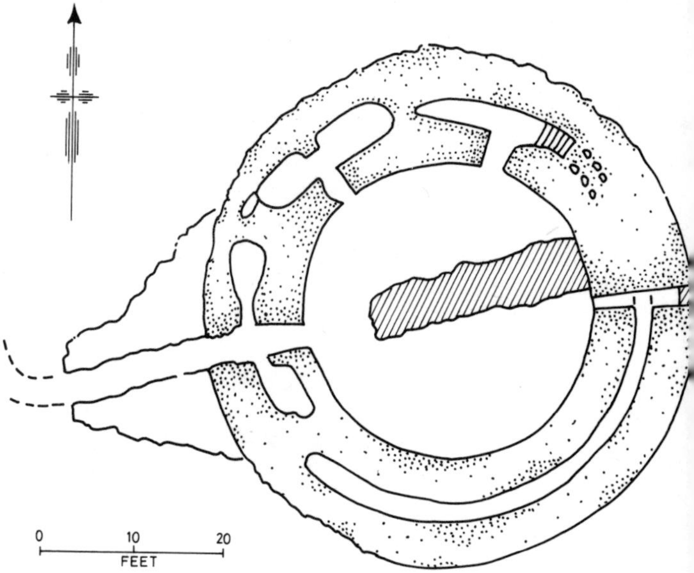


chieftains in the Orkneys who, before they left the south, had been in contact with the Empire. At the same time, the Orcadian submission implies the survival in the far north of a feeling of insecurity and general apprehension with regard to the Romans which, as we have seen, was characteristic of the general atmosphere among the Iron Age peoples of the south-west at this time.

We can now turn to the broch culture in a little more detail. The broch itself was essentially a circular stone castle tower with an internal diameter of between 25 and 35 feet. The lower portions of the massive walls, which may be 12 to 15 feet thick, may contain as many as four rooms hollowed out of the masonry and disposed around the circular courtyard rather like the cells in a courtyard house. Sometimes the chambers were not separated from each other, but instead, inside the massive wall, would run a corridor or passageway, very often with a stairway leading up to a wall-head walk or gallery, defensive or otherwise, running around some 6 or 8 feet above the ground. The brochs were roofed over by frames of light timber resting on pillars erected in the courtyard. The majority of these stone houses or defended farmsteads were small in size but, on the other hand, some possessed cylindrical towers that rose as high as 40 feet above the ground in some instances. The courtyard usually had a well and a hearth near its centre and, in the case of the very tall brochs, there

*Fig. 29*

Plate 26

would be no roof as such, but a verandah roof some 6 to 8 feet above the ground would provide shelter around the sides. The brochs are usually located in positions of natural strength, frequently near the coast, the tower itself being surrounded by an enclosure very often of considerable extent. This enclosure contained smaller buildings, usually round or oval huts, forming, possibly, the homes of some of the chieftain's retainers.

Plate 25

It is clear that the people of the broch culture adapted their economy to the physical environment with the same success as they adapted their habitations. They supported themselves primarily by intensive farming which was at the same time subsistence farming—barley being their main crop. Saddle and flat rotary querns were used to grind the grain, and these were of the same type as the querns found in the south. The bones of Celtic short-horned cattle, sheep, goats and pigs occur frequently in the broch ruins, together with those of the horse, indicating, therefore, that these people were mixed farmers relying equally on cereal and pastoral production. The location of many brochs and wheel-houses along the coast emphasizes the importance of maritime enterprise as a supplementary source of livelihood. The broch itself is often situated beside a secluded little haven along the coast, suitable for harbouring light craft, which were most probably coracles and curraghs. These small craft were not only used for fishing and whaling, but also for local communication between one site and another. We know that the broch-dwellers, in addition to catching large whales, relied heavily on stranded whales for blubber and bones for making several of their larger implements. They also engaged in fowling.[7]

The broch-dwellers used the whole specialized textile equipment of the Glastonbury culture: whorls of stone, bone and pottery; bobbins; long-handled weaving combs and slotted lengths of bone. They presumably brought the tradition of using these with them—an aspect of their culture which suggests, as previously noted, that they must have arrived with their womenfolk. To amuse themselves at home in the long winter nights they played with the same peculiar parallelepiped bone dice as are frequently found in the Somerset lake-dwellings. They hunted the deer with spears, but for the smaller game they relied upon hollow bone dart-heads as was customary in the south.

*Fig. 30*

Bronze and iron were worked in the brochs and wheel-houses, as furnaces, crucibles and moulds have been found, but metal was so

*Fig. 30 Early Iron Age bone combs from Scotland; A, Boreness cave, Kirkcudbright; B, Langbank Crannog, River Clyde (National Museum, Edinburgh)*

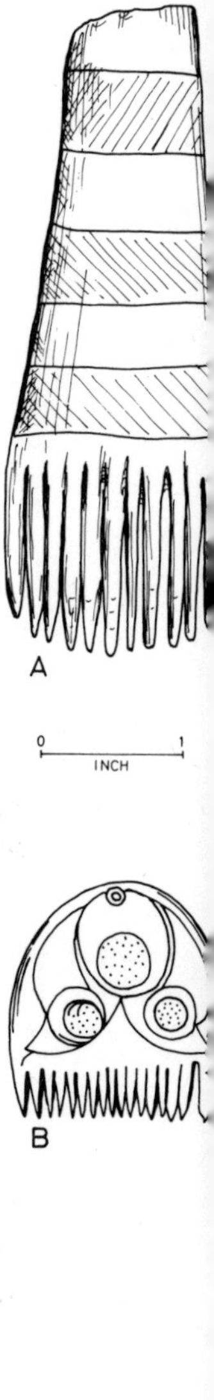


scarce that most of the tools used were either of stone or bone. One consequence of the scarcity of metal was that in the north there is nothing comparable with the magnificently decorated metalwork so characteristic of the Iron Age B and C cultures farther south. Likewise, there developed in the north a vigorous local school of pottery, but it was not of the Glastonbury type. Most of it was plain and crude compared with the beautifully decorated ware in Somerset. A few decorated pieces do occur, but they recall south-English styles of Iron Age A rather than Iron Age B tradition. Gordon Childe suggests that the south-western chiefs may well have been accompanied to the north by a number of Iron Age A subordinates.[8]

It is easy to see that many of the refinements of the south-western Iron Age B culture seem to have been left behind on the voyage northwards. No safety-pin brooches were worn, but cloaks were sometimes fastened by penannular brooches with knobbed terminals, though more often by bone pins with carved heads, or sometimes by bronze pins. Jet armlets were popular, and for controlling their horses, it would appear that the broch-dwellers used old-fashioned bits with antler cheek-pieces.

Foreign trade was at a minimum. The settlements in the Hebrides and the Western Isles were undoubtedly the most prosperous and, as their population increased, they established a slight trade contact with the Roman Province to the south. The settlements in the poorer areas on the mainland had no such contacts and their standard of living appears to have been lower. They had fewer ornaments for personal adornment and their domestic pottery lacked any form of decoration.[9]

The brochs were by no means the only settlements in the Western Isles and Highlands of the north at this time. In particular, there were frequent clusters of 'wheel-houses' in the countryside around. The wheel-houses were stone buildings laid out very much like the ground floor of a broch with attached underground chambers for the storage of food and other possessions. The wheel-houses belong, no doubt, to an older, perhaps Bronze Age population, but they have yielded remains of broch type, so must have been inhabitated contemporaneously with the brochs themselves. These facts, taken together, betoken a relatively dense population in the north-west at this time.

As Euan MacKie has shown, it would therefore appear that as a result of the uniform back-dating of the pre-Roman Iron Age sites, as revealed by C 14 dates, we must assume most of the population of proto-historic Scotland to have been established as early as the late eighth or seventh century BC, by a series of immigrations which blended with the aboriginal communities to form a diverse series of Late Bronze Age/Early Iron Age cultures. Thereafter, the population remained basically static until the early or mid-first century BC. In Atlantic Scotland, therefore, the multiplicity of cultures indicated by pottery styles makes it difficult to suggest cultural names, particularly since peoples with different cultural origins seem to have intermingled in the forts and settlements. By the time the brochs began to be built, the Atlantic cultures are so varied that they are linked only by their adoption of the tower-fort, and to a lesser extent by a few shared artifacts as we have seen.[10]

There is one final question that may be asked. What induced these mid-first century BC/mid-first century AD refugees to travel so far northward along the old sea-routes? Part of the answer may lie in the contemporary political geography. As they proceeded northwards, the only land suitable for settlement in the southern part of the Irish Sea basin was occupied by those who dwelt for the most part in the great Iron Age B hill-forts that characterized this region. Farther north was the powerful confederacy of the Brigantes that stretched across northern England, and most of southern Scotland from shore to shore, and the Brigantes would permit of no intruders. Still farther north, in Scotland on the eastern side, the Hownam culture with its palisaded sites reached up from the Tyne to the Forth, while most of the rest of Scotland was occupied by the Abernethy culture. These people were another powerful group of hill-fort dwellers, and modern radiocarbon dating indicates that they, like the Hownam people, were long and firmly established. The C 14 dating for material associated with their hill-forts suggests occupation some five centuries earlier than was previously thought. The strongest centres of the Abernethy culture were, however, in the north-east around the Moray Firth, in the Forth–Clyde valley and along parts of the western Atlantic coast. It was, therefore, in the Western Isles, in the Outer Hebrides and in northern Caithness and Sutherland, and in the Orkneys and the Shetlands, that our southern refugees found their first real opportunity to settle; even though, as it now appears, it was sometimes on older sites

*Fig. 28*

such as a midden or a semi-broch. On such sites they erected their well-known stone towers.

We have already noted that much of the settlement in the north indicates a great mixture of cultural groups, even peoples of different cultures occupying the same settlements. This implies that warfare and cultural domination by warlike groups was something curiously unimportant at this time. This atmosphere may, indeed, have facilitated settlement by small groups of strangers. There appears to be some archaeological justification for this opinion in the complete absence of weapons of war—swords, daggers, shields and the like—among the broch-dwellers. There were knives, spears and darts, but these were associated with the hunting and fishing aspects of their economy—only one sword has ever been found among them.[11] They do not appear to have had any external enemies, and it was only towards the close of the first century AD (when the colonists appear to have expanded to the limits of the fertile land available to them) that internal pressures became marked. There was much land-hunger, and inter-tribal and inter-clan raiding of cattle and other goods followed—a tradition that was to live long in the highlands of Scotland. It is for this reason that the brochs developed more and more the character of strongly defended farmsteads. By the fourth century AD serious degeneration occurred and the culture slowly declined. While some brochs continued to be inhabited until the coming of the Norsemen, their day was over. So ended the story of a spectacular civilization set up by refugees building on older foundations in these remote northern lands—a civilization that reproduced a barbaric version of the commercially prosperous and highly artistic Iron Age civilization which they had left behind in their homeland, as they took to the western seaways on the eve of the Roman invasion.

CHAPTER V

# *The Saints and the Seaways*

The thousand years that separated the spread of Iron Age peoples along the western seaways and the coming of the Anglo-Saxons into south-eastern England, following the withdrawal of the Roman troops, provides a classical example of Sir Cyril Fox's famous dictum concerning the relationship of the western seaways to the two major physiographical provinces of Britain, which he termed the highland and lowland zones. He maintained that whenever continental cultures impinged upon the lowland zone of south-eastern Britain, the western sea-routes became particularly active, as on them depended the maintenance of cultural and trade links with the Continent. On the contrary, whenever more peaceful conditions reigned over the lowland zone, the western seaways were less active, and communications with the Continent proceeded by way of the Narrow Seas.[1]

The lowland zone of Britain experienced much disturbance during the native Iron Age culminating in the invasion of the continental Belgae in immediate pre-Roman times. At this period, La Tène (Iron Age B) peoples were, as we saw in the previous chapter, moving freely along the western seaways. Following the Roman conquest in the first century AD, the Imperial power held the lowland zone firmly in its grasp; the western seaways languished and economic and cultural relations with the Continent proceeded peacefully by way of the narrow crossings of the English Channel. When, however, Roman rule collapsed in Britain, the lowland zone once more fell into confusion resulting from the Anglo-Saxon invasions, and the western sea-routes regained their importance. It was along these routes in the so-called Dark Ages that the entire western seaboard of Europe became united anew under the influence of Celtic Christianity in the Age of the Saints.

Christianity made several separate landfalls in Britain. In the first place, it is known to have been present during the period of the Roman occupation; more recently, Nash-Williams[2] has assembled the evidence to show the spread of Gallo-Roman Christianity along the sea-routes from western Gaul into Cornwall, Wales and beyond in the immediate post-Roman period. Finally, it is common knowledge that Christianity was introduced (or re-introduced) into south-eastern England at the hands of St Augustine in AD 597. We have to seek the origins of Celtic Christianity in the fusion that resulted from the contact in western Britain between what remained of Romano-British Christianity (pressed westward by the Anglo-Saxon invasions) and the incoming Gallo-Roman Christianity spreading along the sea-routes. We need to digress for a moment in order to examine a little further the various facets of Christianity involved in this fusion, and to locate, if possible, more precisely, where along the western seaboard such a fusion was most likely to have occurred.[3]

The Christianity characteristic of Britain during the Occupation was, of course, similar to that which had developed in the late Empire on the Continent—a Church ruled by bishops from their metropolitan sees. It was essentially a matter for the Roman towns and villas and not something markedly associated with the army. It may be well to stress in this context, that as far as Britain was concerned, there was a clearly marked south-eastern distribution of Roman towns and villas. For the most part, they lie south-east of a line from the Humber to the Severn, with a marked concentration in the lower Severn–Cotswold region. The latter area is interesting also because we possess considerable archaeological evidence, not only for the presence of Christianity in the region, but also for the long survival of civil life in the towns and villas, after the withdrawal of the Roman troops. In this way the Severn–Cotswold area formed an important 'growth point' for many of the hybrid cultures of western Britain in the Dark Ages. There are fairly clear indications that when the Anglo-Saxon pressure increased this late Romano–British Christianity spread beyond the Severn into what is now western Herefordshire and the Vales of Gwent and Glamorgan.

Meanwhile, new influences emanating from the East were entering the provincial episcopal Church of Gaul. The fame of the Desert Fathers of Egypt and the hermits of Cyrenaica had already reached southern Italy before the close of the fourth century, spreading into southern Gaul, and many Christians sought to emulate the ascetics. The religious viewpoint which St Martin introduced was something entirely new in Gaulish ecclesiastical tradition. That it took deep roots and flourished greatly in southern Gaul is well known. With the onset of the barbarian invasions, it would appear that Gallo–Roman Christians migrated in large numbers by way of the western sea-routes to northern lands. An anonymous author, early in the fifth century, has recorded the fact that refugees from Bordeaux and other cities in south-western Gaul made their way across the sea to southern Ireland, taking with them their culture and the last echoes of classical learning. They might even have been in part responsible for the introduction of the Christianity that was known to have existed in southern Ireland in pre-Patrician times.

When we turn to the inner branches of the sea-routes, that is to those emanating from south-western Gaul and establishing contact with the western peninsulas of Britain, we note equally intense activity. Gallo-Roman Christians, doubtless imbued with the new ideas from the East, left the traditional homeland of Gallic Christianity in the Lyon–Vienne area and spread northwards along these coastal routes. The archaeological evidence for these migrations is to be found in the numerous rough stone monuments, with a funerary inscription in Roman letters, which these early Christians apparently raised as memorials to their dead. Sometimes, the evidence locating the origin and date of this diffusion from southern Gaul is given directly, while at other times it can be inferred from the type of funerary formula employed. One of these memorials, set up at Penmachno in Caernarvonshire in north-west Wales, states that it was erected 'in the time of Justinus the Consul'. Justinus was consul in AD 540, and the use of his name was limited on the Continent to monuments in the Lyon–Vienne area. A frequently occurring formula is the
Plate 28 specifically Christian *HIC IACIT*. This originated in Italy in the late fourth century and came into fashion in Gaul early in the next, particularly in the Lyon–Vienne area. Other Christian formulae employed can be traced to North Africa, thus reminding us of Britain's links by sea with the Mediterranean when continental connections with the Classical World had broken down. These early Christian inscribed stones occur in Cornwall and Devon, and in south-west and north-west Wales, while the Isle of Man, the Galloway peninsula and the Solway area are also involved. The influence of the western sea-routes is unmistakable. It would be natural to expect to find large numbers of these memorials in southern Ireland, but this is not the case. A special consideration operated in Ireland: the island lay outside the limits of the Roman Empire and Latin was not generally known or understood. Southern Ireland has,

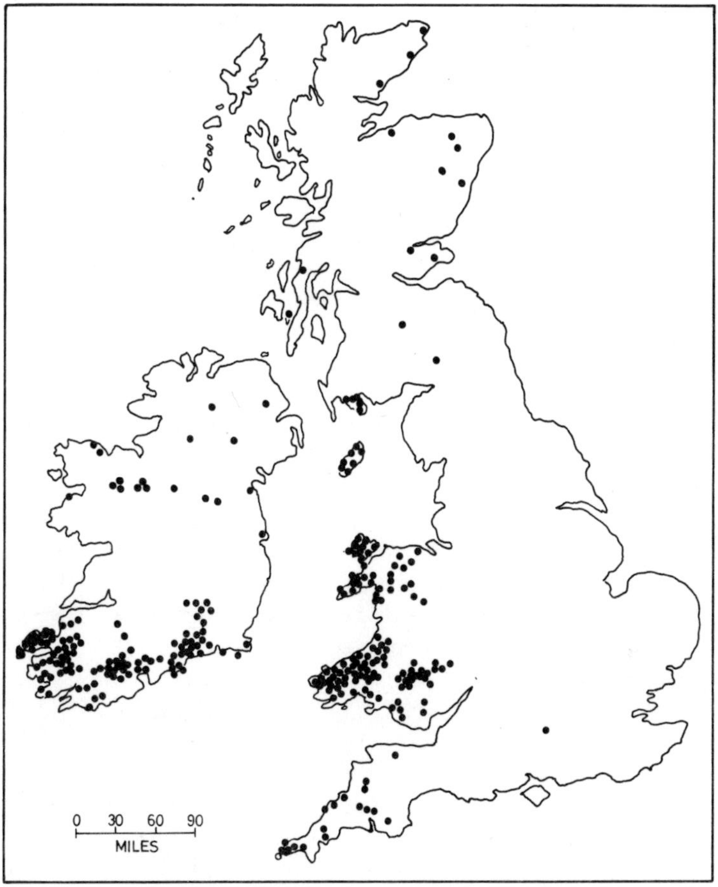


*Fig. 31 Combined distribution of Ogham and early Christian inscribed stones (after Macalister and Nash-Williams)*

however, about 300 stone memorial slabs of similar type to the Gaulish stones, but the funerary inscriptions are in Ogham writing—a form of writing based on a stroke alphabet, evolved either in Ireland or south Wales, by someone who knew Latin. It spread throughout the Celtic world for use on memorial stones. The language used in these inscriptions is old Irish. The script itself consists of twenty letters made of straight grooves and notches carved at the angle of the face and the side of the stone slab. The twenty letters are divided into four groups of five;

the first of each five consists of one mark, the second of two, and so on. The first group is made up of grooves cut on the face of the slab up against the angle; the second group is cut in the same way on the side of the slab; the third cut right across the angle of the face and side and diagonally to it; while the fourth (representing the five vowels) is shown by a series of mere notches on the angle itself. In addition to being cut on memorial stones, Ogham was certainly used in ancient Ireland for carving on short wooden message-sticks, much in the same way as notches on wooden rods were used in counting sheep.[4]

It is now generally agreed that the practice of erecting Ogham inscriptions in Ireland belonged chiefly to the fifth and sixth centuries, though it may have begun in the fourth century and certainly continued into the seventh. It is also found associated with the symbols and carvings of the Picts among whom it remained in use down to the ninth century.[5] Those found in southern Britain are in this way contemporary with the Gallo-Roman inscribed stones, and despite differences in script and language these monuments reflect a common cultural tradition of raising inscribed memorials to the dead. In western Britain there are very many instances of both languages appearing on the same stone— Latin and Ogham. There is, therefore, everything to be said for considering the distribution of the Gallo-Roman inscribed stones and the Ogham stones together, even though the latter in Ireland might never have been used in the first instance in a Christian context. The over-all distribution shows very clearly that the western seaways were in full activity at this time.

Plate 27

*Fig. 31*

Considering the historical background, it would also appear fair to assume that these Gallo-Roman/Irish wanderers were spreading many aspects of eremitical Christianity throughout the western lands. It is especially important for us to note the extent to which these refugees and colonists were able to penetrate inland from the coastal margins. Physical geographical factors, together with the number of immigrants involved, will influence this movement in most cases. The map on the opposite page suggests that the optimum conditions for penetration must have existed in the South Wales area. Here the physical conditions were suitable and there existed a useful network of former Roman roads with important trackways, linking them to the western sea-routes. In other parts of Britain penetration was more difficult. In south-western Scot-

*Fig. 32*

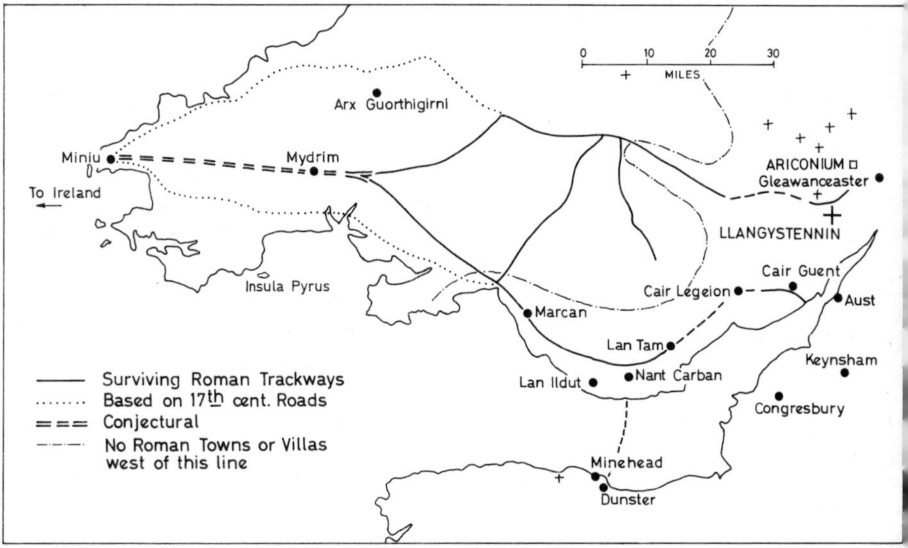


*Fig. 32 Land-ways across south Wales in the Dark Ages (after Crawford). Sites associated with the cult of St Dubricius are indicated by crosses*

land the physical conditions were reasonably suitable, but it would appear that the number of immigrants was small. Penetration from north-west Wales was impeded by the great mountain massifs and the then heavily forested lowlands of the Cheshire plain that lay beyond. In Cornwall and Devon it would appear to have been easier to have used the transpeninsular routes than to have moved inland, either across or around the great mass of Dartmoor. Therefore, all the information we possess cartographically and otherwise points to the fact that penetration eastwards was most easily achieved in South Wales, where the Gallo-Roman-Irish colonists and refugees penetrated into what is now Brecon-shire, western Herefordshire, Gloucestershire and Monmouthshire.

Thus, in the early years of the fifth century, it would appear that at least three facets of contemporary Christianity were converging on the Severn estuarine area. They included the Christian refugees from Roman Britain, carrying with them regional episcopal traditions in Church government; the Gallo-Roman Christians spreading in from the west carrying with them eremitical ideas, and finally Christians with ultimate

Irish associations strongly inclined towards Pelagianism.[6] Celtic Christianity in the Age of the Saints resulted from the fusion of these sub-cultures in this estuarine area. There is no doubt that in the immediate post-Roman period the strongest of these Christian sub-cultures in western Britain was Pelagianism. We know that Pelagius was British, and almost certainly an Irishman, and we have already noted the very strong Irish elements present in south-eastern Wales at this time. The presence of this heresy among the Irish Christians in these parts at this period, is, therefore, extremely likely. Pope Celestine evidently regarded this land as the stronghold of the Pelagian heresy for Prosper of Aquitaine, a good contemporary authority, tells us that in AD 429 he sent St Germanus, Bishop of Auxerre, as his personal representative to uproot the evil. St Germanus made two visits, the one in 429 and a second in 447. We have reason to believe that the second visit, in particular, was directed at western Britain, most likely at the country now forming the Welsh Borderland. In any case, it would appear that his missions were completely successful as we hear little more of Pelagianism in Britain. Meanwhile, the youthful Celtic Church in Wales evolved along lines similar to those found in Ireland at a somewhat later stage. There were three orders of saints or holy men. First, there were the Bishops who possessed a roving, rather than a territorial, commission. Then came the

Plate 36

second order—the holy men in charge of the great monastic houses where the monks were trained; and finally the third order—the most numerous of all—the pilgrim saints or *peregrini*, who roamed over land and sea seeking some 'desert' or lonely place wherein to abide and spend their lives in prayer, praise and meditation.[7]

There is considerable evidence for thinking that St Dubricius (Dyfrig) was a very early saint of the first order in the south-eastern

*Fig. 32*

borderlands of Wales. We have very little information about him that can be considered in any way contemporary, but cross-references to him in one of the earliest *Lives* of the saints suggest that he possessed many of the attributes of an ecclesiastic of the provincial Roman order. He is frequently referred to as *Dubricio episcopo* and *Dubricio papa*, while, with two exceptions (interesting in themselves) all the churches dedicated to

Plate 30

him are gathered in a group in south-western Herefordshire. Equally interesting is the fact that Dubricius is said traditionally to have been a pupil of St Germanus.

The outstanding saints of the second order at this early stage seem to have been SS. Illtud and Cadoc—the heads respectively of the great monasteries of Llanilltud Fawr and Llancarfan in the Vale of Glamorgan. What little detail of a presumably authentic nature that has survived concerning these men suggests very clearly that their religious background was a fusion of the provincial Roman tradition and the eremiticism associated with contemporary Gallo-Roman Christianity.

The saints of the third order seem to have wandered over the countryside, sometimes alone, and sometimes with a small band of followers. At certain places, they would set up one or two beehive cells and possibly a wooden preaching cross. In time, a little church would grow up on the site of the saint's cell, first in wattle and daub, then in timber, and, if the site proved really attractive, ultimately a stone building would be erected. The church would retain the name of its original founder, or frequently that of the founder's patron, and ultimately become one of our parish churches of today. The wandering monk would then move on, establishing more settlements on his journeys until in the end he would retire to a remote solitude, and remain engaged in praise and prayer and in working miracles until his death. It is obvious that, by plotting the distribution of churches bearing the names of these saints, we can get some idea of their respective 'spheres of influence' and the regions through which they travelled. This matter must, however, be treated with the greatest caution as it would be absurd to think that the present-day 'dedications' to Celtic saints are all originally associated with the saint in question, or that they can always be taken to indicate a saint's travels. We know, for example, that many churches were re-dedicated to famous saints in the Middle Ages, so that if we are to be concerned in this chapter with the way in which the wandering saints used the seaways in the Dark Ages, we will be on safer ground if we pay attention to the relatively insignificant and humbler men and women of the third order, who not only spread farthest afield, but whose fame during their lifetime was local, instead of concentrating on the greater saints—the men and women of the first and second orders whose cults were frequently revived in the Middle Ages.[8] With these limitations before us, we can proceed to show how the saints used the seaways. Since it is extremely likely that the Celtic Church had its origin somewhere in the Severn estuarine area, it would be appropriate to consider in the first instance the use of the south-

Plate 34

ern section of the seaways—the sea-routes which linked South Wales with south-eastern Ireland on the one hand, and with Somerset, Devon, Cornwall and Brittany, on the other.

Canon Doble was the first to show that a group of saints commemorated in the Newquay, Padstow and Bodmin area of mid-Cornwall are all in some way associated with each other.[9] The list includes SS. Petroc, Congar, Cadoc, Maugan, Hernin, Carantoc, Brioc, Gwbert and Collen. Their provenance is, however, not confined to mid-Cornwall for there are churches dedicated to all of them in Wales, and to most of them in Brittany. We can select three of the more prominent *peregrini* in this list to illustrate our point: Brioc, Carantoc and Petroc. These saints, or their cults, seem to have originated in South Wales and to have spread across the Channel to Cornwall, where we find their churches in the hinterland of the Camel estuary. From here, they and their followers used the transpeninsular route to the Fowey and thence on by sea to Brittany. Dedications to St Brioc at St Brivaels in Gloucestershire, near the head of the Severn estuary, and to St Petroc at Timberscombe near Watchet in north Somerset suggest that some of these *peregrini* may have taken the shorter crossings further up the Bristol Channel and then moved south-westward along the northern coasts of Somerset and Devon into Cornwall. Of the three examples chosen, the pattern revealed by
*Fig. 33* the dedications to St Petroc is possibly the most representative. Churches bearing his name are found at Llanbedrog in the Llŷn peninsula in
Plate 29 North Wales, at Verwig near the estuary of the Teifi, at St Petrox in south Pembrokeshire, at Timberscombe and Anstey West in Somerset, followed by eighteen dedications both in Devon and in Cornwall. In Brittany, St Petroc has nine churches and chapels dedicated to him. They are mainly in the north of the peninsula. St Brioc's churches follow very much the same pattern: Llandyfriog in south Cardiganshire is dedicated to him in close proximity to the churches of Petroc and Carantoc. Then there is St Brivaels, already mentioned, together with St Breoke, some seven miles north-west of Bodmin, in Cornwall. St Brioc was very popular in Brittany where he has thirteen surviving dedications. They occur in the Morbihan area as well as in the northern parts of Brittany. It is almost certain that Carantoc is patron of Dulane in County Meath under his Irish name of Cairnach. He appears on the Cardiganshire coast at Llangrannog, and in association with a former

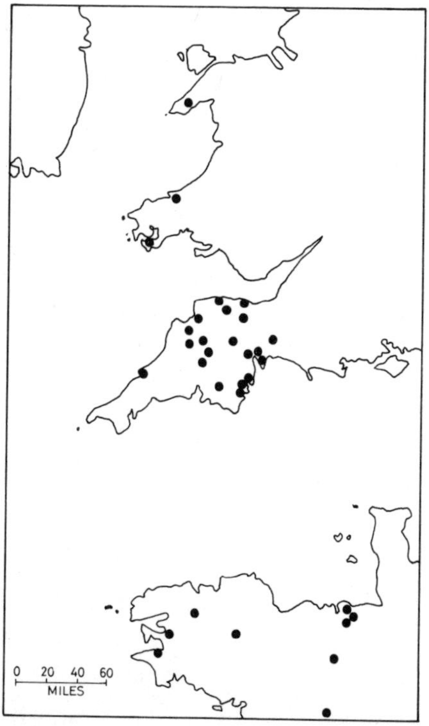


*Fig. 33 Distribution of churches dedicated to St Petroc in Wales, south-west England and Brittany*

chapel in the parish of Llandudoch in the extreme north-east of Pembrokeshire. In Cornwall he is culted at Crantock, while in Brittany, he has churches dedicated to him at Carantec, near Quimper, and at Trègarantec, south-east of Lesneven. This group of Welsh *peregrini* clearly used the western seaways linking Wales to Cornwall, Devon, Somerset and Brittany. On the other hand, we can cite examples where Irish saints arrive in Cornwall and Brittany by the sea-routes and bypass Wales altogether. This would appear to be the case with the famous group of Irish saints led by St Breaca. They appear to have landed on the extreme south-west peninsula of Cornwall, where several churches are dedicated to this saint and her companions. There is no evidence of the presence of this group elsewhere in Britain, but there are churches dedicated to several members of this saintly company in Brittany.

No claim is made for the argument that the saints in either the Welsh or the Irish group were contemporaries, or that they used the same sea-routes at the same time, or, indeed, that they necessarily moved in the same direction. All that is stressed is that most of the churches that carry the names of these wandering monks are located within easy access of the coast, and it is obvious that either they themselves or some of their immediate followers, desirous of honouring their names, did in fact use the sea-routes, linking Ireland, Wales, Cornwall and Brittany in the propagation of their faith.

It is difficult to obtain more precise details of how these combined land and sea journeys were undertaken because hardly any of the *Lives* of the Celtic saints are contemporary with the events they claim to describe. Indeed, many of them were written down nearly 600 years after the saint in question was supposed to have lived, and when all the real facts concerning him had long since been forgotten. There is, however, an important exception in the case of the *Life* of St Samson of Dol. This occurs in a text written early in the seventh century and is, therefore, a document of the greatest importance, as it is completely free from the monkish imaginations of the Middle Ages. In this *Life*, we have a detailed description of St Samson following much the same route as previously described—voyaging along the seaways and making use of transpeninsular crossings. We are told that he was visited at the monastery of Insula Pyrus (Ynys Pyr, now Caldy Island, near Tenby, in south Pembrokeshire) by some 'distinguished Irishmen' who called there on their way home from Rome. He went with them to Ireland and after a short stay he returned to Ynys Pyr taking with him an Irish 'chariot' that he thought might be useful to him in his future wanderings. On his return journey he sailed direct from Arx Etri (Dun Etair, the Howth peninsula, off Dublin) to Insula Pyrus, taking two days over the voyage. Thence he eventually crossed to Cornwall, proceeding to the monastery of Docco (now St Kew, near Padstow). There formerly stood a chapel in Padstow parish dedicated to SS. Samson and Cadoc. After a brief stay in this neighbourhood 'he arranged his journey so as completely to traverse the country'. Though the port from which he embarked for Brittany is not stated, we may confidently identify it with some haven on the estuary of the River Fowey, probably Golant, whose church is still dedicated to him. From the mouth of the Fowey he passed over to

*Figs 34, 35*

*Fig. 34 St Samson sailing to Brittany; detail from a thirteenth-century stained-glass window in the Cathedral of Dol, Brittany*

Brittany, landing in the estuary of the Rance, and proceeded towards Dol. Henceforth Dol was the centre of his activities, though he is known to have visited Paris on a political mission. He achieved great fame as the founder of the monastic Bishopric of Dol, and he and his followers are looked upon as the pioneers of the British settlement in Brittany in the post-Roman centuries. Before leaving the travels of St Samson, two further observations are of interest. We are told that when he left Ynys Pyr for Brittany, he took with him in the boat his Irish 'chariot' (or cart) for the journey across Cornwall. When he was safely landed on that peninsula, his biographer proceeds, 'sending away his ship at the same place (Padstow), he arranged for a cart to convey his holy vessels and books and harnessed two horses to his chariot which he had brought with him from Ireland'. We know that he took the same chariot with him again in his boat when he sailed for Brittany and had it with him later on his journey to Paris. Reverting for a moment to his crossing of Cornwall, we catch a glimpse of his missionary activities. On seeing a large crowd of people worshipping 'an abominable image', St Samson advanced and denounced them, and by performing a miracle, persuaded them to be baptized. To mark this achievement, he took an iron instrument and cut the sign of the Cross on a megalithic standing stone which appeared to be associated with the pagan rites. This is typical of the Celtic West—Sir Cyril Fox's 'Highland Zone'—where cultural assimilation takes precedence over cultural replacement.[10]

As already indicated, there would appear much to be said for considering the journey of St Samson as the beginning of a long process of colonization of Brittany in the Age of the Saints. The British immigrants came mainly from South Wales in the fifth and sixth centuries AD and appear to have made settlements in forest clearings. Their leaders were accompanied by ecclesiastics—the saints—to whom they were often personally related. It was the saints who negotiated settlement sites and other matters with the existing rulers, and also administered to the religious needs of the new-comers. The extensive movements which must have been involved have left few traces behind them for the archaeologist, yet the settlement is well attested by history, linguistic and place-name evidence. It is equally obvious that an extensive use of the seaways was involved, and that the rugged coast of Brittany was especially inviting to the settlers of those days. The *ria* coastline, with its numerous inlets penetrating far inland, was the territory's natural means of access. Equally important is the fact that such submerged coastlines carry with them numerous peninsulas and islands. Islands offshore had a particular fascination as settlement sites for the saints, and it was on islands that they most often made their first landings. Indeed, Largilière has suggested that it was a fixed rule that the saints of the *peregrini* class who came to settle in Brittany first tarried as hermits on the shore (most frequently an island site was selected on which a chapel, bearing the saint's name, is now usually found), and then moved inland to minister to the colonists there.[11] St Paul Aurelian's party from west Wales first landed on the island of Ushant, and it is very likely that Paul's monastery on the Ile de Batz off the north coast of Brittany was founded by him before the settlement at St Pol de Léon itself. Similarly, St Maudez settled on the Ile Modez, north-west of the Ile de Bréhat in the gulf of St Brieuc and established an early monastery there, before proceeding to his life's work in northern Brittany. The distribution of dedications in his name shows a spectacular geographical pattern based on a dispersal from the Ile Modez. Likewise, there was an ancient tradition in the great abbey of Landévennec on the coast of western Finistère that the first settlement of the founder, St Guénolé (St Winwaloe), was on the island of Tibidy

*Fig. 36*

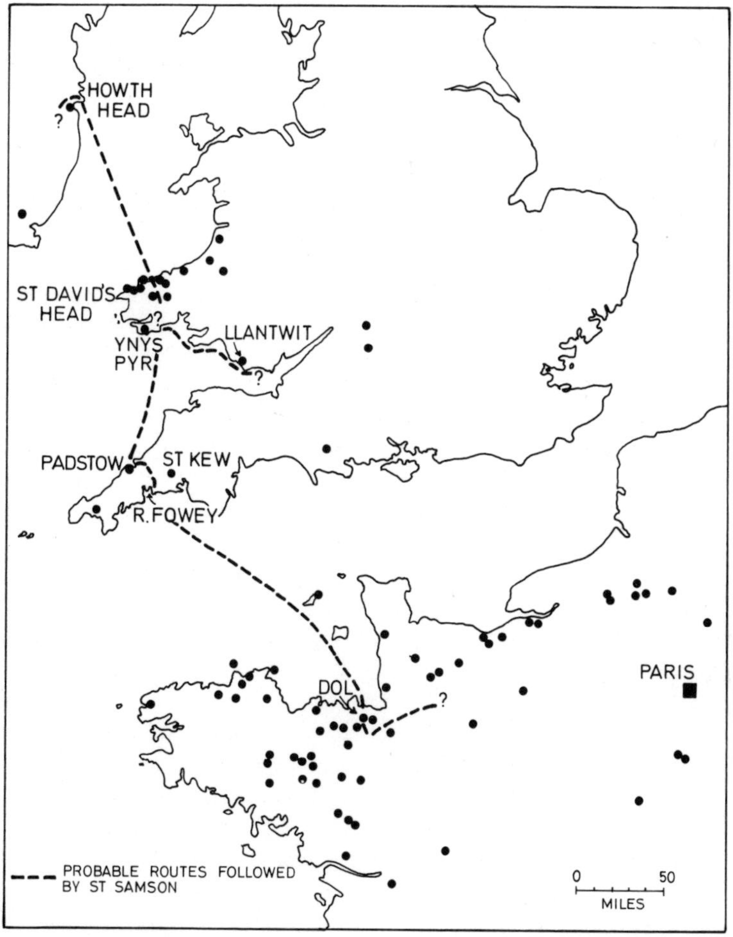


*Fig. 35 The travels of St Samson of Dol*

in a nearby inlet of the sea. Then followed the establishment of Landévennec itself on the mainland and, finally, the spread of the saint's cult from its established base as indicated by the erection of several churches and chapels bearing his name. This great Celtic monastery also had associations with Ireland and dedications to its founder occur in Cornwall and South Wales. The activity that characterized the western seaways in the Age of the Saints is immediately apparent.[12]

Before we leave this southern sector of the main sea-route it is worth considering the close contacts that must have been established between south-west Wales and south-eastern Ireland. We hear of Irish saints as frequent visitors to St David's, and of the saintly children of King Brychan of Brycheiniog (now Breconshire) establishing churches in southern Ireland; while D. A. Binchy, in his study of St Patrick and his biographers, lays great stress on the fact that the first series of Latin loan words in Irish had already been borrowed before the mission of Palladius in 431. These Latin loan words, with the aid of a few native words, were just sufficient to provide the necessary amount of Christian terminology in the initial stages. The borrowed words contained such urgently needed ones as those for Christian, priest and church. There was no word for bishop, no Irish equivalent for the Latin *episcopus*, so the first stratum of Christian loan words must have been established in the Irish language before the first bishop—Palladius—arrived. Binchy maintains that they were unquestionably introduced into southern and eastern Ireland by British Christians almost certainly from south-west Wales. It is, therefore, due to the continued use of the time-honoured sea crossings between South Wales and Ireland that Palladius (who himself is said to have landed at Arklow) was able to minister to the Irish 'already believing in Christ'.[13]

We can now turn to the middle portion of the western seaways which can roughly be described as the Solway province, encircled by Galloway, Cumbria, the Isle of Man and north-eastern Ireland, with an important exit by way of the North Channel. This is the province to which St Ninian and the historic Patrick belong. Before describing their cults, there are several matters of interest for discussion. St Ninian's famous centre was at Whithorn. We cannot but be impressed by the significance of the site especially for those using the main western sea-routes from the south. The south-western peninsula of Scotland lies astride the major route-way so that the voyager from the south would naturally sail into one of the great sea lochs, such as Luce Bay or Wigtown Bay. A little distance inland on the western side of Wigtown Bay lies Whithorn where tradition maintains that St Ninian established his first church—a whitewashed stone building, so different from the churches of the Britons that it was called Candida Casa—the White Church. Bede records that St Ninian on his return from a mission to

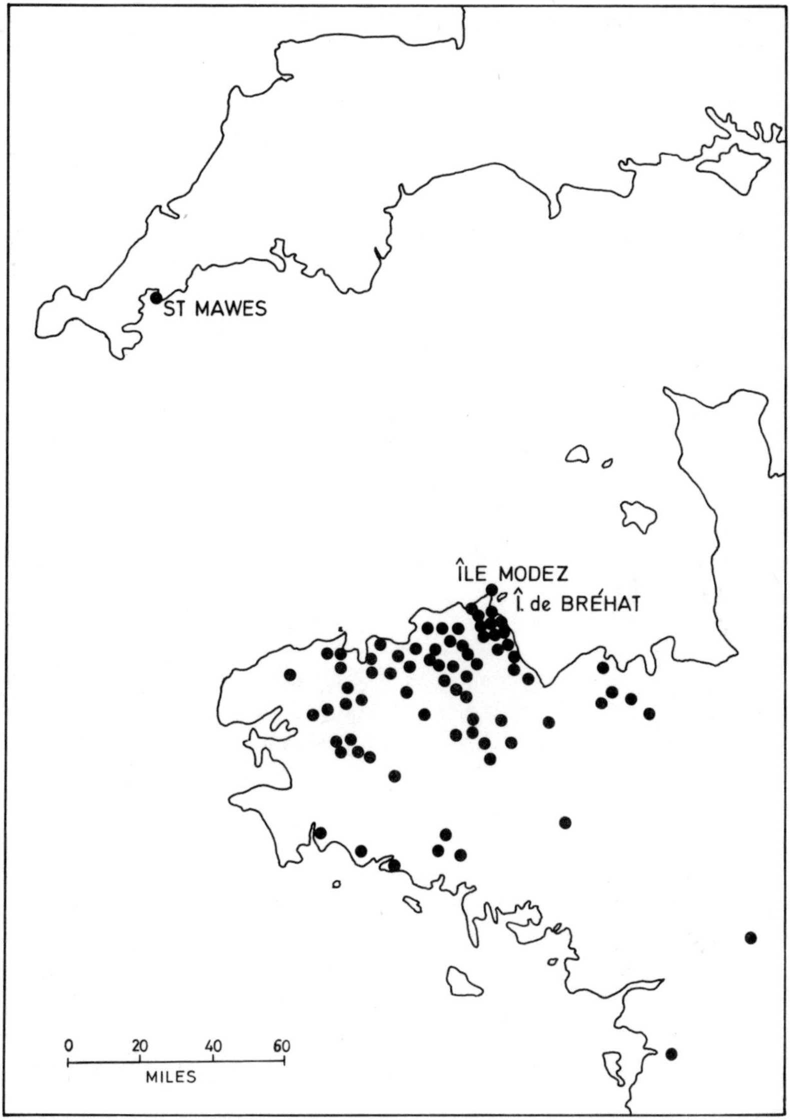


*Fig. 36 Dedications to St Maudez (St Mawes)*

Rome stayed with St Martin of Tours. In this way, Ninian is brought into direct contact with one of the foremost leaders of Western eremiticism. When it came to building his new church at Whithorn, he dedicated it to St Martin. The distribution map on p. 73 shows that in this region there is a clearly marked group of Early Christian inscribed stones similar to those found elsewhere in western Britain. There is nothing, therefore, basically improbable in Bede's story of the links between St Ninian and St Martin. The problems arise when we consider Ninian's supposed visit to Rome and the 'dedication' of his church to St Martin. A visit to Rome was considered to be essential for every early Christian bishop, and Bede would be certain to insert such a visit. But if St Ninian, in fact, did not visit Rome (as seems most likely) there arises the difficulty of linking this early dedication to St Martin in south-western Scotland, with the only other known 'dedication' to the saint at this period, in Canterbury, in south-eastern Britain. We must not, however, forget in this context the importance of the cult of St Martin in Ireland in early Christian times and hence its easy passage across the sea to south-western Scotland.[14] Most scholars now think that the really important point is that the cult of St Ninian was revived by King David I and Queen Margaret in the twelfth century in their efforts to obtain the sanction of ancient tradition for the changes they introduced in bringing the Scottish Church within the full orbit of Rome. It is to this later period also that most of the surviving dedications to St Ninian must be ascribed, thereby making their distribution meaningless in any consideration of his real life-work in the Dark Ages.

*Fig. 31*

Virtually a similar situation exists regarding St Patrick. The few facts we know about him have to be gleaned from his own writings which make it clear that he was a native of Britain—most likely of the Solway area—and that the main centre of his missionary activities lay across the water in north-eastern Ireland, where he would appear to be the founder of Armagh, possessing, like other saints, a local and limited cult in these parts. There is nothing whatsoever in his own writings to suggest that he had ever been in Gaul, and it is much more likely that the ship in which he escaped sailed to Britain and not to Gaul. Most scholars now follow Binchy, who has shown that the origins of the great legend about St Patrick are to be sought in the writings of Tírechán and Muirchú in the Book of Armagh and its derivatives, where the echoes of the historical missions of Palladius and the British Patrick are fused. The works of the latter, as the founder of Armagh were expanded and embellished, and a national hero—the founder of Christian Ireland—was born. As his legend assumed nation-wide importance, churches were dedicated to him in places to which he had never been and it would be manifestly absurd to claim that anything concerning his real work and movements during his lifetime can now be gleaned from a study of their location.[15]

When we come to a consideration of some of the lesser saints of this middle zone of the ancient seaways, a clearer picture emerges. E. G. Towill has been able to examine in some detail the distribution of the cult of St Machaoi who is so closely associated with the famous Celtic monastery of Nendrum on Maghee island in Strangford Lough in Ulster. Towill bases his study on the earlier work of E. A. F. Knight who mentions eleven sites traditionally associated with the saint. Of these, Towill accepts six as being almost certainly genuine, to which he has added a number of others. The resultant distribution brings out very clearly the close interrelationship that must have existed at this time, by way of the sea-routes, between the lands bordering the Solway province. Towill rightly points out that the sea is not a separating, but a unifying factor in the Age of the Saints, and argues that it is unbelievable that the evangelization of Galloway and Ulidia was not accomplished without the closest co-operation between the missionaries concerned. The sea-routes alone can explain how the Galloway peninsula, the Isle of Man, north-east Ireland, Kintyre, and the lands bordering the estuary of the Clyde could be united at this time within a single cultural stimulus. Towill thinks that the famous monastery of Nendrum itself was originally orientated towards Whithorn, rather than towards Armagh, and may well have been founded by St Ninian or one of his associates in the first instance, and then ruled from the middle of the fifth century to its close by St Machaoi, who is generally considered to be the original founder.[16]

*Fig. 37*

Turning to the northern section of the sea-routes, we witness the same intense activity as in other areas in the Age of the Saints. The route that reached back to the days of the Connacht–Carlingford–Clyde culture of Megalithic times was again much in evidence. The movement across the sea from northern Ireland was led by the great Columba who appears to have followed in the wake of the Irish colonists of Dalriada—a territory in western Scotland roughly equivalent to the modern Argyll.

Plate 39 Columba landed on Iona in 563 and from this base emanated a culture whose religious and linguistic aspects were to spread widely in Scotland north of the Forth–Clyde isthmus. Its influence spread south-eastwards, too, reaching not only southern Scotland and the Northumbrian coast, but later most of highland Britain. St Columba's fame spread far and wide and many churches throughout the land claimed association with him, or were otherwise eager to bear his name. We even hear of a Christianized Norseman in distant Iceland dedicating a church there to Columcille in the tenth century. A study of the distribution of churches and chapels bearing the name of the great saint, therefore, raises exactly the same problems as those bearing the names of St Patrick, St Ninian, St David, or, for that matter, St Bride (Bridget) or St Kentigern.

We must turn to St Columba's followers if we wish to study dedication–distribution problems, as it seems more likely that their dedications were established during their lifetime. St Chattan, for example, confined his activities to the Dalriadan culture area, others, like St Moluag seem to have operated in the territory of the Picts, while St Maelrubha kept
*Fig. 37* more strictly to the sea-lanes around the Western Isles. These distributions have an interest not only in the way in which they reflect the use of the sea-routes, but also in the way they reflect, in the Age of the Saints, the re-emergence of the major culture areas of Scotland very much as they were in prehistoric times.[17]

We have now shown the use of the western seaways by *peregrini* from Sutherland to Finistère. The story would, however, be incomplete if we were not to mention the voyages of the *peregrini* far beyond these limits into the dark and stormy waters of the North, on the one hand, and into the brighter and warmer lands of the South, on the other. We will examine the southern end of the sea-route first of all. We remember that during prehistoric times the sea-routes reached into the western basin of the Mediterranean sea, including even the North African coasts. The major routes followed the Straits of Gibraltar as well as the Narbonne–Carcassonne land-crossing. There is abundant evidence that they continued in use down to the Age of the Saints and beyond. There is also direct evidence for the expansion of the Celtic Church into north-west Spain. It is well attested by the presence of the Celtic monastery of Santa Maria de Bretoña near Mondoñedo in Galicia. No one knows exactly when, or by whom, it was established, or whether the stimulus came from

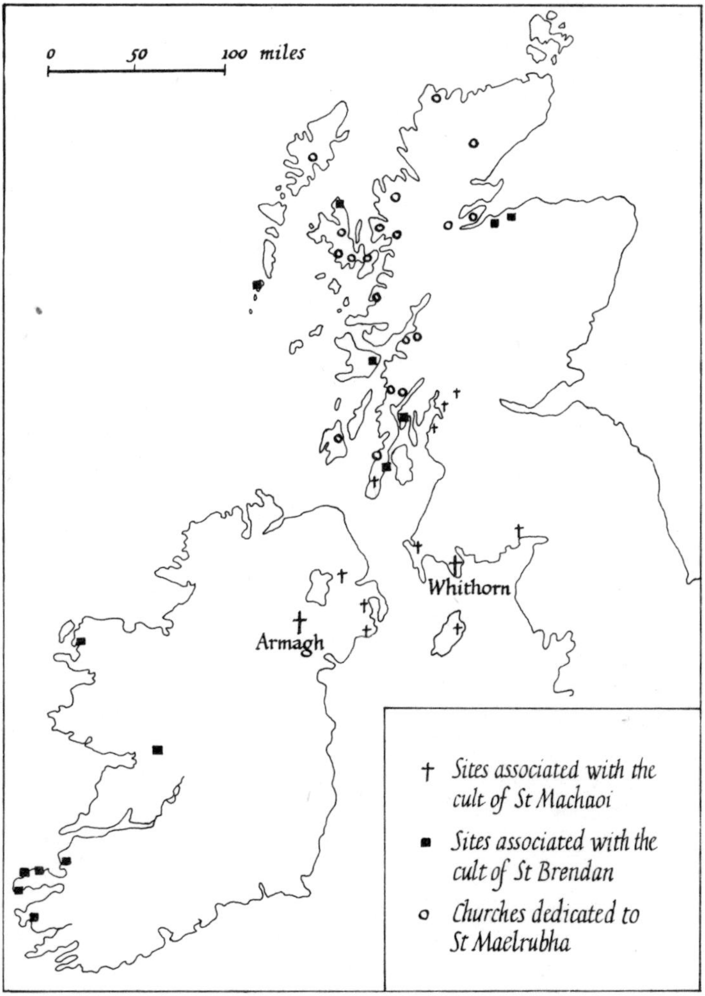


*Fig. 37 Distribution of sites associated with the cults of saints in the north*

Ireland or Britain, or even from Brittany. All we know is that the church and monastery were included in the episcopate of Bretoña in a list dating from Suevic times, and that one of their bishops was named Mailoc—sufficient evidence, if necessary, of a Celtic association.[18] How long the links between the Celtic Church of Galicia and the major centres in north-western Europe lasted, we do not know. They could not, in any case, have survived the Arab conquest of North Africa and Spain in the late seventh and eighth centuries. The Arab conquests of Bordeaux and Aquitaine, although less lasting, must have severed completely the old connections of this area with the Celtic lands, for they resulted in the virtual cutting off from the Celtic world of the southern section of the great sea-route. It is true, however, that with the recession of the Arab tide, direct relations between north-west Spain, south-west France and the Celtic lands to the north once more took shape, but they never again assumed the dominant role they played in the Early Christian period. While the southern portions of the western sea-routes were cut off by the spread of Islam, the northern sections remained unmolested until the coming of the Vikings. Thus, in the eighth and ninth centuries in particular, British, and especially Irish, *peregrini* moved into the stormy, empty waters of the North. They reached not only the Orkneys and Shetlands, but succeeded in establishing their primitive Christian settlements in the Faroes and in distant Iceland as well. When St Columba visited the court of King Brude near Inverness, the king, at the saint's request, was able to give instructions for the safety of Cormac and other ecclesiastics sailing in northern waters. As things turned out, these instructions saved Cormac's life when he landed in the Orkneys. Adamnán, St Columba's biographer, tells of another voyage of Cormac in which he was under full sail before a southerly wind for fourteen days and nights, holding a straight course towards the north until he seemed to pass beyond the limits of human journeying and beyond the hope of return. It is possible that on this occasion Cormac visited the Shetlands, perhaps the Faroes and, possibly, Iceland itself.

In the *Imrama*, or travel tales, of the Irish saints there occur many passages which seem to reflect experiences in high latitudes with blowing whales and volcanoes belching fire and smoke. The best known Irish *Imrama* records the travels of St Brendan in search of an ideal earthly Paradise or Land of Promise.[19] We find churches dedicated to this famous Irish saint and seaman throughout the coastal zone of western Ireland and Scotland. Here are 'the Seas of the Oceanic Border' as described by the British geographer Sir Halford Mackinder. We have already referred to these coastlands in another context—they were, above all, the natural abode of intrepid seamen. We can, if we so desire, leave aside the hagiological literature and the *Imrama* of St Brendan and turn

*Fig. 37*

to the more sober contemporary literary evidence. This shows that the Irish *peregrini* not only knew of Iceland and the Faroes but actually lived in these islands for sixty or seventy years before their discovery by the Northmen. In the *Liber de Mensura orbis Terrae* written in the year 825 by an Irish monk named Dicuil we hear about the islands that lie north of Britain, based on information gleaned from the *peregrini* themselves. In a famous passage, Dicuil says, 'There are many other islands in the ocean north of Britain . . . on these islands hermits who have sailed from our Scotia (Ireland) have lived for roughly a hundred years. But even as they have been constantly uninhabited since the world's beginning, so now, because of Norse pirates, they are empty of anchorites, but full of innumerable sheep and a great many different kinds of sea fowl. I have never found these islands mentioned in the books of scholars.'[20] It is generally accepted that Dicuil was speaking here about the Faroes, which appear to have been discovered by the Irish saints about AD 700, and lived in by them until about the second decade of the ninth century. There can be little doubt that towards the end of the eighth century Irish monks reached Iceland also. Written records which exist show that when the first Norse arrived in Iceland, there were already Irishmen resident there. They were Christians and they refused to live with the heathen Vikings, so they departed, leaving behind their Irish books, bells and croziers by which their nationality and character were established. These were the *papar*—the monks and anchorites. From place-name evidence it is clear that there was a sprinkling of these *papar* over much of the south-eastern part of the island, which is the most likely landfall for ships coming from the south.

We have sought in this chapter to describe a great Celtic thalassocracy reaching from Iceland to Spain and united under a single cultural stimulus. The seventh century was the age of the greatest achievements of the Celtic Church, and the Emerald Isle shone like a beacon in the darkness of contemporary Europe. Irish monks were not only reaching Iceland in the north, but were encircling the British shores and penetrating the Continent by ways of the great estuaries of the Gironde, the Loire, the Seine and the Somme, and establishing churches and monasteries throughout Central Europe. Among them was probably the greatest Irish missionary of all—St Columbanus, whose influence reached beyond the Alps into Italy itself.[21]

CHAPTER VI

# *The Seaways in Reverse*

The close of the eighth century AD saw the beginnings of a vast movement of peoples—raiders, plunderers, settlers and traders from the Scandinavian lands—a movement which, in time, was to affect Europe from Rouen to Reykjavik, and from Wexford to Kiev. Of the three Scandinavian groups, it was only the Norwegians (the Norsemen) and the Danes who raided and settled in Western Europe, since the Swedes were mainly interested in Eastern Europe. These great sea-warriors were collectively known as the Vikings, a term which has often been loosely used, but originally appears to have been applied to the Norsemen, since they came from the numerous creeks and bays along the Norwegian coast known as fjords or *viks*.

The causes of this great exodus have often puzzled historians, and there can be little doubt that they are many and complex. Some emphasize the political factors, including the reaction of the older elements in Scandinavian society to the growing power of royalty; others see a great increase in population in these countries at this time and a consequent pressure on the land, leading to a great exodus of the younger men in search of new homes. Others, again, see behind these movements vast enterprises organized for the combined purpose of piracy and trade. The love of adventure and the thrill of battle alone cannot be overlooked. To be a Viking—and one might coin a phrase, 'to go viking'—was a trade or a profession, a means to the good life or, at least, to a living. Its three main elements, trade, piracy and land-taking, were often closely blended, as had happened with other people many times before and was destined to outlast the particularly turbulent times we have come to associate with the 'heathens' of the Viking Age.[1]

The great migrations for which these people are so famous could in the eighth century be undertaken with confidence, for by then the arts of shipbuilding and seamanship were more advanced in Scandinavia than in other parts of Europe. Thus, the Vikings could accomplish the long sea voyages, not only to the islands of Britain and the shores of northern France, but to far-off Iceland and Greenland, and even America itself. They also voyaged extensively southwards entering the

Mediterranean sea and penetrating up the great rivers of Russia. Much is known of their ships, not only from the Norse Sagas, but also from the remains of actual vessels. It was a common custom for a chieftain to be buried in his ship, the whole grave being covered with a mound or *how*. Several such vessels have been discovered by archaeologists, the most famous being those of Gokstad and Oseberg on the shores of the Oslo fjord and that at Sutton Hoo in East Anglia; more recently, five Viking ships scuttled in the eleventh century to block a narrow fjord near Roskilde in Denmark have been salvaged.[2] Viking ships were shallow, narrow in the beam, and pointed at both ends. In this way they were suitable for handling in creeks and bays, while they could easily be run up onto the beaches. Each ship had but one large heavy square sail and, when a naval battle was in progress, it depended for its movement on its oarsmen. The number of the latter varied with the size of the vessel, but on an average each ship had ten rowers on either side. Since these ships would often have to be rowed both day and night against a contrary wind, many more men would be needed, while others would be required to fight. The Gokstad ship, for example, was an oak vessel with seats for sixteen pairs of rowers and was 78 feet long and 16 feet broad amidships. We have records of far larger Viking ships than this—vessels carrying up to sixty pairs of rowers are known to have existed. Various representations of these ships (as for example on the Bayeux Tapestry—the Norman vessels in which are based on Viking prototypes) show the decorated shields of the warriors hung outside the bulwarks, and the vessel being steered by an oar on the starboard side.[3] The bow and stern rose high above the water, the former looking very grim, being carved as a serpent's, or as a fierce-looking dragon's head. At the end of last century an exact model of the Gokstad ship was made, and in 1893 it was sailed across the Atlantic in less than a month, leaving Norway on 30 April and reaching Newfoundland on 27 May after a stormy crossing. The captain and crew were full of praise for the very skilful way in which a vessel like this and all its equipment was contrived.[4]

Plate 42

Plate 54

Plate 41

The Norwegians who first appeared as the plunderers of the island monastery of Lindisfarne, lying off the Northumberland coast, in 793 and of Iona in 795, had some years previously left the coastal provinces of Norway in search of new homes in the islands of north and north-west Britain. Their first settlements in the Shetlands and Orkneys seem to have been carried out peacefully. They appeared as farmers and fisher-men. But these islands were obvious stepping-stones, not only to Caithness and the east coast of England, but especially for expeditions to the Outer Hebrides and the chain of islands off the Scottish coast that led naturally to Ireland and the lands around the Irish Sea. In this way, the long-established western sea-routes came to be used in reverse and Norse culture began to spread freely along them to the South. It is not surprising that these Norwegian settlers in the islands of northern Britain should have sought supplies and treasure wherever they could, but after the first few raids, they seem to have left England to the Danes and directed their efforts to their new island homes, and to Ireland in particular, which, with its indented coastline and navigable rivers was easily accessible to sea-borne rovers.[5] In this chapter we shall be concerned with the Norwegian raiders off the western coasts of Britain, but we must not overlook the fact that the Danes who settled mainly on the eastern side of England did eventually come through the English Channel and even across northern England and raided, not only the lands forming the Western Approaches to Britain, but also found themselves in conflict with Norsemen in Ireland who had arrived by the western route. Like-wise, the Norse from Ireland and the Danes from their bases on the north coast of France participated greatly in movements which involved the *Fig. 38* southern section of the western sea-routes—routes which led these sea-farers into France, Spain and the Mediterranean lands. First of all, however, we must return to a more detailed consideration of the use made by the Norsemen of the northern section of the seaways.

If the Norse chose to settle in the Orkneys and Shetlands and the Western Isles off Scotland because these islands were on their main route southwards, they were even more attracted by a physical environment very similar to that which they had left behind in south-western Norway. The techniques of fishing, farming and bird-catching, which they had developed at home, could be used in these islands with little or no adaptation. Ireland, however, had much more to offer. The physical conditions were much more attractive, and there were the rich monas-teries which housed tempting and accessible stores of wealth. Ireland, therefore, soon became their major objective.

They handled the situation in their usual way; first came raiding, then the establishment of permanent fortified bases, from which further

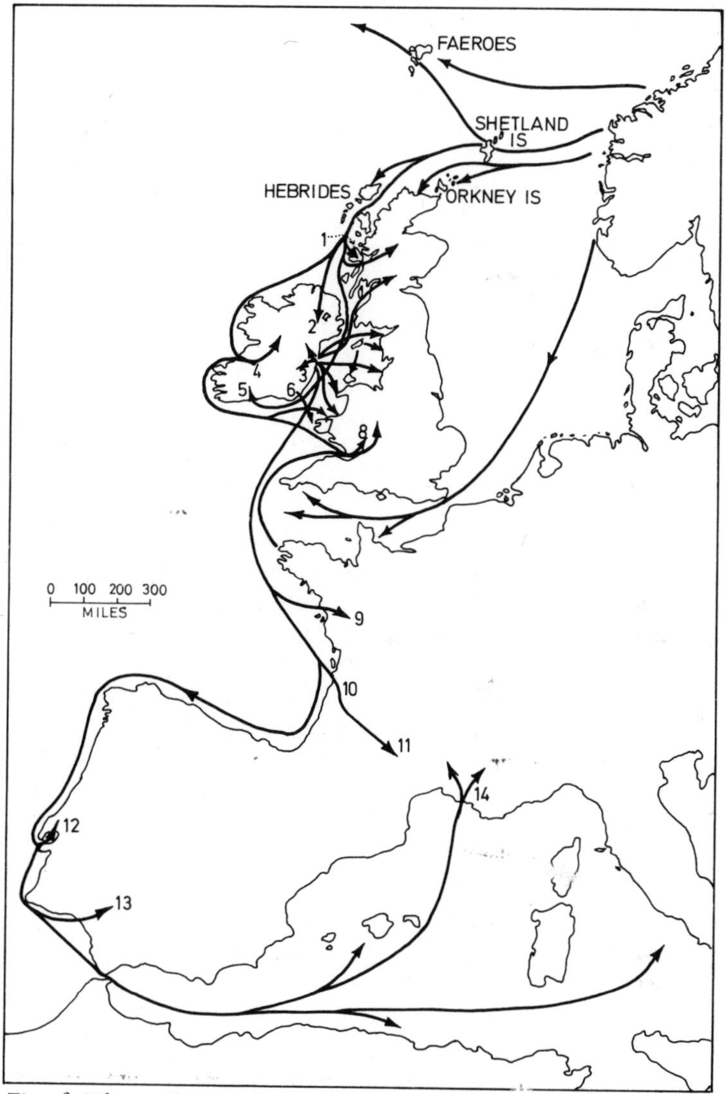


*Fig. 38 Viking raids along the western sea-routes. 1 Iona, 2 Armagh, 3 Dublin, 4 Limerick, 5 Cork, 6 Wexford, 7 St David's, 8 Archenfield, 9 Nantes, 10 Garonne, 11 Toulouse, 12 Lisbon, 13 Seville, 14 Rhône delta*

raiding took place, and finally they became permanent settlers. The Irish coast suffered sporadically from raiders ever since the first attack in 795 on the small island of Lamber, off-shore, just north of Dublin. It was the suddenness of these raids and the inability to tell where the next one would fall, rather than their over-all effect on the economy, that struck terror into the hearts of the Irish. The monasteries, for obvious reasons, suffered most, and we have a vivid picture of one poor monk seated in his little hut near the coast describing in verse how glad he was that the terrible storm raging outside would at least prevent the pirates from approaching the shore that night. His Gaelic verse in translation reads:

Plate 46

> The wind is boisterous tonight
> The white hair of the ocean is tousled.
> I do not fear that there may come across the Irish sea
> hordes of fierce Vikings.[6]

So grim had the position become by 820 that the *Annals of Ulster* could record that 'the sea spewed forth floods of foreigners over Erin, so that no haven, no landing place, no stronghold, no fort, no castle might be found but it was submerged by waves of Vikings and pirates.' It was in response to this situation that many of the characteristic tall round towers of the Irish monasteries were erected. These towers combined the functions of a watch-tower, a belfry, and a place of refuge for the monks, where at the same time were stored the monastic treasures. Some towers reached 100 feet in height, with doorways always several feet above ground level.

By the middle of the ninth century new arrivals, apparently direct from Norway, appeared off northern Ireland led by a great warrior-chieftain—Turgeis. They appeared to be bent on permanent settlement. Armagh—a city of great prestige—was captured by them, and the great harbour strongholds of Dublin, Dundalk, Wexford, Waterford, Cork and Limerick were established at this period. There was certainly a deeper penetration inland than had ever been experienced before, for the sack of the great monasteries of Clonmacnois and Clonfert is laid at Turgeis's door. From the harbour bases extensive raids were carried out on all the lands surrounding the Irish Sea.[7]

The situation was further complicated in 850 when a Danish fleet put into Carlingford Lough. The Danes might very well have come from north-west England or even around by way of the English Channel. In any case, in the following year they overran the Norwegian base at Dublin. They appear to have been fighting both the Norse and the Irish indiscriminately, but gradually they were defeated. In 853 the Norse made a re-entry into Ireland on a large scale with a royal fleet under the command of Olaf, son of the King of Norway. The remaining Danes soon left for Britain and Olaf settled into Dublin. Thereafter followed a period of comparative peace which is said to have lasted for forty years. The year 914 seems to have initiated another period of Norse activity, and in 922 there was further settlement in the south-west. Many authorities attribute the settlements at Cork and Limerick to this period. The Norsemen in Ireland were not finally defeated until the Battle of Clontarf in 1014. Thereafter, we can say that Celtic and Scandinavian cultures in Ireland entered upon a period of fusion, producing during the next two centuries some remarkable achievements in Celtic–Norse Christian art.

Neither the historical events just recorded, nor the fascinating cultural fusions that resulted, form, in themselves, the main theme of this book. We must revert to the part played by the sea-routes, not only in bringing about this situation, but, by the use of the cross-channel routes, as of old, in rediffusing these hybrid cultural developments throughout the Celtic lands. Before concentrating on the cross-routes, it should be noted that there is much evidence to suggest that the Norsemen in their southern progress into Ireland used not only the inner Western Isles–North Channel route, but also the western oceanic route—the route-way that once carried the Connacht–Carlingford–Clyde culture in megalithic times, and St Brendan the Navigator in a later age.

Let us look first of all at the long-established Irish-Strathclyde crossing. In 865 the *Annals of Ulster* record that Olaf (who had settled a decade or so earlier in Dublin) together with another Norse chieftain named Audgisl raided the land of the Picts in Scotland, while four years later Olaf, with the assistance of yet another Norse chieftain, besieged Dumbarton on the Clyde, and after four months succeeded in capturing it, enabling the raiding party to return to Dublin 'with two hundred ships and a great spoil of people—of English, Britons and Picts'.[8]

Farther south, the traditional links between northern Ireland and north-west England are clearly indicated at this period by the mixed Norse–Irish secondary settlement established on the English side of the Irish Sea.

It is well illustrated by the recorded settlement of Ingimund and his followers (most likely from the Carlingford Lough area) in the Wirral peninsula in the year 912. Throughout north-western England, one of the results of this immigration is the large number of place-names combining the Irish word *airghe* (a shieling) with a Norse personal name, as in Goosnargh.

*Fig. 39*

North-west Wales was also raided by the Norse from their Dublin base. Viking remains in the form of weapons, ornaments and coins have been recorded in Anglesey and on the Arfon coast, not to mention such obvious Norse place-names as Great Orme's Head, Priestholm and Bardsey. Anglesey would also appear to have been raided by Vikings based on the Isle of Man. Sea-contacts between Man and north-west Wales are very well known, and are much in evidence throughout prehistoric times. The Isle of Man, by virtue of its central location, was in contact with other areas around the Irish Sea at this time. We shall return later in this chapter to a consideration of the full significance of the Isle of Man in the Age of the Vikings.

Further south we find abundant evidence of Scandinavian raiders and traders from their bases in Ireland and elsewhere making their presence felt in South Wales. This is yet another reflection of the continued use of this well-known cross-route in the Irish Sea. The Norse imprint in this area remains strong in place-names, such as Swansea and Womansby, and, more particularly, in the names of islands and navigation points along the north shores of the Bristol Channel. We have Skokholm and Caldy, Flat Holm and Steep Holm and many others besides. By 914 the Vikings were moving far inland. In this year they captured a bishop at a spot as far removed from the coast as Archenfield in Hereford; but soon there came a respite. This was due to the fact that between 918 and 952 South Wales was ruled by a powerful king (Hywel Dda—Howell the Good) who kept the raiders at bay. His death, however, was a signal for renewed activity. First, the Norse of Dublin and then those of Limerick, together with their compatriots from Man, descended on South Wales. The raids increased in number and violence after 980. The cathedral of St Davids—a very obvious target—was sacked four times between 982 and 989, and Norse armies offered their services to one scuffling Welsh prince after another.[9] Later on, small well-defended marts were set up on the coast, and Norse merchants maintained a brisk trade in Welsh slaves, horses, honey, malt and wheat in exchange for Irish (or Irish-imported) wines, furs, hides, whale oil, butter and coarse woollen cloth.[10] The final settlement phase, as strongly suggested by place-names, seems to have taken place in southern Pembrokeshire and in the Vale of Glamorgan.[11]

With the sea-routes again in full activity, one would have expected to find references to Irish–Norse contacts with both Cornwall and Brittany. Little is known of these. Between 836 and 842 the southern coast of Cornwall was severely tested by Danish raiders, but appears to have put up a very stubborn resistance and little is heard of Danish or other Scandinavian settlement in Cornwall and Devon thereafter.[12]

Although this chapter is called *The Seaways in Reverse*, it would be unwise to think that there was no movement whatsoever in a northerly direction. For example, we hear of King Edward the Elder early in his reign repulsing a powerful fleet of Vikings from Brittany which had entered the Severn and plundered extensively in the English Border counties and South Wales before moving on to Ireland. These movements are strongly reminiscent of similar contacts between the Severn estuarine area and Brittany in Megalithic times. Likewise, there was an important migration from Ireland northwards to Iceland in the second half of the ninth century. We know that the Norse colonization of Iceland began about 870 and while many of the colonists came directly from Norway a large number were Norsemen who had earlier settled in Britain, some of them having Irish wives or slaves. We know, too, that several famous Icelanders in the tenth century had Irish names and that some even had Irish nick-names. Here then is an illustration of seafaring activity directed once again, as in the Age of the Saints, almost to the northernmost limits of the western sea-routes.[13]

We cannot leave the story of the seaways in Northern waters in Viking times without referring once again to the unique position of the Isle of Man as a focus of ways in the Irish Sea basin. While it might well have received much of its Norse culture directly from the sea, it is equally clear that much came from northern and eastern Ireland. It was certainly in close touch with north-western England and the Solway Firth area during the Hiberno–Norse colonization of these territories. Its contacts with Anglesey and north-west Wales are equally well known and we have already noted that Norse settlers in Man joined their colleagues in raids on St David's in Pembrokeshire. In Viking times, therefore, as in all earlier periods when the western sea-routes were in full activity, the Island in virtue of its position acted as the hub of a number of radiating routes. In this way, it became a significant base for Norse activity in the Irish Sea. The famous *Orkneyingers Saga* frequently mentions that the Vikings would set out from the Island in the spring or early summer to raid neighbouring coasts, after which they would 'fare back to Man' in the autumn before the winter storms began.[14]

Plates 44, 45

After the final defeat of the Norse in Ireland at Clontarf, it became clear that the main sources of Norse activity lay in the Western Isles of Scotland, and in the Isle of Man, and gradually Man became the centre from which these scattered territories along the great sea-route were administered. In this way the Kingdom of Man and the Isles evolved. It was Godred Crovan (King Orry)—a typical Norse warrior-chief, he had become King of Man in 1079—who was really responsible for the union of Man and the Isles into one kingdom. He also devised an ingenious political system to administer his great thalassocracy, echoes of which still survive in the constitution of the House of Keys—the present Manx Parliament. Except for brief intervals, his descendants ruled this sea-state (or the major part of it) until 1265. Meanwhile, one of Godred's descendants, King Olaf I (1113–53) formed during his reign a bishopric of 'Man and the Sudreys' which was placed under the Archbishop of Trondjheim in Norway. Sudreys was another name for the islands off western Scotland, to distinguish them from the Nordreys or Northern Isles which included the Orkneys and Shetlands. Later, the word Sudreys was changed to Sodor; so the bishopric became known as the bishopric of Sodor and Man. It persisted in the territorial sense down to the fifteenth century, although it was then administered by the Archbishops of York. At the present time, although there is no longer any connection politically or ecclesiastically between Man and the Isles, the title of Bishop of Sodor and Man is still retained by the Manx bishop as a reminder of Norse days—clearly forming yet another echo of a one-time maritime empire based directly on this portion of the ancient sea-route.

It is worth while taking a final look at this northern area on evidence based on place-names. The over-all picture is shown on the map on the opposite page, which bears striking testimony to the story of the Norse colonization of Celtic Britain by way of the western sea-routes. The most

*Fig. 39*

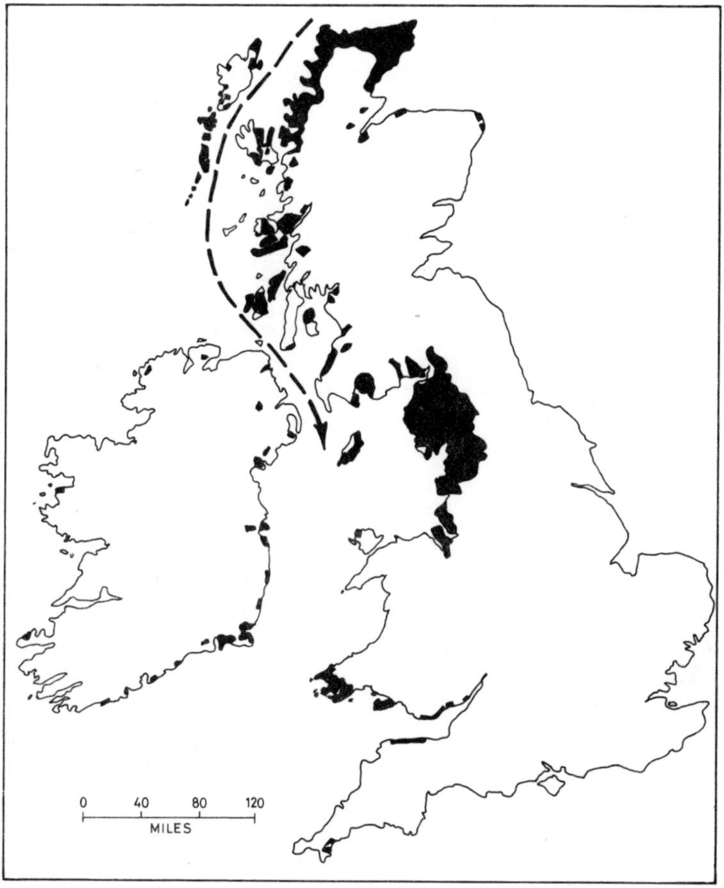


*Fig. 39 Distribution of Scandinavian place-names along the western seaways (after Taylor and Collingwood)*

numerous and distinctive place-names encountered are those ending in -*by* (a Scandinavian term for a farm or homestead), so that Sulby originally meant Sul or Sol's farm; -*thwaite* (a clearing or paddock) as found in Garthwaite, and Ickenthwaite in north-west England; -*holm* (an islet) and -*wick* (originally *vik*, meaning a creek) as in Burryholm, Gateholm, Fishwick and Goodwick. In spite of the spectacular evidence brought out by the map, we should remember that little is known of the date when these names were first given. It could as well have been the

Ostmen of Dublin in the twelfth century, as the Vikings in the tenth, who perpetuated our -holms and -wicks, our -eys and -bys. Great care is needed, therefore, in putting forward arguments in favour of heavy Scandinavian settlement in any area, based on place-names alone, unless their occurrence is strongly supported by archaeological or contemporary literary evidence.[15]

We can now turn our attention to the southern section of the great sea-route used very largely by the Danes who came across the southern North Sea and along the north coast of France towards Brittany, but also frequented by the Norse who came in all probability from Ireland and not direct from Norway. In this way, the movement of both Danes and Norse together would appear to indicate that they sailed and ravaged along the entire western seaways from north to south.

As early as 799 Danish pirates raided various small islands lying off the coast of Aquitaine in southern France. As in the North, this was a presage of colonization which the future would not belie. As the Carolingian Empire grew weaker and became rent with internal strife, so did the Viking raids and the penetration of the countryside increase. The second phase which followed raiding and preceded settlement is well illustrated by the Viking occupation of the island of Noirmoutier at the mouth of the Loire. Here was an ideal site for the establishment of a fortified mart: as an island, it was easy to defend and relatively free from assault. Noirmoutier was also the centre of a considerable trade in salt and wine from the Loire valley and, indeed, had been important in the Age of the Saints, for we remember that they, like the Vikings, had a marked predilection for island sites.[16] In 842 the Norsemen made a well-documented appearance in this part of France. A fleet of 67 ships of the men of Vestfeld (the historic region of Børre, Oseberg and Gokstad in Norway—but coming now in all probability from Ireland) appeared unheralded off the mouth of the Loire. At this time there was rivalry in France between Charles the Bald and the rebel Count Lambert. An interesting geographical side-light on the story is that the Vikings are said to have come at Lambert's invitation and that it was French pilots in his employ who took them through the sandbanks and shallows and uncertain watercourses which in high summer were judged to be an absolute protection against naval assault. Having obtained an easy entry in this way the Norsemen proceeded to the sack of Nantes which was more than the count had bargained for. The Norwegians were, however, driven off and withdrew to Noirmoutier. Contrary to Norse practice, they settled here for the winter 'as if they meant to stay for ever', as the chronicler put it. This is the first recorded instance of a Viking force using a winter base outside their homeland. Hitherto, it was the practice for the leaders to have their men and ships out in the late spring and early summer and to fetch them home again in autumn. 'To go Viking' was originally a seasonal occupation; but the winters were warmer on the French Atlantic coast and the sea never froze over—so why go home at all? Later on, the practice of wintering especially on islands in lands of temperate climate became more frequent, as we know from the occupation of Thanet in 850 and of Sheppey in 855, and we have already referred to wintering in the Isle of Man as a well-nigh regular custom.

We must now follow Norse progress still further southwards on the time-honoured routeways. In the middle of the ninth century a fleet, said to be composed of as many as 150 ships, entered the Gironde estuary in southern France and plundered up-river almost as far as Toulouse. Civil war raged at the time in this part of France, too, between Charles the Bald and Pepin, over the kingdom of Aquitaine. The raid was said to be in support of Pepin, and whatever happened it is significant that his own town of Toulouse was not sacked. The fleet returned down the river intact and is next heard of off the coast of Asturias in northern Spain. Opposition here was very strong and the raiders suffered heavily both by land and sea. A depleted, though still formidable, fleet escaped around Cape Finisterre and proceeded southwards to Lisbon. After several skirmishes in this area they continued southwards to the mouth of the Guadalquivir. Having established their camp on the island of Qubtil (now Isla Menor) nearby they then proceeded up-stream and attacked Seville.

It would appear that the Moors who had but recently conquered these parts of Spain, were stronger than the French of Charles the Bald. Abd-al-Rahman II alerted his allies in Tangier of the danger with the result that the Norse were forced to come to some agreement with this able and powerful Sultan. It was arranged to send a deputation, accompanied by gifts, to 'the great Northern King' who is also referred to as 'King of the Majus'. The king in question is difficult to identify under this title, but if the Vikings were Norse then he might very well have been

Turgeis, at the time the most important Viking chieftain in Ireland; this identification is all the more likely since he is said to have ruled over one big island in the ocean (which might be Ireland itself), that nearby there were other islands (the western isles of Scotland?), and that three days' journey away was the mainland (Norway itself?) where, too, the king held power.[17] If, therefore, this great expedition was mainly an Irish-based Norse fleet (as most modern scholars now believe), then we cannot but comment on the details of the old sea-routes that emerge. For example, there is the entry into the estuary of the Gironde—used by the Cornish tin traders and the Megalithic people before them—and there are contacts with north-western Spain, reminiscent of the previous associations of this territory with the Celtic lands in the Age of the Saints. In chapter VII we shall see that thousands of medieval pilgrims entered the Gironde estuary and proceeded overland, or continued the journey by sea, to the great shrine of St James at Compostela in north-west Spain.

We do not know whether 'the great Northern King' ever received his Moorish gifts, but it is certain that later in the ninth century Norsemen under Bjorn and Hastein with a fleet of 62 ships raided Spain and North Africa and attacked the Italian coast, and possibly proceeded still further eastwards into the Mediterranean. Some Negro prisoners associated with the expeditions (who were probably slaves of the Moors in the first instance) are known to have ended their days in Ireland! Bjorn and Hastein's fleet certainly raided far afield in southern France and in the Mediterranean, and they, too, like their compatriots elsewhere, based themselves on an island off-shore. This time it was the island of Camargue near the mouth of the Rhône.

We have now traced the Norsemen and their colleagues throughout the whole length of the western sea-routes from Iceland and Greenland in the Far North to the sunnier shores of Africa and the Mediterranean lands in the south.

Modern scholars have attempted a reassessment of the contribution of the Vikings to Western civilization. Most contemporary writers were, very naturally, extremely hostile to the Vikings, and concentrated almost exclusively on the violent aspects of Scandinavian activity. Most of these accounts were written by ecclesiastics who were primarily concerned with recording and decrying the activities of the Heathen, who regarded the Holy Places of Christendom simply as treasure-houses fit only to be plundered. From these sources has been built up the popular conception of the Viking Age as characterized solely by turbulence and destruction. The fact is, however, that, although they plundered and engaged in slavery, the plunder was not always of precious objects of silver and gold. They pillaged largely for food and cattle wherewith to sustain themselves. At the same time, they engaged in much straightforward trading, and some of the fortified marts they set up could, and did, blossom into permanent settlements, given favourable conditions. The local kings and princes might, indeed, have welcomed the establishment of these coastal markets as they would keep them in touch with the outside world. Even the destruction of wooden buildings by the Vikings prepared the way for the more extensive use of stone, and by their encouragement of urban life they may be said to have prepared the way for the coming of the culture of Medieval Europe, especially in the remoter areas of the western margins of the continent.[19] They made a great contribution to metalworking, shipbuilding and stone carving (as witnessed by the finely sculptured Celtic–Norse crosses) alongside of the quickening of trade relations. They possessed genuine aesthetic sense, which showed itself especially in metalwork. Silver was greatly coveted by them wherever they went, whether as pirates, traders or mercenaries. Some used it to buy food or fine clothing (in which they were greatly interested), others used it to buy loyalty, but some worked it into very beautiful objects like brooches and rings, and other objects of personal adornment.[20] Above all, however, they had the great capacity of adapting themselves to the local culture in the areas into which they spread. This was done by a process of cultural assimilation.

Plate 43

In the Isle of Man is to be seen a Runic inscription set up by a priest named Iuan; incised beneath the inscription are both the Runic (Norse) and the Ogham (Irish) alphabets.[21] The Vikings thus furnish an example, to add to many others, of the fact that when two outlooks or civilizations come together they may produce results far beyond the summation of their respective traditions.[22] This was certainly true wherever the Vikings settled, and it is nowhere more clearly in evidence than in the Celtic lands whose cultures owe so much to peoples who, throughout the ages, have frequented the western seaways.

Plate 40

CHAPTER VII

# *The Pilgrims' Way*

The veneration of the saints has been a feature of Christianity from the earliest times, and a desire soon arose among the pious to visit the places with which a particular saint had been associated during his lifetime. It was believed that the saint had an earthly home or homes, where, even after death, he continued to exercise his power, blessing those who sought his intercession by prayer and alms-giving, and inflicting his curse on those who infringed his rights. Normally, his cult began at his tomb, the focal sacred place associated with him, and the one from which he was most likely to manifest his powers in a striking manner. Where the whole body of the saint was not preserved in his tomb, some relict of his, such as his head, or arm, or even finger-nails, might serve as a focus

Plate 47

of veneration. The medieval mania for relics made this state of affairs very common so that by the fifteenth century pilgrimages became extremely fashionable and relics were in great demand.

This conception of pilgrimage was, however, somewhat different from that which had grown up in the Celtic Church in the Age of the Saints. The Celtic saints were absorbed by a great desire to 'go on pilgrimage' as a sort of penance in itself tied up with the eremitical monastic concept. They voyaged overseas at the mercy of the elements, often with neither sun nor stars to guide them. The whole picture is vividly portrayed in the well-known story of the three Irish pilgrims who landed on the shores of Cornwall in their frail skin-covered craft. They were subsequently brought into the presence of King Alfred who questioned them concerning the purpose of their journey. They explained to the king that they were 'on pilgrimage for the love of God, they cared not whither'.[1] This search for some secluded spot in the midst of the ocean gave way to a voyage in search of the ideal earthly Paradise or Land of Promise, as recorded in the *Imrama* or travel tales of great voyagers like St Brendan.[2]

With the passing of the Age of the Saints and the dominance of the Medieval Church, these conceptions of pilgrimage became fused and the pious flocked to the shrines of the great figures in the pantheon of Celtic Christianity. Among such shrines were the most ancient pilgrim centres in the Celtic West. They included, for example, St David's, where the patron saint enjoyed a pre-eminence almost as significant on the patriotic level as on the religious; and Whithorn in Galloway, where St Ninian is said to have dedicated his famous church to St Martin of Tours. Pilgrims in their hundreds flocked to the holy well of St Winifred in Flintshire as Plate 48 well as to the famous shrine of St Beuno at Clynnog Fawr in Caernarvonshire. Equally attractive was Bardsey Island—the reputed burial place of twenty thousand saints. Then there was the wooden equestrian figure of Derfel Gadarn (Derfel the Mighty) in his church at Llandderfel, near Bala in Merioneth, and the equally famous shrine of Penrhys in Glamorgan.[3] More adventuresome pilgrims sought the merits of a visit across the Irish Sea to St Patrick's Purgatory, on an island in Lough Derg in western Ireland, while the greatest prestige of all was reserved for a pilgrimage to the shrine of St James at Santiago de Compostela in north-west Spain.

Before proceeding further to describe the renewed activity on the western seaways associated with the movement of pilgrims to and fro from one sacred place to another in medieval times, mention should be made of the ever present attraction for the faithful of a pilgrimage to the Holy Land, in particular to the Holy Sepulchre itself in Jerusalem. Unfortunately for the Christian pilgrim in the Middle Ages, the Holy City itself was in the hands of the Infidel, and peaceful pilgrimages were well-nigh impossible. A substitute had to be found which took the form of a visit to Rome, to the shrine of St Peter. So much, indeed, was it the accepted fashion to go on pilgrimage in the Middle Ages that certain shrines gained added prestige, when for example, in the twelfth century Pope Calixtus II decreed that two journeys to St David's in Wales, or to the shrine of St James at Compostela in north-west Spain, were to be regarded as the equivalent of one to Rome.[4]

Pilgrimages to Rome, important as they were, lie rather outside the scope of this study, for it was the continental rather than the maritime routes that were mostly used by the pilgrims. We return, therefore, to a closer study of some of the great shrines already named, that lie along the western margins of the Continent. We shall be particularly concerned with the use made by pilgrims of the western sea-routes in their visits to these sacred places. *Fig. 40*

Beginning in the north with St Ninian's famous centre at Whithorn, we recall the circumstances of its origin and remember the great revival of this saint's cult at the hands of King David I and his Queen when they became the first monarchs to rule all Scotland, and dedicated themselves to the furtherance of the interests of the Roman Church, especially by claiming the authority of ancient tradition for the changes they introduced. It is in this context that pilgrimages to Whithorn increased considerably. The pious gathered to worship at the famous marble cist, said to contain the bones of the saint. Throughout the whole of the Middle Ages, there appears to have been no abatement whatsoever in the cult of St Ninian. In 1428 King James I granted a general protection to all strangers entering Scotland on pilgrimage to St Ninian's church, and royal visits were paid to his shrine. As late as 1516 the Regent Albany granted safe conduct to all visitors hailing from England, Wales, Ireland and the Isle of Man by land or water to do homage to the saint.[5] The reference to these four territories clearly reflects the part that must have been played by the seaways in carrying pilgrims to the shrine of St Ninian, and at the same time indicates once more the part played by the sea-lanes in maintaining the cultural unity of the lands bordering the North Irish Sea basin.

Particular attention must be drawn to the sanctity of Bardsey Island lying off the tip of the Llŷn peninsula in North Wales. Islands offshore have always attracted primitive navigators and we have seen that at no time was this more so than in the Age of the Saints. In the case of Bardsey, we have not only an island off-shore, but one situated at the end of a peninsula that jutted out into the main sea-route running through St George's Channel. Its geographical situation was ideal, and it is not surprising, therefore, that it was the reputed burial place of twenty thousand saints, including Beuno, Padarn, Dyfrig and Derfel Gadarn. It is worthwhile noting in passing that the last-named was the son of Hywel ab Emyr of Brittany, and, perhaps, we should not overlook the implication of the link along the seaways between Brittany and Bardsey in this connection. The reputed vast concentration of burials, of which not the slightest trace now remains, meant in the Middle Ages that the island enjoyed an almost limitless reputation for sanctity. Indeed, one ancient document mentions the fact that the island became 'a second Rome', in virtue of so great a concentration of holiness within so small a compass. It was the obvious venue for pilgrims from far and near and there still exists in the Vatican Library a list of the indulgences specially

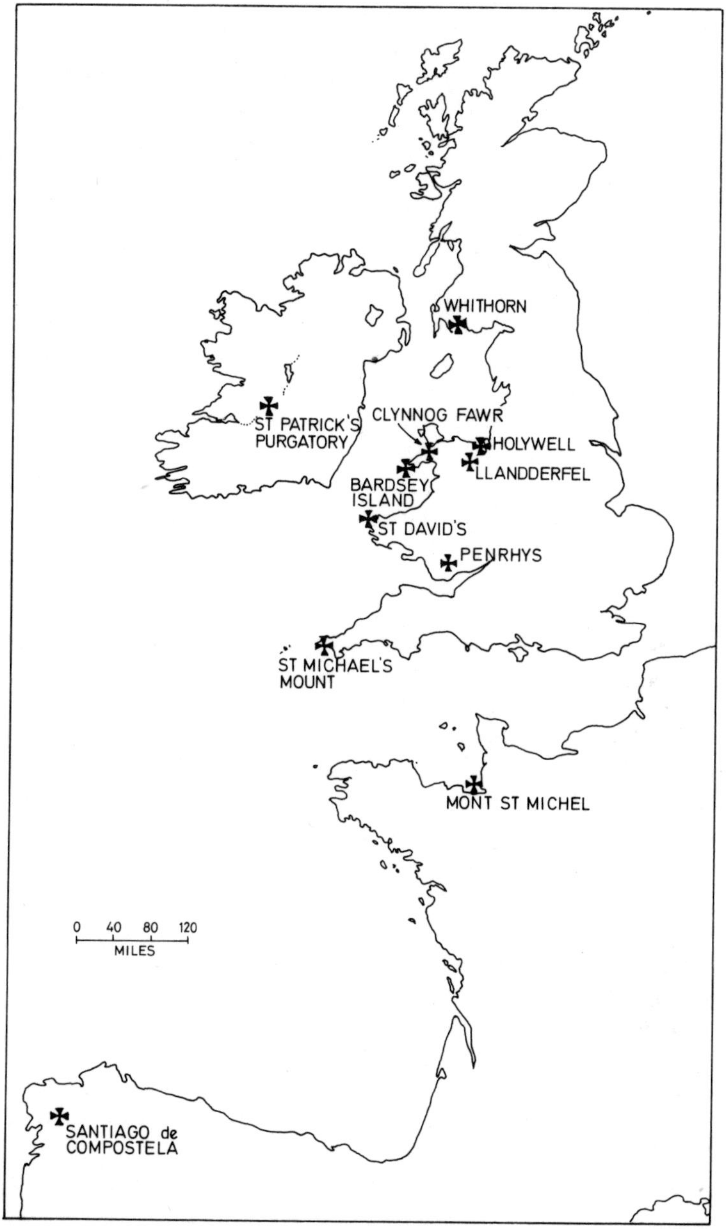


*Fig. 40 Important sites of medieval pilgrimage*

granted to pilgrims going to Bardsey. The holiness of the island is frequently mentioned by the Welsh poets and more than one of them refers feelingly to the terrors of the short, but stormy, sea-passage between the island and the mainland.[6] Indeed, the noticeable falling-off, towards the close of the Middle Ages, in the number of pilgrims visiting the island may well be due to the fact that latter-day pilgrims preferred the easier and more comfortable journeys to the many shrines that were by this time readily accessible to the devout.

We must not, however, over-emphasize this aspect as it would appear that, even at the close of the Middle Ages, there was a constant flow of pilgrims across the stormy and dangerous Irish Channel to St Patrick's Purgatory on the Shannon. The most important point to note here is that the popularity of this pilgrimage indicates, apart from its devotional significance, the continued use of the crossing of the Irish Sea throughout the Middle Ages, reflecting as it does a situation which appears to have been well developed ages before. We should not overlook, either, the wide catchment area from which pilgrims are known to have journeyed to this spot. Lombardy, Florence, Lucca, Rimini, Hungary, France, Spain and Holland as well as Britain are mentioned.[7] It may well be that this wide catchment area is closely associated with the medieval wine trade, for Ireland is known to have imported wine from southern France, Spain and Italy in medieval times, and the ships engaged in this trade almost certainly used the Shannon estuary for entry into the western interior. More will be said later about Irish and other pilgrims utilizing the facilities offered by ships engaged in this trade in their voyages to well known shrines on the European mainland.

Reverting once more to the main routeway through the Irish Sea, we come to the Dewisland peninsula of Pembrokeshire, which like the Llŷn peninsula in North Wales juts out like a gigantic pier-head into
*Fig. 41* the main traffic route of the Irish Sea. It differs in shape from the narrow tapering peninsula in the north, presenting in contrast a more rectangular land mass. The land forming the peninsula is, broadly speaking, a plateau some 200 feet in elevation with isolated upstanding hill masses of igneous origin. The streams were rejuvenated by a pre-glacial uplift so that their courses are now deeply incised into the plateau surface. The main drainage channel is that of the River Alun. In its upper reaches it flows in a W.S.W. direction, then, as the valley develops, the river

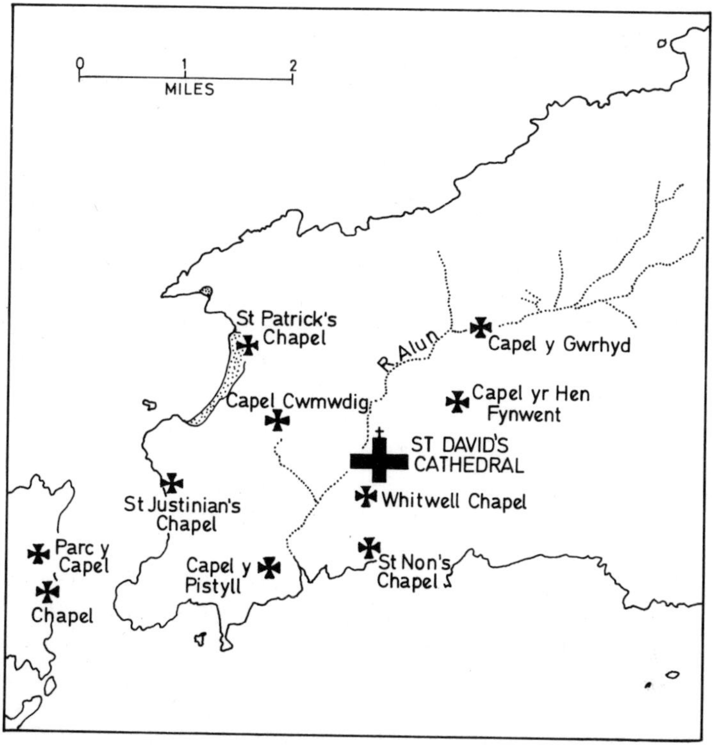


*Fig. 41 Site of St David's cathedral with subsidiary chapels*

occupies a deeply incised, narrow, winding dell, which stands out in sharp contrast to the upper portion of the valley on the plateau surface. It is near to the spot where the valley begins to deepen that the cathedral of St David's now stands, on the site where, presumably, St David located his original cell.[8] The cathedral houses the relics of the saint, which were the object of pilgrimage throughout Celtic and Medieval times. The site possessed distinct physical advantages—it was protected from sea-raiders by being carefully hidden below the plateau surface, yet, at the same time, it could maintain direct access to the sea—the chief highway of communications in early times. Moreover, ancient routes by land and sea converged on it. The sea-routes through the St George's Channel brought the Dewisland peninsula into direct contact, not only with south-eastern Ireland across the water, but also with the Cornish peninsula to the Plate 38 south, and the Llŷn peninsula to the north. Thousands of pilgrims journeyed to St David's along these sea-routes. Like the Celtic saints before them, they were frequently at the mercy of winds and tides and several alternative landing places are indicated. The distribution map shows the location of a large number of medieval chapels (some of which may date back to the days of the saints) situated near to the many bays and inlets around the peninsula. They are all tributary to the cathedral which would appear to be placed at the focus of a number of trackways leading inland from the alternative landing-places. George Owen, the distinguished historian of Pembrokeshire put the matter succinctly nearly three hundred and sixty years ago—'there were formerly', he said, 'several chapels about St David's which all belong to the Mother church, dedicated to several saints . . . all the chapels are near to the sea side and adjoining the places where those that come by sea commonly landed. They were placed here to draw the devotion of the seamen and passengers when they first came ashore: other pilgrims us'd likewise to come to them.'[9]

In addition to the sea-routes many important overland routes converged on St David's, making it a veritable hub of communications in early times. The late O. G. S. Crawford suggested that a very useful reconstruction of the land-routes to St David's and its harbour, Porth Mawr, (which was nearby) could be obtained by plotting the known Roman roads (still available as trackways in the Dark Ages and later), and adding to them John Ogilby's routes numbered 66, 91, 77 and 15 on the Ordnance Survey Map of XVIIth Century Britain.[10] These routes clearly pass by many ancient sites and their western portions are marked by many memorial stones known to be associated with the Dark Ages. The resultant pattern is shown on the plan on p. 75. Two major trackways are indicated: first, a northern one following the north coast of Pembrokeshire and passing through Nevern and thence turning eastwards in the vicinity of the Teifi valley and so on into southern Breconshire, Monmouthshire and Gloucestershire. Secondly, a southern route, marked from St David's towards Haverfordwest, Narberth, Whitland, across the Tâf estuary to the Pilgrims church at Llanfihangel Abercowin. It can be traced thence crossing the Tywi below Carmarthen, and on to Cydweli and the South Wales coastal plain through Neath and Bridgend towards Newport and the Severn estuary which is crossed

Plate 35

at the Aust Ferry. Crawford stresses the important link-road formed by the stretch of Roman road in the mid-Tywi valley from Llanymddyfri to Carmarthen and thence following a third land-route via Meidrim and the flanks of the Prescelly hills to St David's. There is abundant archaeological, as well as proto-historical, evidence for the use of these routes between south-eastern Ireland, St David's and the south-eastern borderlands of Wales in the Dark Ages and at later times. It was along them that medieval pilgrims from all parts of Wales and the British Isles journeyed to St David's. We have interesting evidence of the fact that pilgrims from Devon and Cornwall, and possibly even from Brittany, landed in the neighbourhood of Cydweli and reached St David's by the southern (transpeninsular) route. Plate 49

It is interesting to note that, although St David's had been celebrated in this way as a holy place for pilgrims for centuries, it is not until after 1450 that we hear specific mention of its being connected with the veneration of the Virgin. Other indications of its late popularity are its close association with St Anne. It is only in the fifteenth century that the veneration of the Virgin became widely extended to her mother, and the chapel of St Mary at St David's is known to have possessed at this period a very detailed representation of the Holy Family and of St Anne and Joachim which proved a great attraction for pilgrims. Equally significant was the fact that the Reformation iconoclast, Bishop Barlow, left the statue of St David undisturbed at his shrine.[11]

We have frequently mentioned the attraction for both saints and pilgrims of islands, peninsulas and sheltered waters in their journeys to and fro across the seas. Equally attractive appear to have been 'mountains rising from the sea'. This was especially the case with the famous and spectacular Mont Saint-Michel, the upstanding rocky islet, 165 feet high, off the coast of Normandy, united to the mainland by a narrow causeway, and its counterpart, St Michael's Mount, four hundred yards off-shore in Mount's Bay, Cornwall. Like Mont Saint-Michel, the latter is united with the mainland by a natural causeway passable only at low water. This is the important site we have already heard of in connection with the Cornish tin trade. The cult of St Michael in the West does not belong to the Age of the Celtic saints and seems to have gained popularity in the fifth or sixth centuries when the Archangel is alleged to have appeared to a shepherd on Monte Gargano in Apulia in Plate 50

Italy. St Michael in this way became closely associated with mountain sites. Early in the eighth century, there was a further alleged apparition on the summit of Mont Saint-Michel in Normandy and an oratory was established here by St Aubert in obedience to a command given on this occasion. As can be imaged, the place soon became the resort of pilgrims from France, Britain, Ireland and Italy, and land and sea-routes converged here as at St David's. In 996 Richard I, Duke of Normandy, founded a Benedictine monastery on the site in place of the original oratory. With the coming of the Normans to south-west England, we find that Robert of Mortain gave St Michael's Mount in Cornwall to Mont Saint-Michel in Normandy and the association between them continued until the time of Henry V. Like its counterpart in Normandy, the English Mount became an equally famous resort of pilgrims, benefitting greatly, not only from the many pilgrims who used the sea-routes and, in particular, the transpeninsular tracks across Cornwall, but also from the deliberate encouragement given to pilgrims to visit the Mount by Pope Gregory in the eleventh century. The two sites were in this way closely associated with each other and would appear to have acted as landmarks for pilgrims crossing and re-crossing this section of the Channel linking Cornwall with Normandy and Brittany. It is significant also that the arms of the abbey of Mont Saint-Michel have representations of scallop shells set on a chief azure with its fleurs-de-lis, which are the royal arms of France. It owes its right to use the royal arms to the fact that it was one of the royal abbeys of France.[12] The important feature, however, is that the scallop shell is very definitely a pilgrim's badge, belonging properly to those who had visited the famous shrine of Saint James at Compostela, of which we shall have more to say later. Nevertheless, the presence of the scallop shells on the arms of Mont Saint-Michel would appear to link it definitely with the pilgrim route-ways that utilized the full length of the western seaways throughout the Middle Ages.

The shrine of Saint James at Compostela in north-west Spain was, after Rome itself, one of the greatest pilgrim attractions of the Middle Ages. We cannot overlook the fact that the Galician area had a very long tradition of contact with the sea. The physical setting of the Galician coast was eminently attractive to early mariners: it constitues one of the
*Fig. 42* best examples in western Europe of a *ria* coastline formed by the submergence of the lower portions of valley-ways giving broad inlets of

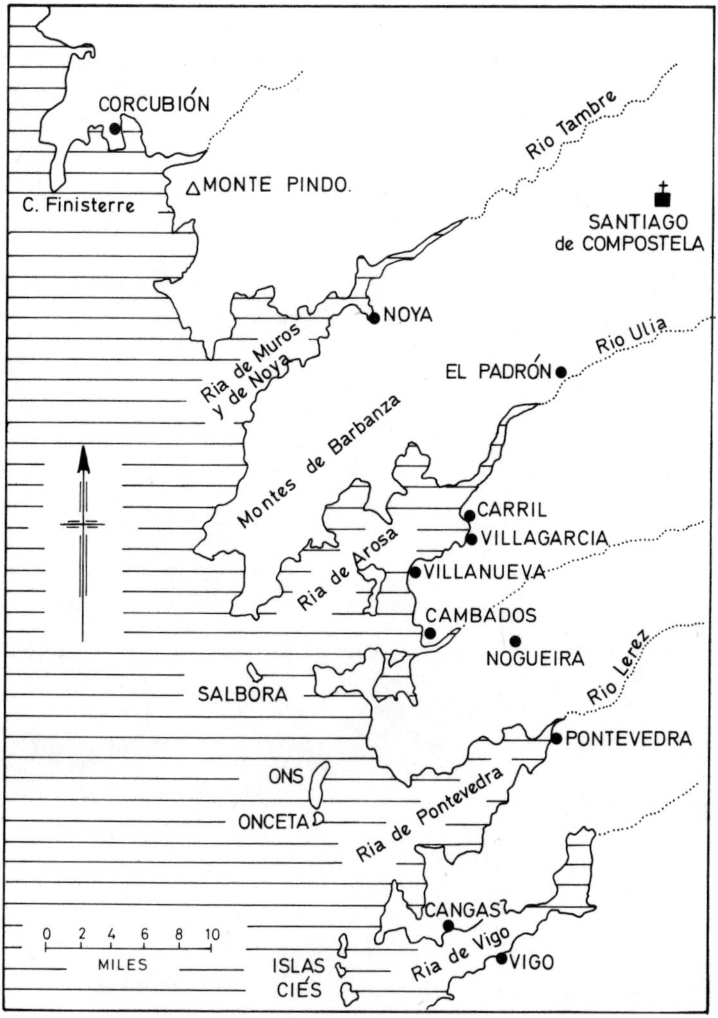


*Fig. 42 The 'Rias Bajas' of Galicia (after Naval Intelligence Handbook 1941)*

sheltered water, with isolated hills, which once flanked the original valleys, protruding as rocky islands offshore. Santiago itself lies between the Noya and Arosa rias which offered sheltered anchorages for storm-tossed ships from remotest antiquity.[13]

The area abounds in megalithic remains and its main attraction then and at later times was the presence of many mineral veins, of which tin ore was the most important. These rich deposits were much sought after by prehistoric prospectors—traders who used the western sea-routes in their intensive commercial activity. It was customary to land in any of these drowned estuarine inlets, and for routeways to develop leading up to the plateau above. At a focus of these route-ways important centres must have developed in prehistoric times. We think that this was true of Santiago, as it was of Carnac in Brittany and St David's in Wales.

Santiago de Compostela rose to importance in the early Middle Ages following upon the supposed discovery of the tomb of St James the Apostle in the ninth century. The legends surrounding this remarkable story are many, the basic one being that the saint came to Spain and preached the Gospel at Padrón, which is one of the ports tributary to Santiago, and subsequently returned to Jerusalem, where he was afterwards put to death by Herod. After his martyrdom his disciples took his body and carried it to Joppa where they found a large ship ready to sail, and in seven days arrived at Padrón. As soon as they had landed they placed the body of the saint upon a large stone, which was already hollowed out like a tomb, and placed another stone on top of it, whereupon immediately the stones, miraculously, took the body into themselves. These stones (possibly megalithic) were known in the Middle Ages as Barca and Patronon. This and similar legends were resurrected in the eighth and ninth centuries during a period of dire peril for the Christians in north-west Spain. The country was being overrun by the Moors, and Christianity survived only in this remote north-western corner. There was a great need to produce a patron saint for the Christians in their holy war against Islam, and with this end in view the burial place of St James in north-west Spain was miraculously rediscovered. The legends associated with the rediscovery of the tomb are many and varied. The official version states that some important personages noticed a mysterious light by night in a copse and reported the matter to Bishop Theodomir in 812. He himself came and saw the lights and after excavating at the spot, discovered there a small church which contained a marble tomb. The bishop informed the King of Asturias, who restored Plate 51 the church in honour of so great an Apostle and moved the bishopric of Iria to Compostela, near to where the find was made.

Possibly the legend that did most to increase the prestige of Santiago as a centre of pilgrimage is found in the 'Ystorya de Carolo Magno.' This occurs as a portion of a Chronicle written towards the beginning of the twelfth century by an unknown French monk under the influence of the great Abbey of Cluny, possibly at the suggestion of, or certainly to please, Gui de Bourgogne who was a member of the royal house of Léon and Castile, and who had become Pope Calixtus II in 1119. The story, of which various versions exist, begins by relating how St James was the first to preach the Gospel in Galicia and how he returned to Jerusalem and was martyred by Herod when his disciples returned to preach to the Galicians. It then tells how Charlemagne one night saw across the sky a pathway of stars stretching from Frisia to Galicia, where the body of St James was lying unrecognized. Seeing this repeatedly and wondering what its significance might be, he at last saw beside him a warrior who said that he was St James the Apostle and demanded that Charlemagne should set his country free from the Sacracens. The author of the Chronicle interpreted the appellation Compostela quite easily as *Campus stellarum*—the field of stars—with clear reference to the dream of Charlemagne and the Milky Way.[14]

The important feature of this Chronicle is that it appears to have been designed to advertise the sacred shrine and to serve as a useful guide book for visitors. The 'Ystorya de Carolo Magno' was translated into many languages and was widely read. Its great circulation was facilitated by the Cluniac monks, who had many houses throughout western Europe, and ended in making pilgrimages to Compostela exceedingly popular.

We can now examine in more detail some of the sea-routes followed by pilgrims to Santiago. Ireland seems to have sent many, and references to arrangements made for their departure are abundant. It is curious that there are fewer references to pilgrims going from Scotland. This may be due to the fact that Scotland was, throughout the Middle Ages, orientated politically more towards France, and most likely pilgrims to the great shrine at Compostela used the North Sea route to the Continent and completed the journey overland through France. In Ireland, circumstances were different in that almost every port saw pilgrims leaving for Santiago. We hear of them departing from Galway, Wexford, Kinsale and Waterford. Henry de Londres, the second Norman Archbishop of Dublin in the thirteenth century, set up a hospice on the banks of the

Liffey for the convenience of pilgrims awaiting there for fair weather, or a suitable ship, for the voyage to Compostela, while it is recorded that at Dingle some enterprising Spanish merchants, resident in the town, built a church there which they dedicated to St James of Compostela. We even hear of a singularly modern aspect of the visit overseas when restrictions were placed on currency export. At Dublin each pilgrim, before embarking for Compostela, was required to swear on the Eucharist not to take, or cause to be taken, more gold, either in mass or in money, than was reasonably required for the journey![15]

*Fig. 43* Some of the Irish pilgrims may have sailed to Santiago directly, or possibly to Bordeaux and completed the journey, as was the custom, overland. Others are known to have crossed over to south-west Wales and used the transpeninsular route from north Pembrokeshire to Carmarthen Bay and then re-embarked for Cornwall, where they crossed the peninsula on their way to Brittany and beyond. Others might have sailed from the south coast ports direct to Bordeaux. Echoes of the long journey to Santiago are clearly marked in south-west Wales. First of all we have the presence in St Mary's Church, Haverfordwest, Plate 52 (Pembrokeshire) of a sepulchral effigy of the early fifteenth century showing all the appurtenances of a pilgrim; the staff; the *vestis signata cruce*; and the wallet with its scallop shells clearly marked, leaving no doubt whatsoever that this is the resting-place of a Compostela pilgrim. As further evidence that pilgrims who visited Santiago had also used the south-west Wales transpeninsular route, we have a scallop shell embossed on a roof beam of the nave of St Mary's Church, Tenby, and the presence of yet another effigy with scallop shells at Llangynog church in western Carmarthenshire.

*Fig. 43 Pilgrim routes to Santiago de Compostela by land and sea. G Galway, Dl Dingle, K Kinsale, Wt Waterford, Wx Wexford, Du Dublin, P Pembroke, B Bristol, H Harlyn Bay, Iv St Ives, Pz Penzance, St M St Michael's Mount, A St Austell, F Fowey, Sh Saltash, Pl Plymouth, Pn Paignton, D Dartmouth, S Southampton*

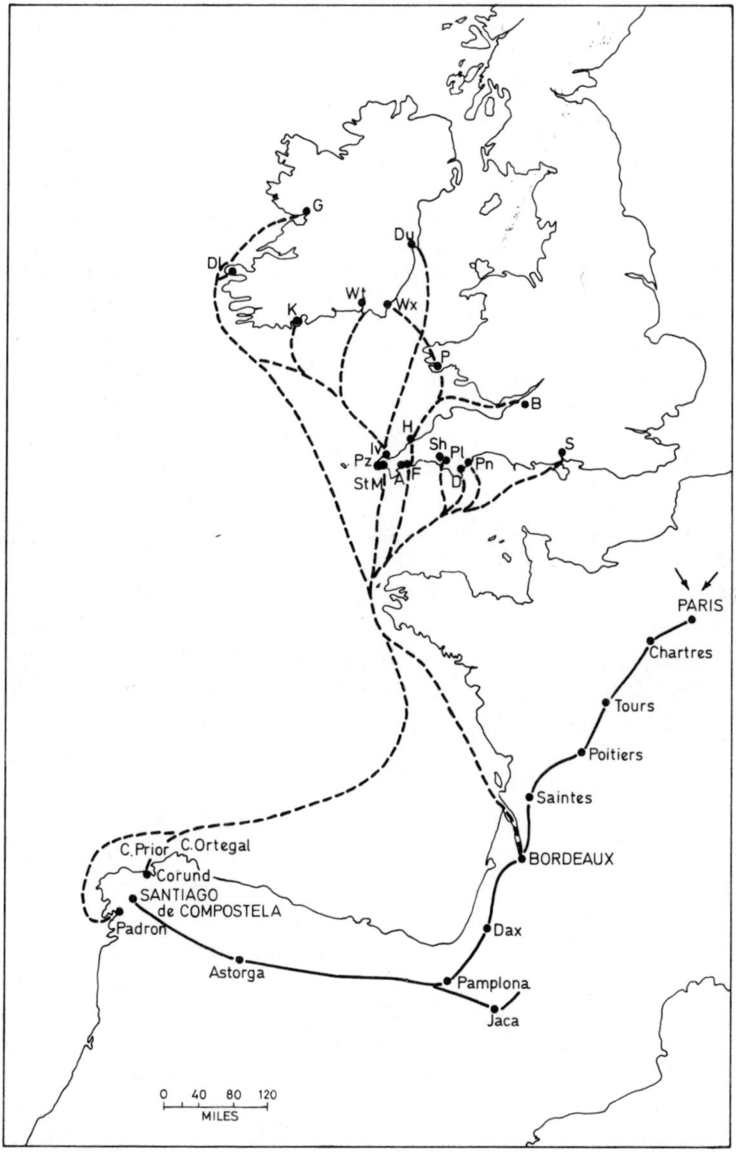
G
Du
Dl
Wt
Wx
K
P
B
H
Sh
Pl
S
Iv
Pz
Pn
StM
A
F
D
PARIS
Chartres
Tours
Poitiers
Saintes
C. Prior
C. Ortegal
BORDEAUX
Corund
SANTIAGO
de COMPOSTELA
Dax
Padron
Astorga
Pamplona
Jaca
0 40 80 120
MILES

Records also exist of Irish and Welsh pilgrims using the trans-peninsular routes across Cornwall both from Harlyn Bay (or the Camel estuary) to St Austell Bay, and from the mouth of the River Fowey (or St Ives Bay) to St Michael's Mount. These were the routes used by the tin merchants of prehistoric times, and later by St Samson on his journey from Wales to Brittany. The records extant for the years between 1413 and 1450 show that ships left Penzance, Fowey, St Michael's Mount and Saltash for Santiago de Compostela. Indeed, there is some evidence to show that ships *en route* for the shrine would assemble in convoy fashion off the south-west peninsula from such widely distributed ports as Pembroke, Bristol, Paignton, Dartmouth, Southampton, Saltash and Plymouth. William Wey who visited Compostela in 1456 left his home in Eton on 27 March and reached Plymouth on 30 April and reports that he sailed then on the *Mary Whyte* past Ortyngerz (Cape Ortegal), Cappyres (Cape Prior) and Insulae Sesarke (the Cisargas Islands). On his arrival at Corunna, he found there both Welsh and Irish ships.[16]

*Fig. 43* In addition to this direct sea-route there was another more attractive route that presented itself. This involved the use of the Gironde estuary, disembarking at Bordeaux and completing the remainder of the journey via Dax and Pamplona by land. The Gironde estuary was, of course, a well known entry and exit route for southern France from Neolithic days. It was extremely popular with British pilgrims when Guyenne was an English possession. So important did the Gironde traffic become that minor ports such as Suloc and Toulais, at the mouth of the estuary, gradually rose in favour. From Bordeaux a network of roads, in addition to the Dax-Pamplona highway, traversed the south-western corner of France, where it bordered on the Spanish frontier. Several guest-houses were established by the Church at intervals along these routes for the entertainment of the pilgrims. The Abbey of La Sauve near Bordeaux functioned in this way and it was clearly a very important centre, for it was here that pilgrims who had travelled by the main overland route across France via Paris, Chartres, Tours, Poitiers and Saintes met those who had journeyed by sea.[17] It was at this abbey that the pilgrim made his will and confession, and received from the abbot the usual equipment of a pilgrim—a staff and wallet which were duly blessed. Often an ass or a horse was given to make the journey less arduous. In the fifteenth century the main tracks from Bordeaux went almost due southwards, crossing into Spain by the lower land at the western extremity of the Pyrenees. This was a far more convenient and safer way of entering Spain than attempting to negotiate the high inhospitable mountain passes further east. Over the frontier other routes from southern France and beyond converged via Jaca on the main route just beyond Pamplona. From this city the pilgrims passed on westwards through Burgos, Léon, Astorga and Lugo to Santiago. There were more hospices along this important highway, and private doors were frequently opened to wayfarers. Of the many hospices, perhaps the most renowned was the one for British pilgrims near Cebreros in the province of Lugo, where the local church was also at their disposal. In Santiago itself on the north side of the Plaza Mayor was the famous Hospicio de los Reyes erected for the reception of pilgrims. It is said that Ferdinand and Isabella devoted a portion of the treasure accruing from the Spanish discoveries in the New World to the erection of this hospice. Having arrived at their destination, the pilgrims ranged themselves before the high altar of the cathedral in companies, according to their nationality. A codex of Pope Calixtus II, dating from about 1140, now in the archives of Santiago cathedral, records that 'Some sang to the accompaniment of the . . . lyre, some to the timbrel, others to the flute, others to the British and Welsh harp and crwth.' When they had fulfilled the round of duties expected of them, the pilgrims retraced their steps to Bordeaux, or returned directly by sea, while others proceeded further either to Rome or the Holy Land.

So detailed is our knowledge of the pilgrimages to Santiago de Compostela that it is tempting to digress and refer to the interesting experiences of individual pilgrims; to tell of their dread of the gigantic Biscayan rollers and the rage of 'the blue white-foam-speckled waves.' Plate 53 The Welsh poets of the period describe the anxiety of lovers, wives and parents at home for the safety of a pilgrim who had left to visit the shrine of St James or possibly Rome.[18] Indeed, considering the dangers and inconveniences to which the pilgrims were exposed, it is not surprising that some shrank from the journey and commuted their vows, or otherwise salved their consciences. One way of doing this was to commission friends, or even professional pilgrims to undertake the pilgrimages for them, by proxy. On the other side of the scale, there were, however, compensations of a lighter character to balance the hardships of the journey. Jugglers and storytellers provided entertainment to while away the weary hours. It should not be forgotten that many of the great romances of the Middle Ages developed from the tales told by pilgrims *en route* to their destinations. The famous *Canterbury Tales* had their origin in this way. All this and much more could form the basis of an interesting chapter of its own, but, it would, nevertheless, be strictly irrelevant to our main theme. There is, however, one further aspect of the story which should not be overlooked, namely the relationship between the pilgrim movement and one of the most important features of the normal trade along the western sea-routes at this time—the well-established wine trade of medieval Europe.

It is well known that in spite of some attempts to cultivate the vine in northern lands, wine and oil (particularly olive oil) were generally lacking in the Celtic lands and had to be imported from the Mediterranean from early times. Evidence of this trade exists certainly from Iron Age times onwards, while Ralegh Radford has drawn attention to the mass of pottery sherds found at the Celtic monastery of Tintagel in Cornwall and at other monastic and civil sites in western Britain and Ireland associated with the Dark Ages. Most of the sherds formed part of amphorae—great wine or oil vessels. No one would suppose that these large coarse vessels were imported for their own sake and not for their contents. Here, therefore, is clear evidence of the wine trade utilizing the western sea-routes in Early Christian times. We have interesting corroborative evidence from literary sources. A passage in the *Life* of St Ciaran of Cluain in Ireland (who died about the year AD 550) mentions, in connection with a great harvest feast to be held at his monastery on the banks of the Shannon, that, by chance, merchants from Gaul had filled the great storage vessel of the monastery with wine just in time for the occasion. This shows that the Gaulish wine merchants were in touch with western Ireland at an early date.[19] The wine trade continued to flourish throughout the Middle Ages and as time progressed, the commercial production of wine, which had once been widespread over Europe, wherever climatic conditions permitted, gradually became concentrated in regions of specialized viticulture. The wines of Poitou, Gascony, Burgundy and the Moselle were well-known in northern Europe in medieval times. In the late thirteenth century, the wines of La Rochelle were pre-eminent, while in the fourteenth they probably took second place to those of Gascony. By 1480 English merchants appeared in force in the wine markets of Bordeaux.[20] The wine ships did not return to the French ports empty; on the contrary, they offered ideal facilities for pilgrims and others desirous of travelling to France. Wherever the pilgrims were landed on French soil, they made for Bordeaux—the gathering-place *en route* for Santiago. As already noted, Bordeaux itself was the great port for the Gascony wine trade, so that in the case of the vast majority of ships, the pilgrims were able to reach the assembly point for the final stages of their journey directly. Bordeaux, therefore, became one of the busiest ports on the Atlantic seaboard of Europe in the thirteenth and fourteenth centuries. Plate 55

In describing the centres of pilgrimage that appealed with such extraordinary power to the peoples of the Celtic fringe of Europe in the Middle Ages, we have sought to emphasize that the routes, which led the pilgrims to their shrines, and which linked Scotland to Ireland, and Ireland to Wales, and Wales, in turn, to Cornwall, Brittany and distant Galicia, were the successors of prehistoric coastwise trade routes and seaways over which saints had wandered ages before.

CHAPTER VIII

# *Aftermath*

The great discoveries of the fifteenth and sixteenth centuries revolutionized the whole conception of sea travel among the maritime folk of the western fringes of Europe. Fundamental changes in methods of sailing, and especially of navigation, became inevitable, while real, newly discovered geographical facts replaced the mythical geography of the great medieval legends. Fantasy gave way to reality. Especially was this the case when the dazzling realities of the newly discovered America often outstripped the most fanciful flights of earlier imagination. Likewise, the major trade routes of the world were re-orientated, and no longer did the mariners hug the coasts, but sailed out boldly onto the open ocean to the fabulously wealthy lands that lay beyond the horizon.

The outstanding feature of the great voyages of discovery was the fact that it was the small fishing communities along the western seaboard of the Continent that supplied the crews of the caravels which encircled the globe and opened up a new era in Europe. The crews of the famous Portuguese vessels came from such insignificant ports as Nazare and Cascais in central Portugal. It was not only from the coasts of Spain and Portugal, however, that intrepid seamen were recruited—they emerged from the myriads of little harbours all along the coastal margins of Western Europe. For example, many historians have suggested that the stormy seas that characterize the Western Approaches to Britain (especially the entries to the Bristol and English Channels) proved an admirable recruiting ground for adventurous seamen. It was in such an environment that men like Cabot, Drake and Hawkins were nurtured, be they acting as discoverers, buccaneers or pirates. Daring Breton sailors took part in early voyages across the water to the Newfoundland Banks. It is significant that many Welsh seamen manned the Bristol ships that set out on the early voyages of discovery, patronized by their kinsman King Henry VII. Among such men were Roger Barlow, who hailed from Slebech, situated along one of the creeks of Milford Haven. He had sailed along the western sea-routes as far south as the Azores and probably had visited the coast near modern Agadir, and accompanied Sebastian

Cabot out of Bristol on his second voyage of discovery in April 1526. He translated the famous Spanish treatise *Suma de Geographie*. This work contains the earliest account of the New World in English, including much material drawn from Barlow's own experiences. It lay neglected in manuscript for nearly four hundred years until it was published by the Hakluyt Society in 1931.

An equally important voyage of discovery from Bristol in the early days was that of Captain Thomas James, whose family hailed from the Breconshire–Monmouthshire borderland. Looking for the north-west passage as a route to the East, he sailed in 1631 into the Arctic Ocean and explored around Greenland and the Hudson Strait. He suffered great hardship and exposure in the Arctic but his daring, skill and perseverance enabled him to bring his ships back again after being ice-bound for many months. In 1633 the Government published his spirited account of this voyage, which in later times was read by S. T. Coleridge who used many of the details as the basis of the *Rime of the Ancient Mariner*.[1] The names of many adventurers from all parts of Atlantic Europe who took part in the great voyages of discovery could easily be added to those already mentioned, but it is not the object of this chapter to enumerate their experiences or to assess their exploits, but rather to show that behind this great activity there continued an unbroken seafaring tradition along the western shores of the Continent.

The New Age brought with it changes in methods of navigation. We know, for example, that Mediterranean sailors in the Middle Ages used an information book for navigators containing details of the coast-line, parts of call, and the time likely to be taken in sailing from one port to another. A harbour book of this kind was called a *Portolano*, drawn up by seamen for seamen—based on experience and personal knowledge. As the arts of navigation developed, additional information was added. The earliest supplement introduced was the Portolan Chart—a sea chart or pilot chart. These were almost entirely the work of Venetian, Genoese and Catalan draughtsmen. The voyages of discovery, in turn, so greatly and so rapidly enlarged the known world that pilot books supplemented by charts proved completely inadequate. A further supplement became necessary giving the declination of the sun and the *locus solis*, to enable sailors to determine the ship's longitude by the meridian altitude of the sun. This necessitated a section containing a calendar and the relevant

Plate 56

tables. Finally, a fourth section was added on astronomy and the theory of the sphere. Very naturally, it was the Portuguese who first printed pilot books containing sailing directions, charts and tables of this kind.

While all these developments in ocean navigation were taking place those who continued to use the western seaways still clung to directional manuals. Indeed, it would appear that North European seamen generally made no use of sea charts until the closing decades of the sixteenth century. William Bourne in his preface to the first native English printed work on navigation, known as *A Regiment for the Sea*, mentions the contempt in which British seamen of the period held their more enlightened contemporaries around the Mediterranean who used portolan maps or 'sheepes skinnes' as Bourne sarcastically refers to them.[2] This evidence points clearly to the fact that we have in the north and west of Europe the survival of the oldest forms of navigation, that taken from written directions alone, and based, in turn, on past experience, which, apart from the fact that it was now written down, must have been the method of navigation used by mariners sailing these seas many millennia before. In 1889 the Hakluyt Society published one of these sailing manuals appropriately entitled *Sailing Directions for the circumnavigation of England and to the Straits of Gibraltar*. Here, indeed, is a manual clearly designed for sailors along the old western seaways. It belongs to the late fifteenth century when the peoples of Western Europe were beginning to know more of the wider ocean and the shores of West Africa. Nevertheless, because we think it reveals so much that is an aftermath of the remote past, it may not be inappropriate to quote a short extract from the manual
Plate 57 indicating the sailing directions given for navigating a portion of the east coast of the Irish Sea. The section of the sea-route described begins near St David's Head in Pembrokeshire and proceeds around the coast of North Wales to the estuary of the Dee. The only feature of ancient sailing that has not survived appears to be the transpeninsular route of the ancients across north-west Wales.

> see goth half tide betwene the smale [the Smalls near St Davids] and Skidwhalles [St Tudwal's] and the bersays [Bardsey]. And it flowith est and west on the mayne londe and at the Ramseir north and south the stremys renne in the sonde and be owten the Bisshoppis and his clerkis north northwest and south south est, sculke holme [Skok-

> holm] and the sone [Sound] of Ramseirs north and south . . . And kepe more nere the Ilonde than the mayne londe till ye be passid the point and thorowe the sande, than no north till ye come at a nothir Rok . . . And than your cours is north northest for to go with barseis stremys . . . An yif ye go to Chestir ye shall go fro the scarris [Skerries] till ye come anens the Castell of Rotlonde [Rhuddlan] . . . And take your saught on the mayne londe of Wales Rotlonde and the Redebank of Chestre watir north and south.[3]

It has already been noted that the New Age was characterized by the fading away of stories of fabulous voyages of discovery and adventure that so pleased the people of old, yet some echoes of these tales are still with us today. We have had occasion to refer to the *Imrama* of St Brendan and his voyages to the Far North. He is also said to have voyaged southwards on the ocean margins of the great western sea-routes to the neighbourhood of the Canaries and the Azores. There he tells of such marvels as self-moving islands and promised lands attainable by the saints alone. Such blind faith was placed in the tales related of him, that his reputed discoveries served as a source of inspiration for a large number of sea charts in the New Age. Today, we know that the Island of San Brandan, which was often referred to as the Lost Island, or the Inaccessible Island, or Non Trubada, through its power of submerging and re-emerging from the bottom of the sea at the whim of the Fates, does not exist, yet nearly all the early ocean charts from the end of the fourteenth century onwards show it to the west of the Canaries and half-way between there and the Azores. The first sea chart that inserts it is the famous Pizigano map which was drawn in 1367 and shows St Brendan with his arms outstretched towards the island that bears his name. The island is also shown on the Weimar map of 1424; on Fra Mauro's map of the world of 1457 and on Martin of Bohemia's famous globe of 1492, and, finally, makes yet another appearance on an extremely important map of the world which came into the possession of Yale University Library about 1960. The map is bound together with a text (which can be dated about 1440) presenting a new manuscript version of John de Plano Carpini's journey to the court of Kublai Khan in the thirteenth century. The map shows among other interesting features both Greenland and Vinland and so the find is now generally known as *The Vinland Map and the Tartar*

*Relation*. The greatest excitement centred around the discovery of this map among both historians and historical geographers, for if it can be proved that the map is of the same date as the text with which it is bound, then here is for the first time a Pre-Columban map of the American mainland proving the genuineness of the old Norse Sagas. On the map—but arousing much less excitement—many fabulous islands are still shown, among them the *Magnae Insulae Beati Brandani* situated, as before,
*Fig. 44* to the west of the Canaries and half-way between them and the Azores.[4]

The excitement caused by the publication of *The Vinland Map and the Tartar Relation* in 1965 serves also as a reminder that the sagas of Eric the Red and his associates are but another facet of the aftermath of the western seaways. Interest in these narratives appears to be recrudescent, for the seventeenth and eighteenth centuries saw several bursts of enthusiasm resulting even in definite action associated with these reputed discoveries. Less than a quarter of a century after the discovery of America, two famous English explorers Frobisher and Davis made important expeditions to the Arctic. The reports of their discoveries and the descriptions they gave of the Arctic coasts had a profound effect on all people of Viking descent, for in those descriptions they quite rightly thought they recognized the lost Greenland of Eric the Red. Could descendants of these distant valiant ancestors be still alive? Would any vestiges be found of that remote lost outpost of the white race at the very limit of North Atlantic waters? King Christian of Denmark organized a series of expeditions to explore the coasts of the rediscovered Greenland and to find out, if possible, what fate had befallen the descendants of the settlers of old. The first Danish expedition to Greenland set out in 1605. They found no men of the white race still living there, but they did find a large quantity of deposits to start archaeological investigations and even Runic inscriptions for the palaeographers. These were taken as sufficient proof of the presence of Viking colonists there in the days of Eric the Red.[5] From that moment, literature on Greenland themes, or of Greenland origin, became widespread, and the cartographer Resen in his map of 1605, now in the Royal Library at Copenhagen, (doubtless seeking to flatter the Danish king) dotted the newly discovered North American coastlands with names taken from ancient Scandinavian literature. This is how, side by side with the real names of lands recently discovered, Resen added others that were entirely fictitious.

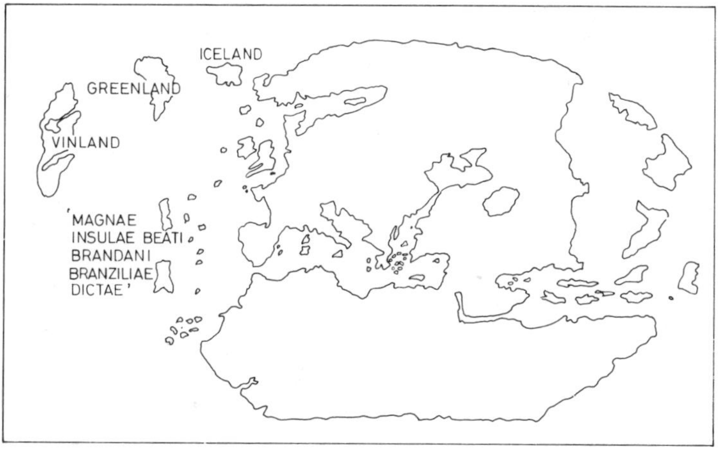


*Fig. 44 The 'Vinland' map (based on G. R. Crone, Geog. Journ. 1966)*

A similar aftermath of ages of contact with the western seas is to be found in many a Welsh legend—none, possibly, so well known as the famous story of the discovery of the New World in the year 1170 by Madoc, son of Owain Gwynedd, a prince of North Wales. The legend in its most elaborate form records that Prince Madoc's expedition crossed the Atlantic in ten ships, and that after discovering a great western continent, he and his party settled down there, resulting, it was believed in later times, in a tribe of Welsh Indians descended from him and his followers surviving in the wilds of America.[6]

The only authentic reference we possess to a son of Owain Gwynedd, named Madoc, in the Middle Ages occurs in a Welsh poem dated about 1440. The poet, however, makes no reference to Prince Madoc discovering America or even to his sailing out over the western ocean; he merely quotes the Prince's love of the sea to justify his own devotion to the craft of fishing. Nevertheless, by Elizabethan times the legend of the Welsh discovery of America in the Middle Ages had taken deep roots and initiated a voluminous literature. The fact that the legend flourished greatly at this period cannot, of course, be dissociated on the one hand from a natural jealousy of the contemporary achievements of the Spanish and Portuguese, and, on the other, from the presence of a Welsh dynasty on the throne, whose monarchs naturally looked with pride on the Celtic past. The Madoc story would be proof that British sailors had discovered America before Columbus or Amerigo Vespucci. Legitimately, therefore, Britain, and not Spain, had first claim on the New World. It is amazing how the legend found its way into the great geographical texts of the sixteenth and subsequent centuries. It appears in the famous *Historie of Cambria*, which the great Tudor geographer Humphrey Lhuyd of Denbigh left unpublished at his death in 1568[7]. Lhuyd was no mean cartographer and was responsible for the first published map of Wales in Abraham Ortelius' great Atlas. In the *Historie of Cambria* he speaks of Madoc's discovery of a new land which he identifies with either Nova Hispania or Florida, and of his return home, and his second departure, and mentions the fact that here was proof that the British people discovered America before the Spaniards. The story was printed by Richard Hakluyt, and discussed by the well-informed and able Peter Heylyn in 1633 in his *Microcosmos: A little description of the Great World.* The legend was accepted in the eighteenth century by Dr David Samwell—a distinguished Welshman and a surgeon in the Royal Navy, who had accompanied James Cook on his voyages of discovery. Even after the most daring, yet unsuccessful, attempts to locate the Welsh Indians (who were supposed to live among the Mandan near the headwaters of the Missouri), belief in the legend continued unabated in both Wales and America. Most amazing of all was the fact that, in the early nineteenth century, Alexander von Humboldt—the acknowledged father of modern geography—who himself was a great traveller in the New World, and who possessed one of the ablest and most critical minds of his age, thought the story worthy of serious consideration.

The most significant feature of the aftermath of the long-established sailings along the western seas is, however, not so much the survival of stories of legendary voyages, but their corollary—the inspiration they afforded to men of courage and imagination to test their accuracy. The Madoc legend, supplemented over the years by an amazing accretion of evidence, purporting to be based on personal experiences, in this way inspired John Evans, a Methodist minister from Waunfawr in Caernarvonshire, to set out, late in the eighteenth century, in search of the lost tribe of Welsh Indians in America.[8] Although Evans would appear to have been stimulated by motives identical with those that had influenced King

Christian of Denmark in similar circumstances, the results of his strange journey provided the most accurate information (all carefully mapped) of the interior of the United States that was available at the time, and laid the basis for the first transcontinental crossing of North America by the famous explorers Lewis and Clark.

John Evans sailed across the Atlantic and arrived in Baltimore in 1792. From there he proceeded to St Louis, which was at that time in Spanish territory. Things went wrong at first and he spent two years in prison under suspicion of being a British agent. When finally released, he proceeded up the Missouri to its head-waters with a party of thirty men and a few Indian guides in August 1795, mapping his route with great accuracy as he went along. He contacted the Mandan Indians and several other tribes including the Paducas, but found no one among them able to speak the Welsh language. After many adventures, he returned in 1797 to St Louis and later accepted a post with the Spanish administration in New Orleans, where he died, a relatively young man, two years later, weakened, no doubt, by the great hardships he had endured.

Meanwhile the strange journey of John Evans had attracted the attention of Thomas Jefferson, then President of the infant United States. The information gathered and mapped by Evans was transferred to the President by Daniel Clark of New Orleans and was, in turn, passed on by the President himself to Meriwether Lewis and William Clark. Although the references to Evans in the journals of these famous explorers are few, they most certainly profited by his work and took his map with them on their great expedition to the shores of the Pacific, as the corrections they made on it clearly testify.[9] The point we have to stress is that Evans was inspired by legends which had their origins in traditions of the sea that reached back in Caernarvonshire to the days when the grey waters of the Irish Sea were as 'bright with Neolithic argonauts as the Western Pacific is today.[10] He laid a trail across an empty continent that in turn was to guide pioneers in their thousands across the prairies to lay the foundations of a nation that has emerged as the greatest republic in the western world.

Before leaving the story of John Evans, it is not inappropriate to mention that in the years before he left Wales to explore the innermost recesses of an unknown continent, his co-religionists were using the western sea-routes in large numbers. The late-eighteenth century saw a great religious revival in Wales which brought into being the Welsh Calvinistic Methodist Church. It so happened that the initial movement had its bases in South Wales and chief among the early leaders was Daniel Rowland of Llangeitho in southern Cardiganshire. People from all parts of Welsh-speaking Wales flocked to hear him preach. As his church was far too small to hold the vast congregations that assembled, they had to meet in the open fields nearby.[11] Those journeying from Anglesey and western Caernarvonshire, in particular, went to Llangeitho along the old western sea-routes, crossing the Llŷn peninsula on foot, if need be, and then embarking for New Quay, or one of the other small ports in south-western Cardiganshire, and walking the remainder of the journey to Llangeitho. We know, too, that Caernarvonshire and Anglesey Baptists also sailed from the Llŷn peninsula over Cardigan Bay to New Quay and other ports for their religious gatherings in north Pembrokeshire at this time, so this section of the western seaways remained very active in this way throughout the eighteenth and early nineteenth centuries.

Plate 58

While we have concentrated on travelling in pursuit of some great objective, or for health or religious reasons, we must not forget that the cause of travelling in every age and in every land is primarily, but not exclusively, economic. The ancient hunter followed game and sought flint for his weapons from the nearest suitable quarry. There is in this context one reason for travelling by sea which is not often mentioned, but which must have had an influence on movement over the western seas from the earliest times, and that is the pursuit of fish.

The basis of successful fishing in these seas rests on the character of the continental shelf underlying these waters; the shelf is very rich in fish food—plankton of all kinds, and the waters over it, being shallow, are admirably suited in modern times for both trawlers and drifters. Britain occupies a central position on this shelf, and this important fact must be regarded as being mainly responsible for the rise of the British fishing industry in the past[12]. Many other countries also share the great advantages of fishing on the continental shelf. Spanish as well as Breton fishermen fish in these important grounds. Boats from San Sebastian, Vigo and Corunna fish regularly in the waters of eastern and western Greenland, as well as around Newfoundland for cod. These fishermen also catch tunny and bonito off Morocco and Madeira and visit south-western Ireland for skate. Likewise, the Breton fishermen on the north coast of Brittany, from St Malo to Paimpol, visit Newfoundland and western Greenland waters as well as the Icelandic fisheries every year. They frequently appear also off the south and south-west coast of Ireland. Equally interesting in the present context is the fishing from the south coast of Brittany. This is based on Groix island opposite the Blavet estuary—an area famous in the Age of the Saints. Here is centred the tunny fishing which extends southwards to the coast of Spain and also utilizes the Biscayan Deepwater area. At the other extremity of the western seas, along the Norwegian coasts, Bear Island, Spitzbergen and Iceland, the U.S.S.R. is the newcomer, and with its modern fishing fleet has established itself as the most important fishing country in the whole area.

Economic activity at the present time along the western seaways is equally clearly shown by a study of the market-gardening industry. In Brittany and the Channel Islands (in spite of their exposed positions) there exists many a deep-sided valley possessing rich soil and protected from the Atlantic gales. With the low range of temperature characteristic of these maritime lands, conditions are admirably suited for the growing of early vegetables. In addition to the produce of Guernsey, the small tidal ports of Brittany, especially Morlaix, Lannion, St Brieuc, Pont L'Abbé and St Pol de Léon, send out early potatoes, cauliflowers, and, possibly most characteristic of all, onions in the later season. For generations the presence of Breton onion men has been an annual feature of most towns and villages in western Britain and Ireland. The onions are sold from door to door in long strings carried on a pole over the vendor's shoulder but behind the individual salesman, there are rented warehouses in well-established locations such as Plymouth, Pembroke, Dublin and Glasgow. Thus the commercial activity of the western seaways is not yet extinct.[13] Plate 61

It is clear, therefore, that the inhabitants of the 'Atlantic façade of Europe' have lived for countless generations in the closest proximity to the sea. Their life is bound up with it and with ships and with those who sail in them. A way of life has developed that is clearly different from that of the peasant, the industrial worker or the city dweller. It is from such a background that the seamen of both the Royal Navy and the Merchant Navy have largely been drawn, in much the same way as Breton sailors laid the foundations of the French Navy and Merchant Service. The coasts of Wales, Ireland, Scotland, the Isle of Man, Cornwall, Brittany and Galicia are studded with coves, each with its little breakwater and its quota of fishing-vessels, while nestling in the sheltered valleys behind Plate 59 lie the tiny villages where the fishermen and their families live. The village is often served neither by a railway nor good roads, but, nevertheless, its inhabitants have a cosmopolitan outlook. The conversation one hears is far more likely to be about some distant port on the far-away highways of the world than about things at home.[14] There is no doubt, too, that the age-old tradition of the sea was deepened in the days of the sailing ships, especially from the sixteenth to the mid-nineteenth century. Plate 60 The schooners, barks, brigs and brigantines of Britain, Ireland, France and Spain literally sailed 'the seven seas'. In their hey-day in the mid-nineteenth century, they crossed to Newfoundland for Canadian timber and visited Casablanca for Mediterranean wheat, and rounded Cape Horn for the natural nitrates of the Atacama desert. While these extensive ocean voyages were certainly important in building up a hardy seafaring tradition, they must not be allowed to mask the fact that underlying this ocean traffic was the local trade in which these small sailing ships participated. Herein lay the tradition of the western-sea trade. The Port Books reveal that such commodities as salt, soap, sugar, candles, tobacco, figs, fish, hops, millinery and glassware were brought into these little harbours in the days of the sailing ships.[15] Milford, Chester, Liverpool, Glasgow, Ayr, Stornoway, Bideford, Poole, Portsmouth, Bristol, Newhaven, Cork, Wexford, Galway, Dublin, Rochelle, Brest, Nantes, St Malo, Corunna, San Sebastian were all equally involved. The landsmen, in turn, came down to the little quaysides with their carts and waggons and distributed the commodities far and wide into the hinterland. When, in the end, the steamship and the ocean liner arrived, the sailors left their little harbours and joined the larger ships that sailed out of the greater ports.

During the period from the sixteenth to the nineteenth century, the nations of the Atlantic fringe of Europe built up great navies. Spain and Portugal, France and Britain were all involved. The growth of large navies, in turn, depended on this same tradition of the sea, that reached back to remote antiquity. Long before the days of the Armada, the coastal fishing-villages of Devon, Cornwall, Wales and Scotland provided the bulk of the sailors for the Royal Navy. We hear, for example, of the little town of Fowey in Cornwall (situated at the terminal of a route-way across the peninsula that had been in use from prehistoric times) taking the greatest pride in having provided no less than 47 ships for King Edward III's navy that laid siege to Calais, compared with the miserable total of just 25 ships provided by the Great City of London.[16] It was from the same little harbours that seamen crowded to the flag whenever invasion by Spaniards or Frenchmen threatened. So too, it was British fisherfolk and officers and men of the Merchant Navy who undertook in the great wars of the present century much of the auxiliary work of the Royal Navy in conditions of extreme danger, be it with the convoys in 1917 or at Dunkirk in 1940. It was men from the little ports who did the hard sea-work to which their lives at sea had inured them, and for which the professional Navy had neither the vessels nor the men. These men possessed what Professor A. J. Marder, the great modern naval historian, has called 'the sea instinct'.[17] In this book, we have attempted to show how tradition, heredity and environment, over many millennia, have combined to perpetuate this 'sea instinct', especially along the shores of Atlantic Europe.

# *Abbreviations*

| | |
|---|---|
| *AA* | *American Anthropologist* |
| *A Arch* | *Acta Archaeologica* |
| *AB* | *Analecta Bollandiana* |
| *AberS* | *Aberystwyth Studies* |
| *AC* | *Archaeologia Cambrensis* |
| *AGR* | *American Geographical Review* |
| *AntJ* | *Antiquaries Journal* |
| *Ant* | *Antiquity* |
| *Arch* | *Archaeologia* |
| *AS* | *The Advancement of Science* |
| *CA* | *Current Archaeology* |
| *C LlGC* | *Cylchgrawn Llyfrgell Genedlaethol Cymru* |
| *DNB* | *Dictionary of National Biography (with supplements)* |
| *GJ* | *Geographical Journal* |
| *JEH* | *Journal of Ecclesiastical History* |
| *JMM* | *Journal of the Manx Museum* |
| *JRAI* | *Journal of the Royal Anthropological Institute* |
| *JRSAI* | *Journal of the Royal Society of Antiquaries of Ireland* |
| *MCS* | *Map Collectors' Series* |
| *NP* | *New Phytologist* |
| *PPS* | *Proceedings of the Prehistoric Society* |
| *PRIA* | *Proceedings of the Royal Irish Academy* |
| *PWCFC* | *Proceedings of the West Cornwall Field Club* |
| *SC* | *Studia Celtica* |
| *SH* | *Studia Hibernica* |
| *TRHS* | *Transactions of the Royal Historical Society* |
| *THSC* | *Transactions of the Honourable Society of Cymmrodorion* |
| *UJA* | *Ulster Journal of Archaeology* |

*References in the Notes on the Text preceded by 'Bibl.' are to numbers in the Bibliography, p. 143.*

# *Notes on the Text*

## CHAPTER I

1 For a general statement, see Glotz, *A.C.* and also Childe, *Bibl.* 4b, especially Chaps. II, III, IV, and V. 15–83.

3 Evans, *Bibl.* 26, 56.

3 A clearly drawn map indicating the presumed coastline of the British area in immediate post-glacial times can be obtained from Peake and Fleure, *Bibl.* 30, 26. Fig. 15. See also fig. 1.

4 Much of the original work dealing with post-glacial climatic conditions has been based on the Scandinavian area associated with the names of de Geer, Liden, Antev, Blytt and Sernander, and others. Modern research, especially that dependent on pollen-grain analysis and radio-carbon dating, has meant that absolute dates relating to post-glacial times are being constantly revised as new evidence becomes available. The diagram on p. 13 has been specially prepared for this work by Dr D. Q. Bowen of the Department of Geography, University College of Wales, Aberystwyth, and represents the situation as envisaged by scholars in 1971.

5 For a good summary statement of the colonization of England and Wales by post-glacial forests, see Godwin, *Bibl.* 28.

6 Based with additions on Clark, *Bibl.* 24a. Map (Frontispiece) and Chap. III 19–53.

7 Thomas, C., 'The Palaeolithic and Mesolithic Periods in Cornwall' *P.W.C.F.C.* II 2, (1957–8), 10.

8 Hencken, *Bibl.* 29, 5–6.

9 Evans and Jope, *Bibl.* 25, 75.

10 Clark, G., 'The Prehistory of the Isle of Man' *P.P.S.* (1935) 75.

11 Clark, *Bibl.* 24a, especially Chaps. IV and V 54–91.

12 Grimes, W. F., 'Guide to the Collection illustrating the Prehistory of Wales' (Cardiff 1939) 8–17.

13 Hencken, *Bibl.* 29, 49. See also Evans, *Bibl.* 33, 151.

14 For Rathlin Island and Tievebulliagh, see Evans and Jope, *Bibl.* 25, 77 (with distribution map Fig. 9) and for Graig Lwyd, Penmaenmawr, see S. Hazzledine Warren, *A.C.* LXXXII (1927), 141.

15 Megaw, J.V.S., 'The Neolithic Period in Cornwall' *P.W.C.F.C.* II 2. (1957–58), 20.

## CHAPTER II

1 Evans, *Bibl.* 33, 182.

2 See especially Daniel, *Bibl.* 31a.

3 For the general argument see Fox, *Bibl.* 41b, 22, Forde, *Bibl.* 35 and Peake and Fleure, *Bibl.* 36b.

4 See note 2 above.

5 Ashbee, P. 'The Fussell's Lodge Long Barrow Excavations 1957' *Arch.* 100 (1966) 47.

6 Renfrew, A. C. 'Colonialism and Megalithismus' *Ant.* (1967) 276.

See Note 5 above.
Daniel, G. E. 'Northmen and Southmen' *Ant.* (1967) 315.
See Note 8 317.
Bray, W. 'Aspects of the Early Metal Age in Sardinia' Ph.D. Dissertation. No. 4177 (Cambridge 1962).
See Trump, D. H. *Pre-Roman Peninsular Italy* (London 1966).
See Note 8. 316.
Evans, *Bibl.* 8, 7.
Childe, *Bibl.* 44, 36.
The argument is well presented in Professor de Valera's work on the western counties of Ireland, see especially de Valera and Nuallain *Bibl.* 37, but reference should also be made to Evans, *Bibl.* 8, 13–14.
Johnstone, P. *'The Ships of Prehistory'* (London 1972). IX.
Lethbridge, T. C. *Boats and Boatmen* (London 1953). III.
Hencken, H. O'N. *Bibl.* 29, 175 (with map). See also A. Berthelot Ed. Festus Avienus, *Ora Maritima* (Paris 1934). 57.
Johnstone, P. *The Ships of Prehistory* (London 1972). IX.
Fox, C. 'A dug-out canoe from South Wales.' *Ant. J.* VI. (1926) 121–142.
Marsden, P.R.V. *A Roman ship from Blackfriar's London* (London 1962) 34–5.
2 Marquis de Folin, *Bateaux et Navires* (Paris 1892). 16
3 Johnstone, P. *The ships of Prehistory* (London 1972) X.
4 Daniel, G. E. *Bibl.* 31b, 127–8.
5 For evidence of this in Wales and Brittany see *Bibl.* 36a, 90–1, and more especially for Brittany–Chadwick, *Bibl.* 3d, 296–7 and Plate 10 indicating a Christianized menhir at Rungelo.

CHAPTER III

1 Fox, *Bibl.* 11, 45.
2 Wailes, B., 'The Bronze Age in Cornwall' *P.W.C.F.C.* II 2 (1957–58) 29.
3 Childe, V. G., 'Trade and Industry in Barbarian Europe till Roman Times' *Camb. Econ. Hist. of Europe*. Vol. I, Chap. I, 13–14.
4 Hencken, *Bibl.* 29, 68.
5 Coffey, *Bibl.* 39. See also Fox, *Bibl.* 41b, 48–49.
6 *Ibid*, especially Fox, *Bibl.* 41 b, 48.
7 Hencken, *Bibl.* 29; 74 and 78.
8 See the map (Plate VI) in Fox *Bibl.* 41b prepared by Miss L. F. Chitty based mainly on the catalogue of bronze implements in the British Museum.
9 For a general account, see Peake, *Bibl.* 43 and also A. Brewis, 'The Bronze Sword in Great Britain', *Arch.* lxxiii (1923), 253–65, and E. E. Evans, 'The Sword Bearers', *Ant.* IV (1930) 157–165 (with distribution map of accessory intrusive Late Bronze Age objects.)
10 See general discussion in Childe, 'Trade and Industry in Barbarian Europe till Roman Times', *Camb. Econ. History of Europe*. Vol. I Chap. I.
11 See Fox, *Bibl.* 41b, 41–42 (with illustrations) 91, and maps by Miss L. F. Chitty, Plates V and VIII.
12 For Maps, see V. G. Childe, *Ant. J.* (1939) 322, and for comment see the same author in *Camb. Econ. History of Europe* quoted above pp. 22–23.
13 Childe, *Bibl.* 44, 71.
14 The original map showing the distribution of socketed axes of 'Welsh' type appeared in

Fox and Hyde *Bibl.* 41c, plate LXXXI facing p. 390. See also R. E. M. Wheeler, *Prehistoric and Roman Wales* (Oxford 1925) 156. Several finds have been made subsequently, but they do not alter the fundamental distribution pattern.

15 Hencken, H. O'N., *Bibl.* 42, 92 and Fig. 26.

16 Diodorus, *Opera* V. 22. The passage is given in translation by H. O'N. Hencken, *Bibl.* 42, 171.

17 *Bibl.* 42, Chapter V.

## CHAPTER IV

1 Strabo, *Opera* iv. 4. 1. See also Childe, *Bibl.* 4a, 244.

2 See Hawkes, *Bibl.* 45a, and 45B.

3 MacKie, Euan. *P.P.S.* XXXI, 1965, 104 and 124.

4 MacKie, Euan. 'Radiocarbon dates and the Scottish Iron Age' *Ant.* XLIII (1969). 22.

5 After describing Claudius' annexation of Britain, Orosius says; 'Orcades etiam insulas ultra Britanniam in oceano positas Romano adiecit imperio'. (Quoted by Scott, *Bibl.* 46b, 104).

6 For Childe's deduction that this means that Orcadian chiefs sent envoys to make formal submission to Claudius, see Childe, *Bibl.* 44. App. ix. 129.

7 Scott, *Bibl.* 46b, 103.

8 Childe, *Bibl.* 4a, 248.

9 Scott, *Bibl.* 46b, 115.

10 MacKie, Euan. 'Radiocarbon dates and the Scottish Iron Age' *Ant.* XLIII (1969). 25.

11 Scott, *Bibl.* 46a, 33.

## CHAPTER V

1 For the general theme, see Fox, *Bibl.* 11.

2 Nash-Williams, V. E. *Bibl.* 18, 4. This important work provides a complete bibliography and corpus with datings of the Early Christian monuments found in Wales. The monuments are divided into four groups according to age, the first group covering the period from the fifth to the seventh centuries. In his introduction to this work, he suggests that the distribution of the monuments belonging to his first group points unmistakeably to influences reaching Wales from the western seas and passing in-land by way of the Roman roads. He thinks this means evangelization from Gaul directed at Wales, as well as at Cornwall and North-western Britain.

3 A general discussion of the situation will be found in Bowen, *'The Settlements of the Celtic Saints in Wales'* (Cardiff 1954), and Bowen, 'The Settlements of the Celtic Saints in South Wales' *Ant.* XIX (1945), 175–186.

4 Jackson, K. *Language and History in Early Britain* (Edinburgh 1953) 151–2.

5 Bray, W. and Trump, D. *A Dictionary of Archaeology* (London 1970) see under Ogham or ogam. 166.

6 For Pelagius, see Ferguson *Pelagius* (Cambridge 1956) and for a discussion of Pelagianism in Britain, see Bowen, *Bibl.* 2c, 63–6 and Bu'lock, *Bibl.* 50, 133–141.

7 The tripartite division derives from the famous *Catalogus Sanctorum Hiberniae* ('The Catalogue of the Saints of Ireland'). For a general discussion, see Chadwick, *Bibl.* 3a, 71–8.

8 Good use has been made of this viewpoint by

B. R. S. Megaw. See his article on 'Who was St. Conchan?'—A consideration of Manx Christian origins' *J.M.M.* (1962–63) VI 79.

Doble, G. H. *St. Petrock: Abbot and Confessor* (Long Compton 1930). See also Doble, *Bibl.* 52.

Bowen, *Bibl.* 49a and also Fawtier, R. *La Vie de Saint Sampson* (Paris 1912).

Largillière, J. *Bibl.* 55.

Bowen, *Bibl.* 2c, 188, and also Chadwick, *Bibl.* 3d, 283.

See Binchy, *Bibl.* 48, 165–6 and Bowen, *Bibl.* 2c, 117–124.

An important paper by Paul Grosjean, 'Gloria postuma St. Martini Turonensis apud Scottos et Britannos', *A.B.* LV (1937) 300–45 should be consulted.

Binchy, *Bibl.* 48, 167–8.

Towill, E. S. 'St. Mochaoi of Nendrum' *U.J.A.* (3rd series XXVII) 1964. 109–29.

Bowen, *Bibl.* 2c, 99–104.

Chadwick, *Bibl.* 3a, 58–59.

Selmer, *Bibl.* 59. See also Bowen, *Bibl.* 2b, 161.

Dicuil, *Liber de Mensura orbis Terrae VII* 17. Ed. Parthney. 44.

The best account of the work of Irish missionaries on the Continent is found in Gougaud, *Bibl.* 14, but see also Fitzgerald, *Bibl.* 53 (with map).

CHAPTER VI

Jones, Gwyn, *Bibl.* 64, 3.

See Sawyer, *Bibl.* 69a, 60 and 67, and also Jones, Gwyn, *Bibl.* 64, 189 especially Note 1.

Armstrong, *Bibl.* 61, especially Fig. 34, pp. 82–3 and also Kinvig, *Bibl.* 66, fig. 22, p. 68.

4 Jones, Gwyn, *Bibl.* 64, 186–190. For a standard account of Viking ships and seafaring see Brøgger and Sheteling, *The Viking Ships—their ancestry and evolution* (English version, Oslo, 1953).

5 Sawyer, *Bibl.* 69b. 86–87.

6 Quoted by Kinvig, *Bibl.* 66, (1944), 70.

7 Jones, Gwyn, *Bibl.* 64, 204–206.

8 Sawyer, *Bibl.* 69b, 87–88.

9 Jones, Gwyn, *Bibl.* 64, 355.

10 Williams, A. H., *An introduction to the History of Wales*, I, Prehistoric Times to 1063 AD (Cardiff 1941), 157.

11 For a general account see Charles, *Bibl.* 63.

12 Jones, Gwyn., *Bibl.* 64, 210.

13 Sawyer, *Bibl.* 69b, 88.

14 Kinvig, *Bibl.* 66, (1944) 72.

15 Loyn, *Bibl.* 67, 89.

16 See Chapter V, especially with reference to St Paul Aurelian, St Maudez and St Winwaloe.

17 Jones, Gwyn, *Bibl.* 64, 214–215.

18 Jones, Gwyn, *Bibl.* 64, 216–217.

19 Evans and Jope, *Bibl.* 25, 96.

20 Sawyer, *Bibl.* 69a, 83, especially Plate VIII; See also Bersu and Wilson, *Bibl.* 62, Plates V, VI, and VII.

21 Kinvig, *Bibl.* 66, (1944), 101, Fig. 29.

22 Fleure, *Bibl.* 9, Chap. 7, 'The Sea Rovers', 153–157.

CHAPTER VII

1 Quoted in Bowen, *Bibl.* 2c, 145–146.

2 Hughes, K., 'The changing theory and practice of Irish Pilgrimage' *J.E.H.* xi (1960) 143 ff.

3 Baring-Gould and Fisher, *Bibl.* 1, II, 333–336, see also Williams, G., *Bibl.* 79, 441 and 490.

4 Jones, G. Hartwell, *Bibl.* 77, 250–251.

5 *Ibid.*, 198.

6 Williams, G., *Bibl.* 79, 494–495. The island would appear to have enjoyed an almost limitless reputation for sanctity.

7 An interesting pictorial map of St Patrick's Purgatory on an island in Lough Derg on the Shannon is given in Gorman, *Bibl.* 74, fig. 37, 56–57.

8 Bowen, *Bibl.* 2c, 217–218, and especially Fig. 52.

9 Willis Browne, *Survey of the Cathedral church of St David's* (1717) 52, copying a memorandum of George Owen, (d. 1613).

10 Crawford, *Bibl.* 51, 190, and especially the map on p. 189.

11 Williams, G., *Bibl.* 79, 491–2 and 494.

12 Jones, G. Hartwell, *Bibl.* 77, 256–257.

13 For a general account of the coastal geomorphology of north-western Spain see R. Way, *A Geography of Spain.* (London 1962), 38.

14 See Peake, *Bibl.* 78, 208–26, and Howes, *Bibl.* 75, 132–150.

15 Jones, G. Hartwell, *Bibl.* 77, 570.

16 *Ibid.*, 254.

17 Crone, *Bibl.* 73. This important article shows Roman and other itineraries, especially those of the Middle Ages from which many of the place-names on the famous Hereford Cathedral Map of the World were derived. The overland route through Western Europe to Santiago de Compostela is clearly indicated. See Fig. 2 p. 450.

18 The long sea journey involved in the pilgrimage to Santiago exercised a strange fascination for the contemporary Welsh poets, especially men like Lewis Glyn Cothi and Rhys Nanmor. The former, for example, wrote a *cywydd* to Gruffydd ab Rhys ab Ieuan of Vranas in the parish of Llandrillo in Edeyrnion when he was on pilgrimage at sea (G. Hartwell Jones, *Bibl.* 77, 255–257). See also Bell, Idris, 'Translations from the *Cywyddwyr*', *T.H.S.C.* 1942, 135–6. Similarly, David Jenkins discusses and publishes a *cywydd* by Lewis Trefnant describing the apprehensions of those left waiting at home for a pilgrim who had left on a voyage to Rome. (*C. Ll. G.C.* viii (1953), 92–94). For contemporary English verse of the same kind, see J. A. Williamson, *The English Channel*, (London 1959), 145 and refs.

19 Radford *Bibl.* 57, 69. Dr Radford refers to the passage in the *Life* of St Ciarán of Cluain on p. 68.

20 See *Camb. Econ. Hist. of Europe* II. (Cambridge 1952). Trade and Industry in the Middle Ages. Chap. IV. 123–4.

## CHAPTER VIII

1 Evans, *Bibl.* 83, 9. The article on Captain Thomas James in the *D.N.B.* casts some doubt on the question of his work being the basis of Coleridge's 'Ancient Mariner'.

2 See *A Regiment of the Sea and other writings on Navigation*, by William Bourne of Gravesend, *c.* 1535–1582. The Hakluyt Society, 2nd Series, No. CXXI. Ed. E.G.R. Taylor, (Cambridge 1963) and for further reference *Journ. Inst. of Navigation.* 23 (1970), 408.

3 See Evans, *Bibl.* 83, 6.

Crone, *Bibl.* 82, 76 together with an outline sketch indicating the main features of the Vinland map. See also Luca de Tena, *Bibl.* 88, 516.

For a general discussion, see Luca de Tena, *Bibl.* 88, 517.

Williams D., *Bibl.* 90, 110–111.

*Ibid.*, 111.

*Ibid.*, 121–123.

Abel, *Bibl.* 81, 335 and 342.

Childe, *Bibl.* 44, 36, already quoted in Chapter V.

For a general account of Daniel Rowland, see D. J. O. Jones, *Bibl.* 85.

See L. D. Stamp and S. H. Beaver, *The British Isles: A Geographic and Economic Survey* (London 1954 and 1961), Chap. XIII. The British Fisheries. (See especially Fig. 132, p. 261 for a general discussion of the distribution of the main British fishing grounds.)

13 Crawford, *Bibl.* 51, 184.

14 Jones, D. Parry, *Bibl.* 86, 56.

15 For a general picture of this trade, see Lewis, *Bibl.* 87, Morgan, *Bibl.* 89, and Hughes, *Bibl.* 84.

16 See Elliott-Binns, L. E., *Medieval Cornwall.* (London 1955), 88.

17 Marder, A. J., *From the Dreadnought to Scapa Flow.* V. (London 1970), 332.

# Bibliography

## GENERAL


1 BARING-GOULD, S. and FISHER, J. *The Lives of the British Saints*, 4 vols., (London, 1907–13).

2a BOWEN, E. G. 'The Irish Sea Province,' *C.A.* 8, (1968).

b — 'The Seas of Western Britain: Studies in Historical Geography' *Geography at Aberystwyth, (Jubilee Vol.)* (Cardiff, 1968).

c — *Saints, Seaways and Settlements in the Celtic Lands,* (Cardiff, 1969).

d — 'Britain and the British Seas, 1902–1968' *The Irish Sea Province in Archaeology and History* (Cardiff, 1970).

3a CHADWICK, N. K. *The Age of the Saints in the Early Celtic Church,* (Oxford, 1961).

b — *Celtic Britain* (London, 1963).

c — *The Colonization of Brittany from Celtic Britain,* (London, 1965).

d — *Early Brittany*, (Cardiff, 1969).

4a CHILDE, V. G. *The Prehistoric Communities of the British Isles,* (London 2nd Edit., 1947).

b — *The Dawn of European Civilization.* 6th Edit., (London, 1957).

5 COLLINGWOOD, R. G. and MYRES, J. N. L. *Roman Britain and the English Settlements.* (Oxford, 1936).

6 DOBLE, G. H. *The Saints of Cornwall,* Four Parts ((Truro 1960; Oxford, 1962; Truro 1964; Oxford, 1965).

7 EKWALL, E. *Concise Oxford Dictionary of English Place-Names* (Oxford, 1936).

8 EVANS, E. E. *Prehistoric and Early Christian Ireland. A Guide,* (London, 1966).

9 FLEURE, H. J. *A Natural History of Man in Britain* (London, 1951).

10 FOOTE, P. G. and WILSON, D. M. *The Viking Achievement,* (London, 1970).

11 FOX, C. *The Personality of Britain*, 4th Edit., (Cardiff, 1947).

12 FOX, C. and DICKENS, B. (Eds.) *Early Cultures of North-West Europe* (Cambridge, 1950).

13 GIOT, P. R. *Brittany*, (London, 1960).

14 GOUGAUD, DOM L. *Christianity in Celtic Lands*, (London, 1932).

15 LEWIS, A. R. *The Northern Seas,* (Princeton, 1958).

16 MACKINDER, H. J. *Britain and the British Seas*, (Oxford, 1902).

17 MOORE, D. (Ed.) *The Irish Sea Province in Archaeology and History,* (Cardiff, 1970).

18 NASH-WILLIAMS, V. E. *The Early Christian Monuments of Wales,* (Cardiff, 1950).

19 DE PAOR, M. and L. *Early Christian Ireland,* 4th Impression (London, 1964).

20 SHAW, R. C. *Post-Roman Carlisle and the Kingdoms of the North-West.* 2nd Edit., (Preston, 1964).

21 WILLIAMS, I. *Enwau Lleoedd,* (Liverpool, 1945).

## CHAPTER I

22 BERARD, V. *Les Phénicians et l'Odyssée* Vol. I (Paris, 1902).

23 BROOKS, C. E. P. *Climate through the Ages*, 2nd Edit., (London, 1949).

24a CLARK, J. G. D. *The Mesolithic Age in Britain,* (Cambridge, 1932).

b — *The Mesolithic Settlement of Northern Europe,* Cambridge, 1936

25 EVANS, E. E. and JOPE, E. M. Prehistoric and Protohistoric Periods. *Belfast in its Regional Setting, Brit. Assoc. Adv. Sci.* (Belfast, 1952).

26 EVANS, E.E. 'The Atlantic Ends of Europe' *A.S.* XV. (London, 1958).

27 GLOTZ, G. *The Aegean Civilization*, (London, 1925).

28 GODWIN, H. 'Pollen Analysis and Forest History in England and Wales', *N.P.* 39, (London, 1940).

29 HENCKEN, H. O'N. *Archaeology of Cornwall and Scilly*, (London, 1932). Especially Chap. I.

30 PEAKE, H. J. E. and FLEURE, H. J. *Hunters and Artists*: Corridors of Time. II. (Oxford, 1927).

## CHAPTER II

31a DANIEL, G. E. 'The Dual Nature of the Megalithic Colonization of Prehistoric Europe' *PPS New Series VI* and *VII.* (London, 1940–1).

b — *The Megalith Builders of Western Europe,* (London, 1958).

32 DAVIES, M. 'The diffusion and distribution pattern of Megalithic Monuments of the Irish Sea and North Channel coastlands' *Ant. J.* XXVI, Nos 1 and 2. (London, 1946).

33 EVANS, E. E. 'Prehistoric Geography', *The British Isles: A Systematic Geography*. Ed. Watson and Sissons. (London, 1964).

34 FLEURE, H. J. and ROBERTS E. J. 'Archaeological Problems of the West Coast of Britain.' *AC* Vol. 70. (Cardiff, 1915).

35 FORDE, C. D. 'The Early Cultures of Atlantic Europe', *AA* Vol. 32. (New York, 1930).

36a PEAKE, H. J. E. and FLEURE, H. J. *The Way of the Sea*, Corridors of Time, VI. (Oxford, 1929).

b — 'Megaliths and Beakers' *JRAI* Vol. IX, (London, 1930).

37 DE VALERA, R. and NUALLAIN, S. O. *Survey of the Megalithic Tombs of Ireland,* II. *County Mayo.* (Dublin, 1964).

## CHAPTER III

38a CHILDE, V. G. *The Bronze Age* (Cambridge, 1930).

b — 'Trade and Industry in Barbarian Europe Until Roman Times' *Cambridge Economic History of Europe.* II. Chap. I. (Cambridge, 1952).

39 COFFEY, G. *The Bronze Age in Ireland* (Dublin, 1913).

40 CRAWFORD, O. G. S. 'The distribution of Early Bronze Age Settlements in Britain'. *GJ* XL (London, 1912).

41a FOX, C. 'An Encrusted Urn of the Late

Bronze Age' *Ant. J.* VII (London, 1927).
b — *The Personality of Britain* 4th Ed. (Cardiff, 1947). Especially for maps of Flat and Hammer Flanged Axes, Cast Flanged Axes, Cordoned and Encrusted Urns, by Miss L. F. Chitty, and of Gold objects by Chitty and Fox.
c FOX, C. and HYDE, H. A. 'A Second Cauldron and an Irish Sword from the Llyn Fawr Hoard, Rhigos, Glamorgan'. *Ant. J.* XIX (London, 1939).
42 HENCKEN, H. O'N. *Archaeology of Cornwall and Scilly*, (London, 1932) especially Chap. III. The Bronze Age and Chap. V. The Prehistoric Tin Trade.
43 PEAKE, H. J. E. *The Bronze Age and the Celtic World.* (London, 1922).

CHAPTER IV

44 CHILDE, V. G. *Scotland before the Scots,* (London, 1946).
45a HAWKES, C. F. C. 'The British Hill-Forts' *Ant.* V (London, 1931).
b — 'The ABC of the British Iron Age', *Ant.* XXXIII, (London, 1959).
46a SCOTT, LINDSAY 'The Problem of the Brochs' *PPS New Series XIII* (London, 1947).
b — 'Gallo-British Colonies. The Aisled Round-House Culture in the North' *PPS* New Series, XIV. (London, 1948).
47 WAINWRIGHT, F. T. (Ed.) *The Northern Isles,* (Edinburgh, 1962)

CHAPTER V

48 BINCHY, D. A. 'Patrick and his Biographers' *SH* No. 2. (Dublin, 1962).
49a BOWEN, E. G. 'The Travels of St Samson of Dol, *Aber S* XIII (Aberystwyth, 1934).
b —'The Irish Sea in the Age of the Saints', *SC* IV (Cardiff, 1969).
50 BU'LOCK, J. D. 'Early Christian Memorial Formulae' *AC* CV (Cardiff, 1956).
51 CRAWFORD, O. G. S. 'Western Seaways' in *Custom is King*, (London, 1936).
52 DOBLE, G. H. *The Cornish Saints,* especially Part IV (Oxford, 1965): *The Saints of the New Quay District.*
53 FITZGERALD, W. *The Historical Geography of Early Ireland,* (London, 1925)
54 HILLYGARTH, J. N. 'Visigothic Spain and Early Christian Ireland', *PRIA* 62 (Dublin, 1962).
55 LARGILLIÈRE, J. *Les Saints et l'organization chrétienne primitive dans l'Armorique Bretonne,* (Rennes, 1925).
56 LETHBRIDGE, T. C. *Herdsmen and Hermits —Celtic Seafarers in the Northern Seas* (Cambridge, 1950).
57 RADFORD, C. A. R. 'Imported Pottery found at Tintagel, Cornwall', in *Dark Age Britain (Ed. Harden) (*London, 1956).
58 RICHARDS, M. 'The Irish Settlements in South-west Wales,' *JRSAI* XC. Part II (Dublin, 1960).
59 SELMER, O. O. *Navigatio Sancti Brendani* (Paris, 1959).
60 THOMAS, C. 'Cornwall in the Dark Ages,' *Archaeology in Cornwall 1933–1958. PWCFC* II No. 2 (Truro, 1957–58).

61 ARMSTRONG, R. *The Early Mariners: A History of Seafaring* (London, 1967).
62 BERSU, G. and WILSON, D. M. *Three Viking Graves in the Isle of Man*, (London, 1966).
63 CHARLES, B. G. *Old Norse Relations with Wales*, (Cardiff, 1934).
64 JONES, GWYN *A History of the Vikings*, (London, 1968).
65 KENDRICK, T. D. *A History of the Vikings* (London, 1930).
66 KINVIG, R. H. *A History of the Isle of Man*, (1st Edit. Douglas, 1944, 2nd Edit. Liverpool, 1950).
67 LOYN, R. H. 'History from the End of the Roman Occupation to the Norman Conquest,' *The Cardiff Region: A Survey. Brit. Assoc. for the Adv. of Science.* (Cardiff, 1960).
68 MEGAW, B. R. S. and E. M. 'The Norse Heritage in the Isle of Man' in *Early Cultures of North Western Europe.* (Cambridge, 1950).
69a SAWYER, P. H. *The Age of the Vikings*, (London, 1962).
b — 'The Vikings and the Irish Sea' in *The Irish Sea Province in Archaeology and History*. (Cardiff, 1970).
70 STENTON, F. M. 'The Historical Bearing of Place Name Studies: England in the Sixth Century. *TRHS* Series 4, XXI (London, 1939).

## CHAPTER VII

71 Admiralty Naval Intelligence Division Geographical Handbook Series, *Spain and Portugal* Vol. I. *The Peninsula*. BR 502. (London, 1941).
72 CONDRY, W. M. *Exploring Wales*, (London, 1970).
73 CRONE, G. R. 'New Light on the Hereford Map' *GJ* 131. (London, 1965).
74 GORMAN, M. (Ed.) *Ireland by the Irish* (London, 1963).
75 HOWES, H. W. 'The Cult of Santiago at Compostela', *Folklore* 36 (London, 1925).
76 HUGHES, K. 'The changing theory and practice of Irish Pilgrimage' *JEH* XI. (London, 1960).
77 JONES, G. HARTWELL *Celtic Britain and the Pilgrim Movement.* Y Cymmrodor. Special Publication (London, 1912).
78 PEAKE, H. J. E. 'Santiago: The Evolution of a Patron Saint', *Folklore* 30, (London, 1919).
79 WILLIAMS, GLANMOR *The Welsh Church from Conquest to Reformation.* (Cardiff, 1962).
80 WRIGHT, J. K. *The Geographical Lore of the Time of the Crusades.* (New York, 1925 and 1965).

## CHAPTER VIII

81 ABEL, A. H. 'A New Lewis and Clark Map' *AGR* I (New York, 1916).
82 CRONE, G. R. 'The Vinland Map Cartographically Considered; A Review'. *GJ* 132 (London, 1966).
83 EVANS, O. C. *Marine Plans and Charts of Wales.* Map Collectors' Circle, *MCS* VI. No. 54 (London, 1969).
84 HUGHES, H. *Immortal Sails* (London, 1946, Republished 1969).
85 JONES, D. J. O. *Daniel Rowland* (Llandysul, 1938).

86 JONES, D. P. *Welsh Country Upbringing* (London, 1948).

87 LEWIS, E. A. *The Welsh Port Books 1550–1603*. Cymmrodorion Record Series, XII (London, 1927).

88 LUCA DE TENA, L. 'The influence of Literature on Cartography and the Vinland Map'. *GJ* 132. (London, 1966).

89 MORGAN, D. W. *Brief Glory*. (Liverpool, 1948).

90 WILLIAMS, D. 'John Evans's Strange Journey'. *THSC* (London, 1948).

# *Sources of the Plates*

The following persons and institutions kindly permitted use to be made of photographs taken or owned by them and their help is most gratefully acknowledged.

Plate 1, Miss M. H. Bigwood; 3, 29, Miss E. R. Payne; 4, 9, 10, 12, 21, 27, 28, by permission of the National Museum of Wales; 5, 7, 23, 25, by permission of the Department of the Environment, Crown Copyright Reserved; 6, courtesy of the Commissioners of Public Works, Ireland; 15, photo Malcolm Murray; 11, 13, 37 courtesy of the Trustees of the British Museum; 26, A. J. Bird; 30, Hereford City Library; 32, 33, courtesy of the National Museum of Ireland; 31, Bord Failte photo; 35, J. K. St Joseph, Crown Copyright Reserved; 38, 48, 49, National Monuments Record; 41, Sunbeam Photo Ltd; 43, A. T. A. Stockholm; 45, the Manx Museum; 44, University College, London, courtesy of Professor D. M. Wilson; 52, Studio Jon Ltd.; 53, courtesy of the Trustees of the Ashmolean Museum; 55–7, photo Peter Davy; 58, J. Ll. Jenkins; 60, the National Maritime Museum, Greenwich; 61, Ronald Davies. Plates 2, 8, 14, 16–20, 22, 24, 34, 36, 39, 40, 42, 46, 47, 50, 51, 54, 59 are from originals in Thames and Hudson archives.

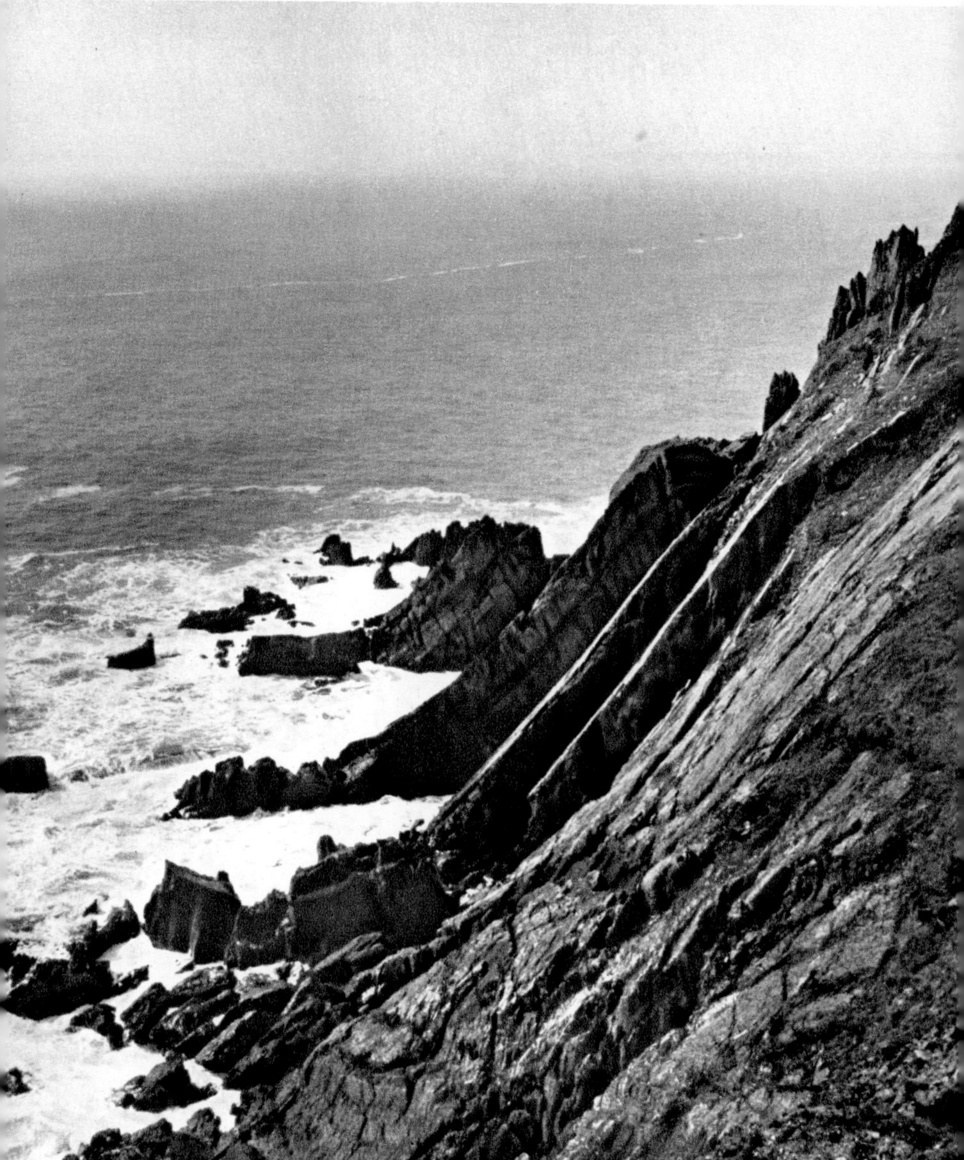

1

2

4

3

6

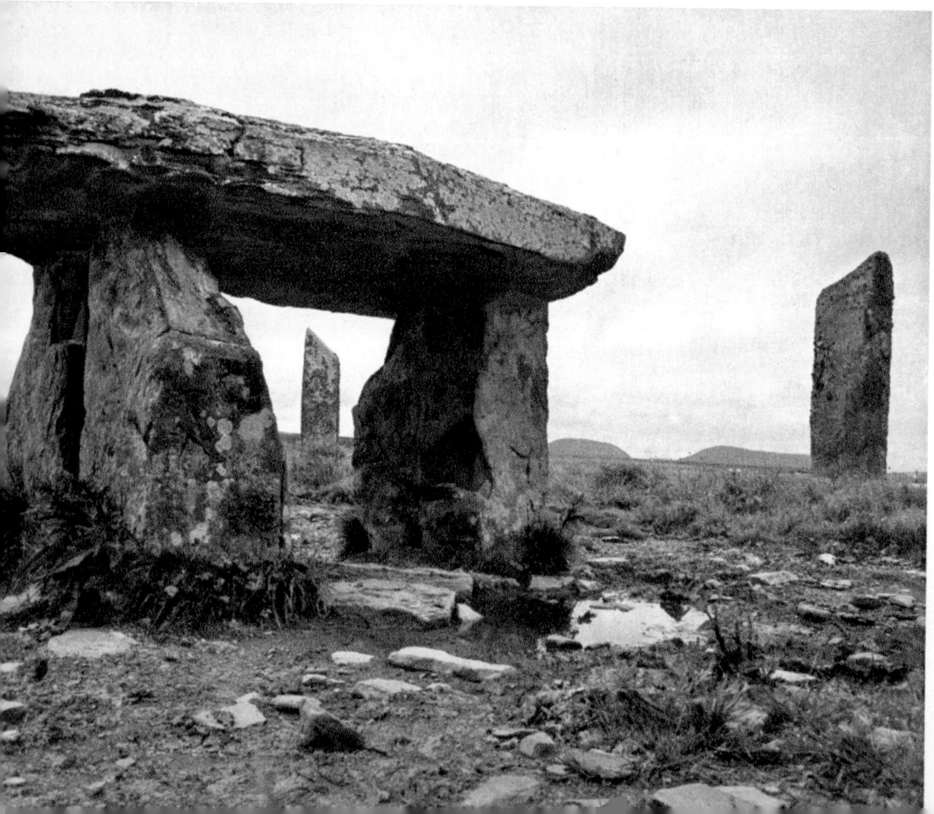

7

9

10

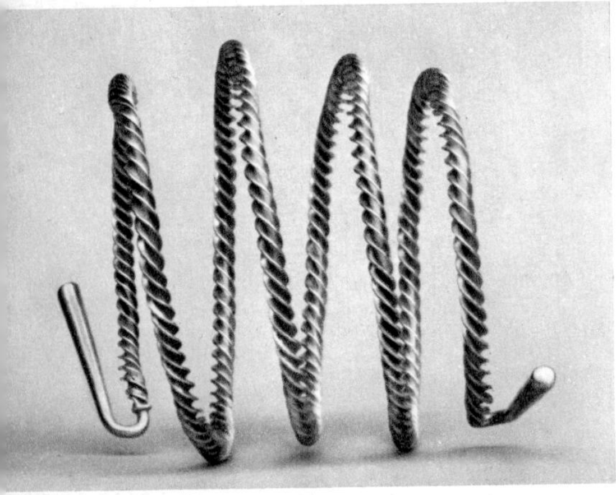

11

12

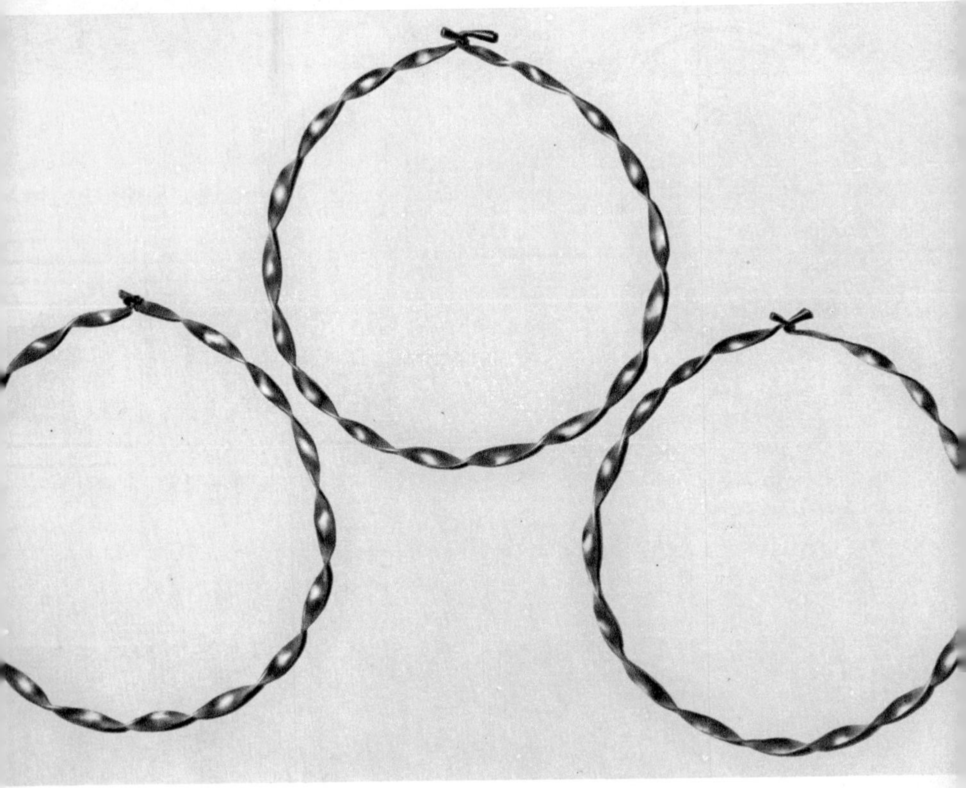

13

14

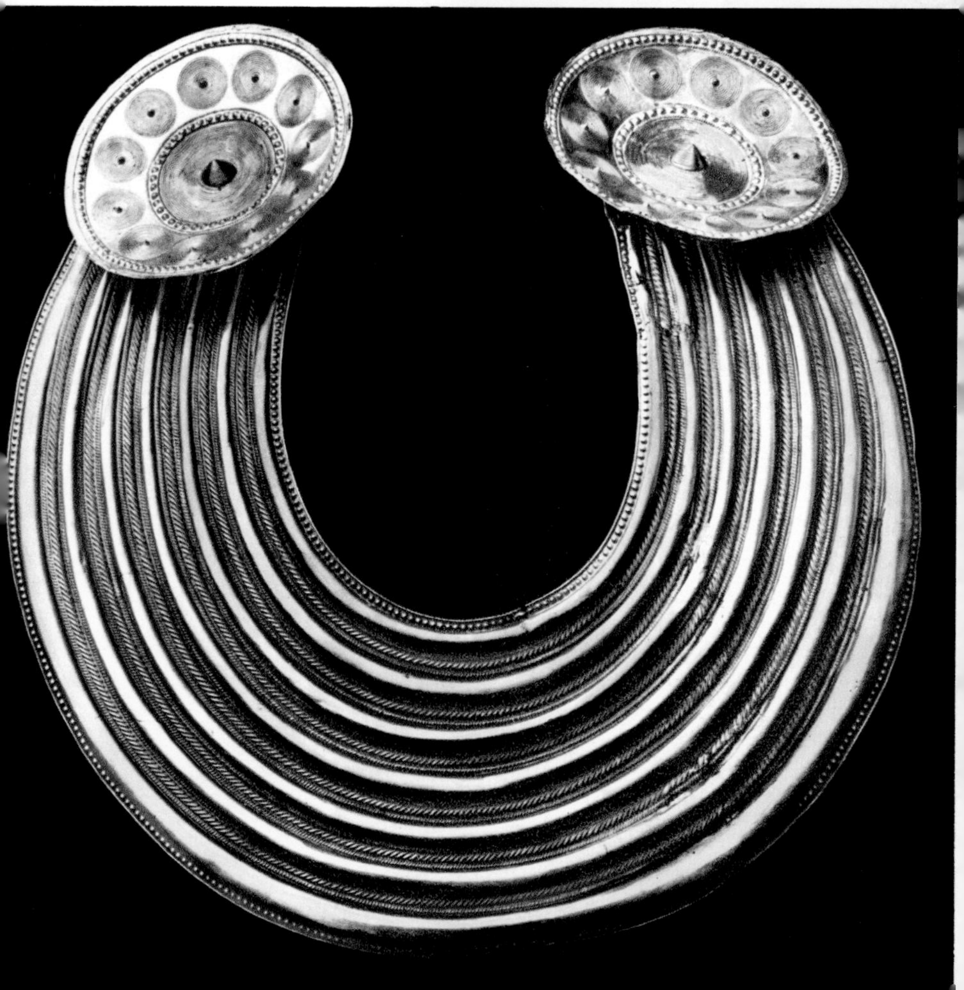

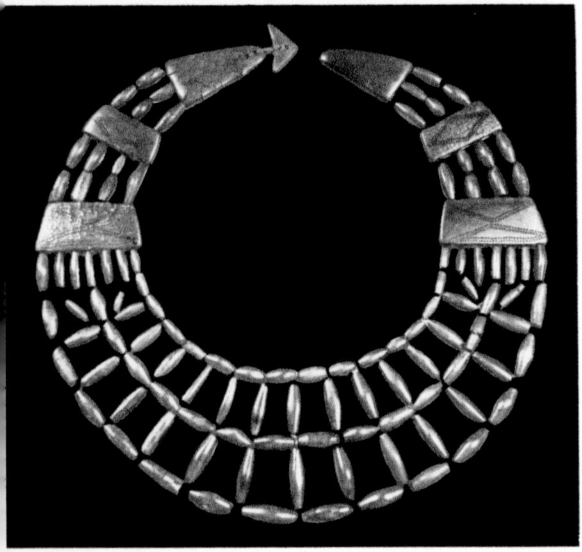

15

17

16

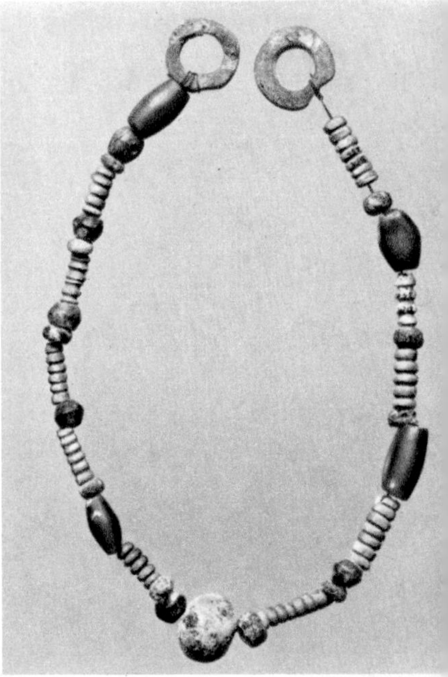

18

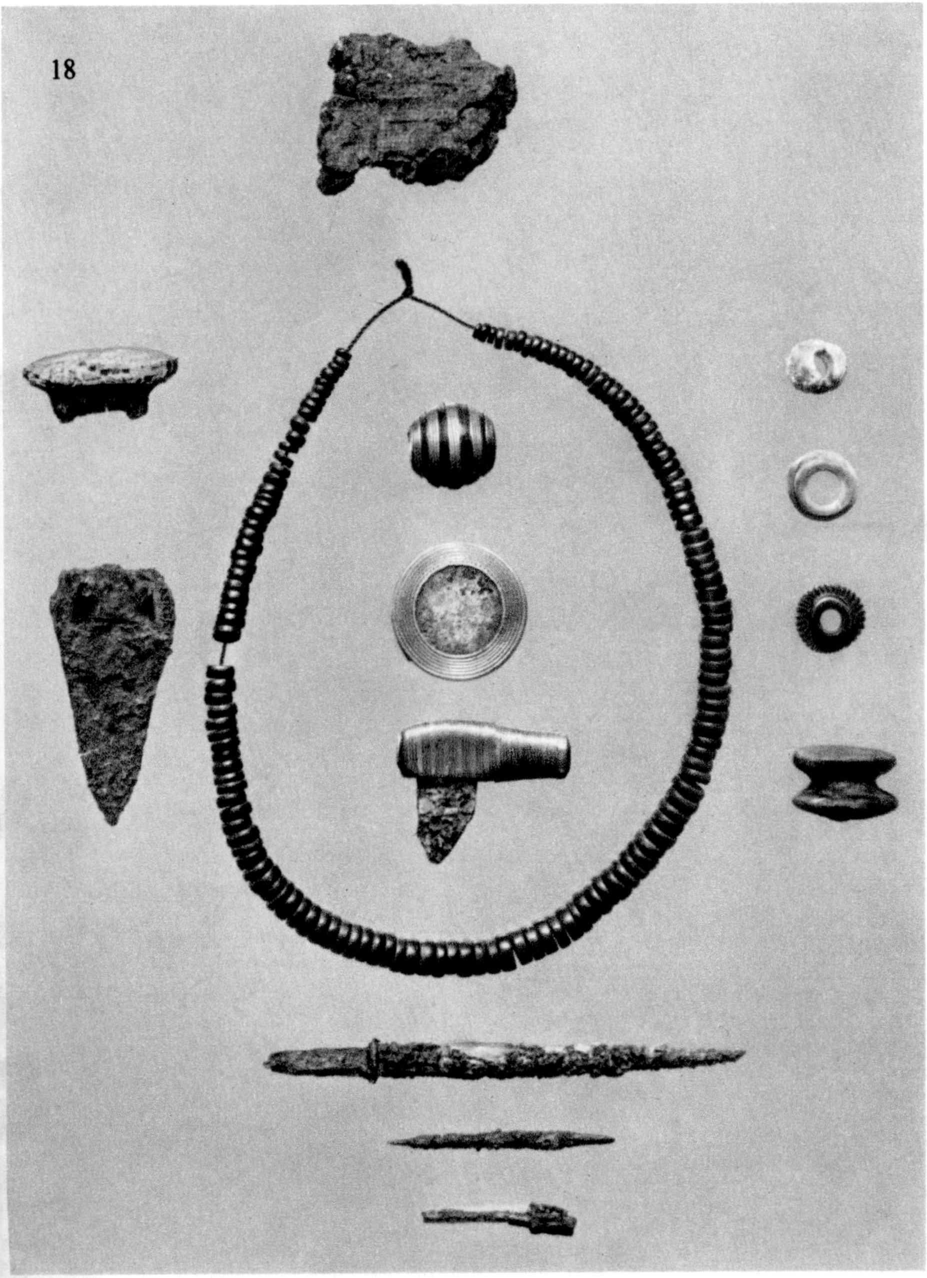

19

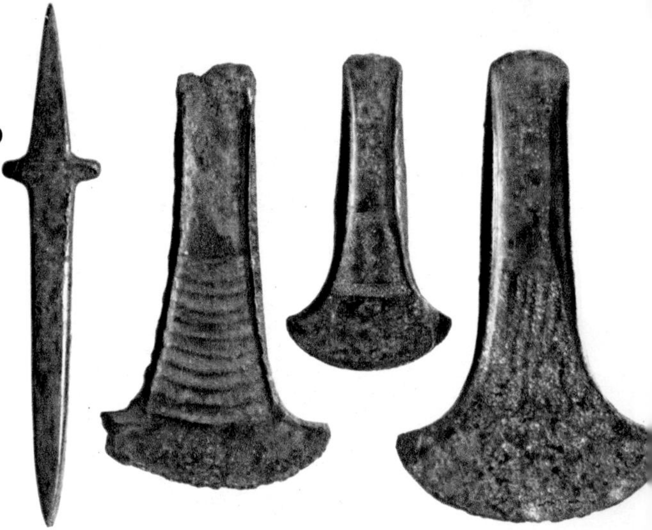

20

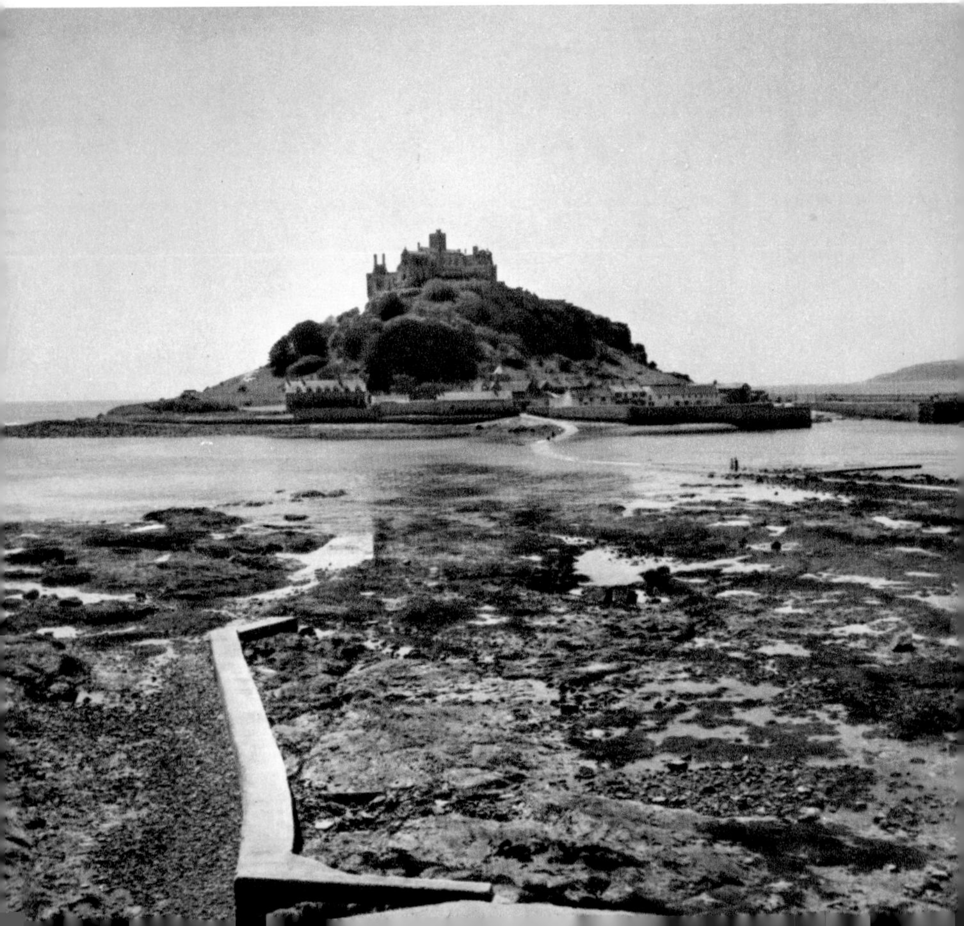

21

22

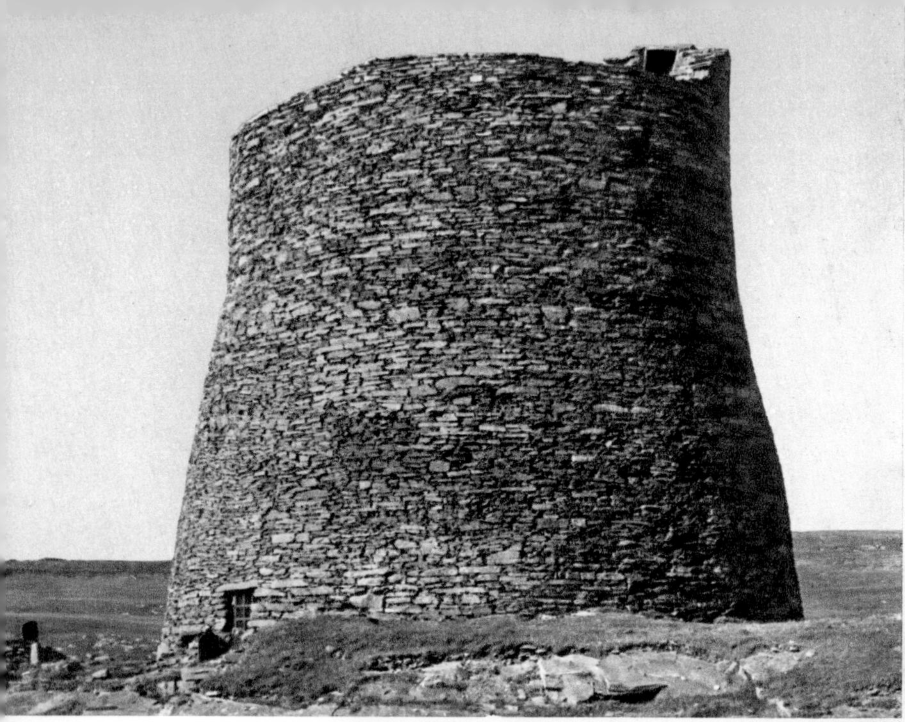

23

24

25

26

27

2

29

30

31

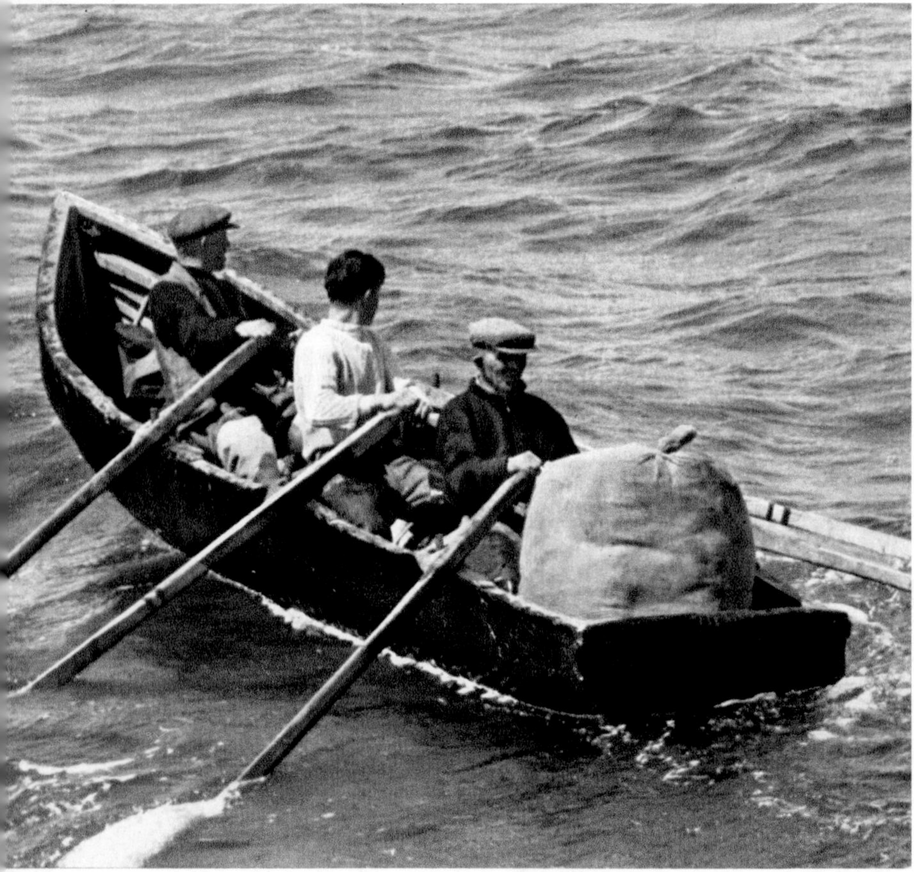

32

33

34

35

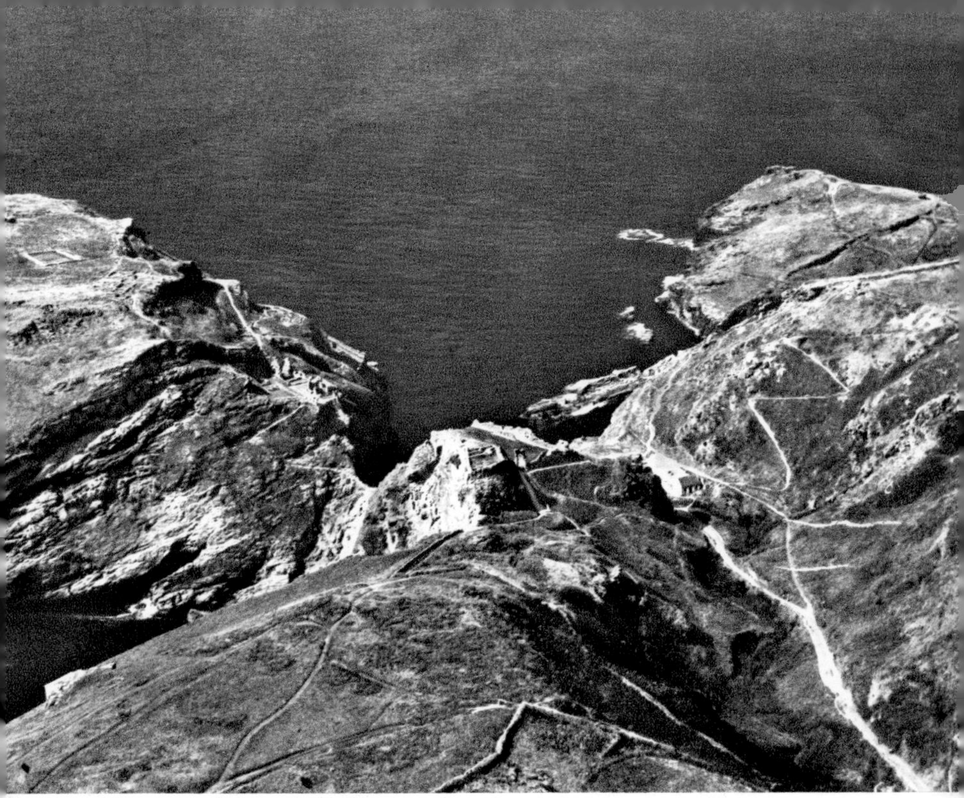

36

37

38

39

40

41

42

43

44

45

46

47

48

49

50

51

53

52

54

55

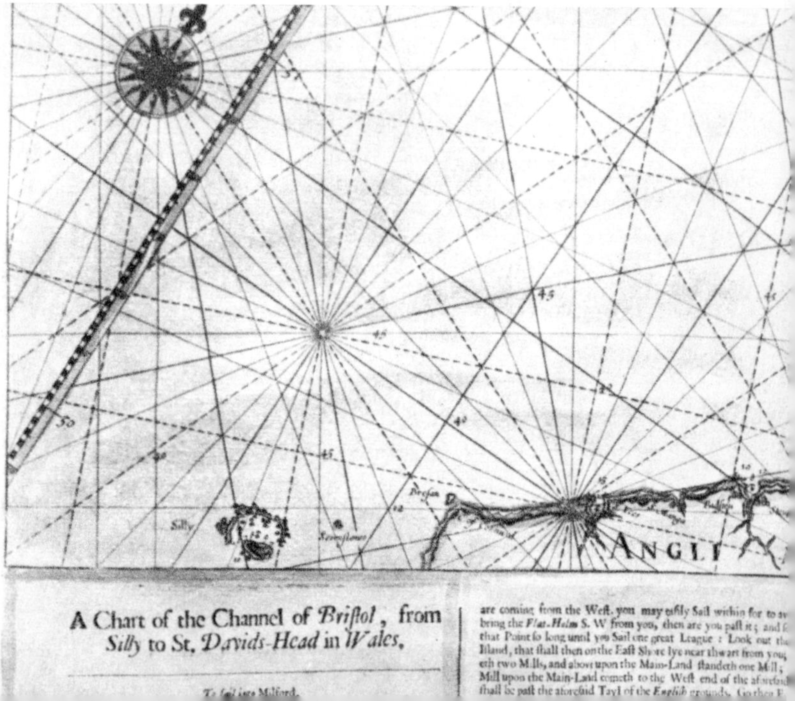
A Chart of the Channel of Bristol, from Silly to St. Davids-Head in Wales.
Silly
ANGLI

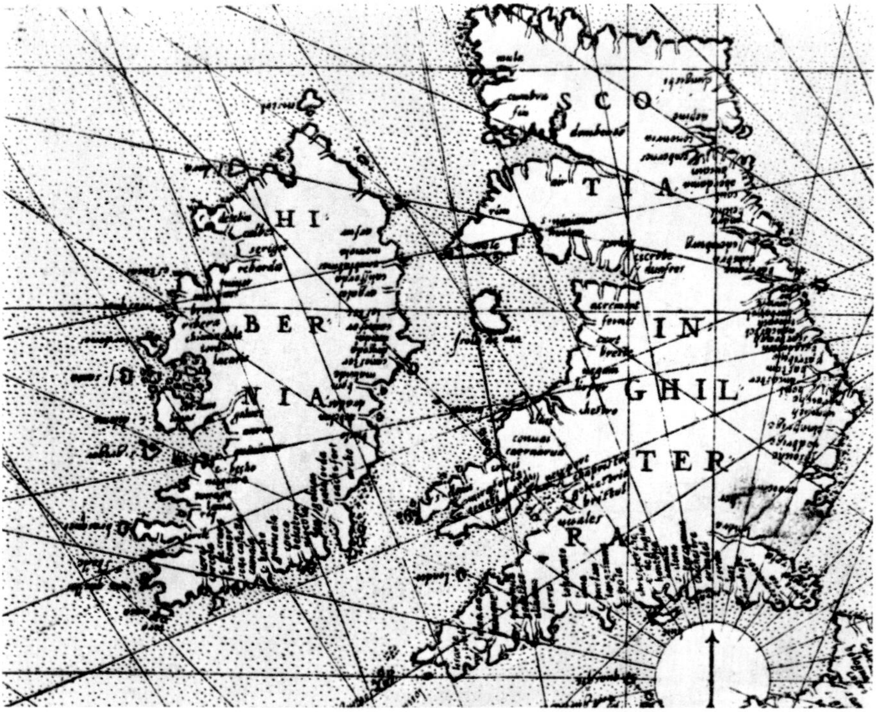
SCO
TIA
HI
BER
NIA
IN
GHIL
TER
R

56

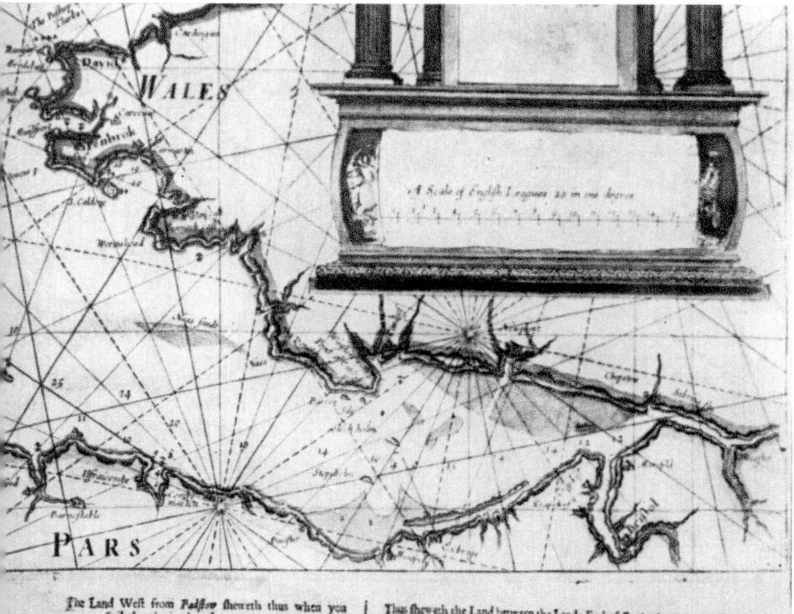
WALES
PARS
A Scale of English Leagues 20 in one degree
The Land West from Padstow sheweth thus when you Sail along by it, three Leagues from you.
Thus sheweth the Land between the Lands-End of England and the Island Brefham; and it is about five Leagues Long.

57

59

58

60

61

# *Notes on the Plates*

1 The Nab Head, St Bride's Bay, Pembrokeshire is a well known Tardenoisian site within easy access of the sea for fishing and of the beaches for the acquisition of flint pebbles. There is a complete absence of stratification, but the finds indicate a Late Tardenoisian industry with scrapers, microliths, triangles, crescents and the microburin. The site is famous in that it incorporates Maglemosian elements as indicated by the presence of tranchet picks and perforated stone hammers associated with many tiny shale discs pierced as if for a necklace. (*Arch. Camb.* 1926, 86–110; W. F. Grimes, *Guide to the Prehistory of Wales, Cardiff.* 1934, 13–14).

2 The coastline at St Ives Bay, Cornwall. The Bay on the north coast of the peninsula was a natural attraction for early navigators, who did not relish the voyage around Land's End, but preferred to send their cargoes across the narrowest and most level part of the peninsula that lay between St Ives Bay and St Michael's Mount. This transpeninsular route was used throughout prehistoric times and continued in use in the Age of the Saints, and even later when Irish and Welsh pilgrims passed this way while on pilgrimage to the shrine of Santiago de Compostela in Spain. The story of the Holy Virgin Hia (better known as St Ives) tells of her negotiating the ocean on a leaf.

3 Sand dune coast at Little Furzenip, Castlemartin, South Pembrokeshire. Evidence of submergence along the South Wales coast in Mesolithic times is well authenticated. Underneath the peat, found at the present low water mark, occur old land surfaces, from which pebbles, cores and flakes have been recovered. Implements of this type have been obtained from such a surface in the area shown in this picture. Many of the implements were unfinished and are thought to have come from a temporary chipping floor and to represent the work of hunters actually engaged in the search for game. (A. L. Leach, *Proc. Geol. Assoc.* XXIX 1918, 52).

4 Tardenoisian flints from Aberystwyth, Cardiganshire. The implements come from a flint chipping floor near the coast at the junction of the Rheidol and Ystwyth rivers immediately south of Aberystwyth. Access is readily available to an abundant supply of flint pebbles from the storm beach nearby. Cores and flakes are well represented, while there are many flint scrapers of end- and discoidal type, together with small geometric crescents and triangles. The microburin is also present. The stratigraphical evidence indicates a post-Palaeolithic—pre-Neolithic date for the industry. (R. Thomas and O. T. Jones, *Journ. Roy. Anth. Inst.* 1924, 73–89).

5 The entrance to the Megalithic passage grave of Bryn Celli Ddu in the parish of Llanddaniel Fab, Anglesey, North Wales. The monument consists of a circular mound of earth and stones some 12 feet high and approximately 160 feet in diameter. Inside

the mound was a polygonal burial chamber and the passage-way by which the latter was entered. After excavation, other features were found to be concealed by the mound, in particular, a large stone with incised spiral and sinuous ornament—a decoration which can be matched with that found on stones in Spanish and Breton Megaliths.

6 Labbacallee, a wedge-shaped gallery grave at Fermoy, Ireland is the largest of all the wedge-shaped gallery graves of the Megalithic Age in Ireland. It is situated about 4¾ miles north-west of Fermoy in County Cork. It is 20 feet wide at the western end, and 11 feet at the eastern end. There are three capstones which cover the entire gallery, but originally the whole was covered by a cairn of stones. In front of the gallery on the western side are the remains of an antechamber. Inhumation as well as cremation burials, accompanied by burnt animal bones and sherds of pottery, have been found in this grave. Much local folk-lore is associated with the site. (*Bibl.* 8, 81–2).

7 Ballymacdermot Court Grave, near Newry, Northern Ireland. The picture shows the forecourt and entrance to the gallery. The monument is a well-preserved wedge-shaped cairn, some 90 ft long by 40 ft wide at the forecourt end. The base of the cairn is composed of large granite blocks. There are three chambers; the end chamber yielded fragments of cremated bones and sherds of pottery, while fragments of a flat-bottomed vessel were also found in the forecourt area. The site has also yielded a few flint flakes. The pottery evidence suggests that this monument is a late example of its class.

8 Standing stones and chambered tomb at Stenness, Orkney, Scotland. The chambered tomb is of the Orcadian Passage Grave type, now without its original cairn. The interesting feature at Stenness is the presence nearby of standing stones. The whole may represent a megalithic cemetery, as the monoliths may mark the site of individual graves. On the other hand, they may have a ritualistic significance as monoliths have sometimes being found in the centre of burial chambers as at Bryn Celli Ddu in Anglesey. Another view, frequently held, is that they are merely 'pointers' to the chambered tomb itself.

9 Megalithic chambered tomb, St Lythan's, Glamorganshire. This is one of several megalithic chambered tombs found in the Vale of Glamorgan, South Wales. They are generally thought to belong to the Severn–Cotswold type. In spite of their westerly position in relation to the main concentration of these tombs in England, it seems improbable that they represent direct colonization from southern Brittany. The St Lythan's chambered tomb does not contain an axial transepted gallery of the type found in the Wessex country and so the general inference is that it belongs to a group of tombs which are the result of secondary colonization from across the Bristol Channel. (R. J. C. Atkinson, 'The Cardiff Region' *British Assoc. Handbook* 1960).

10 This fine menhir, 12 feet high, is found in a field called 'Cae Carreg Fawr' (the field of the Great Stone) in the parish of Llangyndeyrn in southern Carmarthenshire. It is traditionally said to mark the site of a battle. There are several standing stones in the area, especially north-west of Llangyndeyrn Mountain, on the slopes of which are many stone tumuli or cairns. The purpose of these

standing stones is uncertain, but they may have been sepulchral memorials, and there is ample evidence that such monoliths are closely associated with the remains of the Megalithic culture.

11 A gold spiral arm-ring from Stanton, Staffordshire. It is an Irish export of the Middle-Late Bronze Age (*c.* 1000 BC), made up of four gold torques each twisted round to form a long armlet. It is possible that this attractive ornament could be worn more loosely coiled around the neck.

12 A hoard containing three gold ribbon torques was found while ploughing a field at Heyope, Knighton, Radnorshire. They are of very simple structure, being little more than ribbons of gold twisted into a necklet. Similar torques were common in Ireland in the Middle-Late Bronze Age (*c.* 1000 BC), and these Welsh ones undoubtedly derive from there. There must have been, however, some people wealthy enough in South Wales at this time to be able to buy these charming, but expensive, ornaments. They are now in the National Museum of Wales, Cardiff. (C. H. Houlder and W. H. Manning, *South Wales* London, 1966, 50).

13 A gold collar of the Late Bronze Age from Cintra, Portugal. This magnificent collar consists of heavy gold loops, each engraved with geometric designs. Two of the loops are provided with trumpet-like terminals or cusps. The clasp by which the collar was fastened around the neck of the wearer is clearly indicated. This ornament is almost certainly of Irish gold, while its provenance, 14 miles W. N.W. of Lisbon on a southern projecting peninsula of Portugal, emphasizes its maritime location, indicating that it was almost certainly associated with trade along the Atlantic sea-routes linking Ireland with south-western Portugal.

14 A gold collar found in 1932 at Gleninsheen, Ballyvaughan, Co. Clare, Ireland. It was discovered in a small fissure in limestone rock where it must, presumably, have been hidden. Although belonging to the Bronze Age, it is in a remarkable state of preservation. The collar which is about 12 inches in diameter has a boss or disc at either end which is beautifully ornamented. Collars were popular ornaments among the Celts. They were used, not only for personal adornment, but appear to have had a positive, though ill-defined, socio-religious significance and they often appear on images of gods. This collar is now in the National Museum in Dublin.

15 A jet necklace from Poltalloch, Argyll, Scotland which may be dated to the Early Bronze Age. It represents the most popular form of necklace found in Scotland at this period, consisting of two or three strings of long barrel-shaped beads connected at intervals by flat spacers. The spacer is a bead perforated with several holes, usually parallel, designed to keep the several strings of a necklace at the proper distance apart. They were cut to various shapes and diagonally perforated so that the necklace is broader on the throat than behind the neck where it is fastened.

16 A bell-beaker from the West Kennet long-barrow, Wiltshire. It was found inverted and almost intact in the uppermost layers of the filling of the north-west chamber of the barrow. It is $7\frac{1}{2}$ inches in height and beakers of this type are so named from their similarity in shape to a church bell. Bell-beakers normally occur associated with inhumation burials in individual graves, and at other

times as secondary burials in existing long barrows. The body was invariably placed in a fully contracted position on its side with the beaker or other articles disposed around. Now in Devizes Museum.

Reconstructed necklace from a Wessex culture grave at Upton Lovel, Wiltshire, with beads of amber, shale and blue faience of segmented and quoit forms. The quoit beads are ¾ inch in diameter. Until recently, it was thought that the faience beads indicated trade contacts with Egypt, but some archaeologists now incline to the view that they are more likely to be of indigenous origin. The necklace is now in Devizes Museum.

18 Objects of gold, bronze, faience and amber from a woman's grave of the Wessex culture, Manton, Wiltshire. Included among the objects, which are now in Devizes Museum, is a fragment of textile and below it three bronze awls. On the left a bronze knife blade with a bone pommel, on the right shale and stone beads. A string of shale disc-beads encircles another shale bead with gold inlaid bands; an amber disc in a gold mounting and a pendant in the form of a miniature halberd with gold-plated shaft and bronze blade. The knife-blade on the left is 1¼ inches long.

19 A hoard of three flanged axes and a punch, from Westbury-on-Trym, Gloucestershire. With the beginning of the Middle Bronze Age (about 1500–1000 BC) the flat bronze axe with its expanded cutting edge was succeeded by the flanged axe in which the sides were hammered, or (later) cast upwards to form flanges. These examples were found in a traders' or founders' hoard and such hoards often contain both new and unfinished weapons, old broken objects, pieces of scrap and waste, moulds, and sometimes tools for metal working, as in the case of the punch illustrated here.

20 St Michael's Mount, Cornwall, at low tide. The mount itself is an upstanding rock some 400 yards offshore in Mount's Bay. It is connected with the mainland by a natural causeway passable only at low water. The Mount certainly attracted the attention of primitive navigators and the identification of the famous tin-exporting port of Ictis with St Michael's Mount is more or less accepted among British scholars. Diodorus says that during the ebb of the tide, the intervening space is left dry and the natives carry over the tin to this island in abundance in their waggons. An Abbey was established on the summit of the Mount in the Middle Ages, when it was an appendage of the great Norman Abbey of Mont Saint-Michel across the Channel. (*Bibl.* 42, 176).

21 Late Bronze Age cauldron from Llynfawr, Glamorganshire. An important Late Bronze Age hoard was discovered near the shores of Llynfawr at the head of the Rhondda Valley, Glamorganshire, and nearby, if not actually with the hoard, two bronze cauldrons, one of which is illustrated here. It consists of thin bronze plates rivetted together to form a squat globular body with everted rim to which were attached by means of staples a pair of large rim handles. The origin of these cauldrons is thought to be associated with certain Mediterranean *situlae* and their distribution in Western Europe (with a concentration in Ireland) suggests that they were diffused by the Western Atlantic seaways, rather than by the continental route. (E. T. Leeds, *Archaeologia*, LXXX, 1930, 1–36).

22 These Bronze Age shields come from two hoards in Scotland. The larger shield is from Auchmaleddie, Aberdeenshire, and the smaller from Yeyholm, Roxburghshire. Defensive armour in the form of circular shields or bucklers of hammered bronze first appear in the Late Bronze Age. The hemispherical boss about 4 inches in diameter at the centre of the shields should be noted. The hollow behind the boss is spanned by a strap of metal which serves as a handle. The round shield does not appear to have been introduced into Britain from Central Europe; a derivation from the Eastern Mediterranean by way of the Atlantic sea-routes would be more likely.

23 An external view of the broch of Mousa in the Shetland islands. This is the tallest and best preserved of the brochs, which were essentially circular castle towers. The internal diameter of the Mousa tower is 22 feet while, near the ground, the walls themselves are 15 feet thick. Resting on such massive foundations, the tower rises to a height of 40 feet above ground level.

24 Interior view of the Broch of Mousa showing the massive stone masonry of which the broch is built. Out of the 15 feet thick ground floor walls, four circular chambers have been contrived, used presumably as dwelling rooms, each with access to the central courtyard. The tower was apparently roofless and open to the sky, but the interior central courtyard was sheltered by a verandah roof running around the inner tower wall six or eight feet above the ground.

25 The Dun Troddan broch, near Glenelg, western Inverness-shire, Scotland. It stands on good agricultural land: saddle and flat rotary querns are among the commonest broch relics showing that their original inhabitants must have relied greatly on crop growing. Dun Troddan broch is also within easy access of the sea at Glenelg Bay, off the Sound of Sleat; a tiny cove or harbour dominated by the broch would become an easy landing place for the coracles and small skin-boats of the broch dwellers. In this way, they added fishing to their food resources, while sea travel doubtless gave them some contact with the outside world.

26 Dun Telve broch, near Glenelg, Western Inverness-shire, showing interior structure. The massive walls of the broch are hollow—the two faces of the hollow portion being tied together at intervals by horizontal transverse slabs as shown in the picture. In the interspace, a stairway winds up clockwise from the ground floor, thereby giving access to a number of stepped galleries.

27 The stone of Sagranus at St Dogmael's Pembrokeshire, inside the church, standing against the west wall of the nave. It is a rough pillar stone with two gate hanger holes in the face. The inscriptions on these memorial stones commemorate the burial of priests or prominent laymen. In some cases, the inscription is in Latin alone, sometimes in Ogham (the contemporary Irish stroke-script) and sometimes in both Latin and Ogham as in this case, commemorating the same person. The Ogham script is used on the left angle of the face of the stone reading upwards SAGRAGNI MAQI CUNATAMI (*the stone*) *of Sagragnus, son of Cunatamus.* The Latin is in two lines reading vertically downwards SAGRANI FILI CVNOTAMI (*the stone of*) *Sagranus, son of Cunotamus.* It can be dated to the fifth or early sixth century AD (*Bibl.* 18, 384).

28 The Bodvoc Stone was found on Margam Mountain in Glamorganshire, South Wales, and has a Latin inscription in four lines reading vertically downwards BODVOC HIC IACIT FILIVS CATOTIGIRNI PRONEPVS ETERNALI (S) VEDOMAVI. *(The stone) of Bodvoc. Here he lies son of Catotigirnus (and) Great-grandson of Eternalis Vedomavus.* The name Bodvoc is met with on early British coins of the first century BC found in the Oxfordshire—Gloucestershire region and as a potter's stamp on Roman Samian vessels in Gaul in the mid-second century AD. The Bodvoc stone may be dated 400–650 AD and is now housed in Margam Abbey Museum. (A. Fox *Arch. Camb.* 1939, *Bibl.* 18, 36 and 229).

29 St Petrox's church, Castlemartin, South Pembrokeshire is a representative parish church with distinctive South Pembrokeshire characteristics, especially the tall prominent tower of military appearance. The dedication to St Petrox (Petroc or Pedrog) is the chief feature of interest. Churches bearing his name are found at Llanbedrog in the Llŷn peninsula in North Wales; at Verwig near the estuary of the Teifi; here in South Pembrokeshire; at Timberscombe and Anstey West in Somerset, with seventeen further dedications in Devon; and six more in Cornwall, while in northern Brittany, he has eight churches and chapels dedicated to him. The late Canon Doble has shown that St Petroc was one of a group of Celtic saints with dedications in these areas, indicating that these *peregrini* must have made full use of the sea-routes linking the peninsulas of north-western Europe in the Age of the Saints. (*Bibl.* 2c, 70).

30 The church of St Dubricius, Hentland, Herefordshire. The *Life of St Dubricius* (who undoubtedly was one of the founders of the Celtic Church) records that he established a famous school at Hennlann (now Hentland) 4 miles W.N.W. of Ross in Herefordshire. This is undoubtedly a genuine tradition, for several of the most famous Celtic saints are described as *magistri* in great monastic schools. The Hennlann in the *Life of St Dubricius* is called *Hennlann Dibric* in a list of churches headed *De Terra Ercycg*. The modern Hentland, with its church still carrying the name of St Dubricius, is near to the former Roman town of Ariconium, from which the little Celtic kingdom of ERCIC or Erging (now Archenfield) seems to have got its name.

31 The curragh is the traditional sea-going fishing craft made of tarred canvas stretched over a frame-work of wooden laths. They are in direct line of descent from the prehistoric skin-boats of Western Europe and are still quite common along the south and west coasts of Ireland. Despite their flimsiness, they can in skilful hands survive an Atlantic gale. Irish and Scots literature teems with stories and legends of the long voyages made by these curraghs. Particularly fascinating are those associated with Celtic saints such as Brendan and Cormac.

32 A Boyne coracle, or river curragh. The river curragh used for netting salmon on the river Boyne is the only example of the river-coracle type of basket boat now existing in Ireland. In construction, it resembles the Welsh coracles, but the method of putting the framing together is very different. The body of the Boyne coracle consists of an open framework of hazel laths, oval or

slightly ovoid in plan. It measures about 6 feet in length by 4½ feet in beam. Overall is drawn a tanned oxhide laced to the wickered gunwhale at short intervals. At mid-length is a wooden seat. The coracle is generally manned by two men; one kneeling at the fore end and paddling over the bow with a short broad-bladed paddle, while the other sits facing the stern and attends to the net.

33 This delightful piece of gold ornament representing a ship's hull 18.5 cms long, complete with mast and oars, was found at Broighter, Co. Kerry in Ireland, by a ploughman in 1891. It was part of a hoard containing, in addition to the boat, a gold collar, two twisted torques, two chain necklaces and a hanging bowl. The hoard can be dated to the second century BC. The straight rim of the gunwhale with little sheer, and the short curved stern may be noted, indicating that the ship is clearly in the skin-boat tradition and, therefore, ancestral to the modern large curragh.

34 An aerial view of a monastery on Inishcaltra (Holy Island) close to the shore in Lough Derg, Co. Clare, on the Shannon. A scatter of monastic buildings; a round tower 80 feet high but lacking its top; the ruins of four churches; and traces of enclosures may be seen. Island sites were beloved of the Celtic saints, and the monastery of St Colum of Terryglass on Inishcaltra is no exception. By far the most striking group of recumbent grave slabs found in Irish monastic cemeteries is to be seen on Inishcaltra. The graves date from the seventh to the eleventh centuries.

35 Porth Mawr (the Great Harbour), alternatively known as Whitesands Bay, is some 2½ miles from St David's on the north Pembrokeshire coast. Nearby is St David's Head, and the sandy foreshore and the great sweep of the bay make it an attractive landing place. It was, doubtless, of considerable importance in prehistoric times for traffic between South-west Wales and Ireland. A twelfth-century document which clearly incorporates earlier material records that Marchell (the mother of Brychan Brycheiniog—the fifth century eponymous King of Brycheiniog—now Breconshire), travelling from Breconshire to Ireland to marry Amlach, an Irish Prince, embarked at Porth Mawr. Contacts between St David's and Ireland were very marked in the Age of the Saints and this harbour was much used. In 1922 excavations revealed the ground plan of a medieval chapel, dedicated to St Patrick, on the shores of Whitesands Bay, just a few feet above high water mark.

36 An aerial view of Tintagel Head and Castle, Cornwall. It includes the site of a Celtic monastery believed to date from about 500 AD excavated in 1933 and 1934. The buildings are of the usual Celtic monastic type. Four graves of the monks cut out of the solid rock were found. An interesting type of Dark Age pottery was discovered on the site which suggested a possible connection with southern Gaul at this date. (C. A. R. Radford, *Arch. Camb.* CXI (1962) 7 ff. See also official guide to *Tintagel Castle.* H.M.S.O. (London, 1939).

37 The Celtic monastic site at Tintagel, Cornwall, yielded a considerable quantity of interesting pottery which subsequent research has shown to be largely of Mediterranean origin. The most important class of pottery includes fragments of brick-red

ware often with impressed crosses of Chris-tian origin. Similar pottery is found at other sites in the British Isles; in the Eastern Mediterranean; North Africa; Southern France and near the mouth of the Loire in Western France. Its distribution affords tangible evidence of trade between the Mediterranean and the Celtic world, indi-cating the importance of the western sea-routes at this time. (*Bibl.* 57, 59–70).

The Cathedral Church of St David's in North-west Pembrokeshire stands presum-ably on the site of St David's original cell in the valley of the River Alun. The land forming the Dewisland Peninsula is a plateau some 200 feet in general elevation into which the rivers have been deeply incised. The cathedral, situated on the valley floor, is thus carefully hidden below the plateau surface. On the other hand, the river provides direct access to the sea—the chief highway of movement in the Age of the Saints—while at the same time, the winding sunken valley hid the great church from pirates and other raiders who frequented the western seas. (*Bibl.* 2c, 216–218).

Iona Cathedral as it was in 1850. The cathedral is situated on a tiny island off the coast of Mull in western Scotland, and is famous as the landing-place of St Columba in 563. Here the saint established his first church, and Iona, in consequence, is sometimes referred to as Icolmkill—'the island of the church of Columba'. Columba was following in the wake of his fellow-countrymen, who in the fifth century moved from Northern Ireland and settled in western Scotland. From Iona, Celtic monks chris-tianized Pictish Scotland until they were expelled by Nechtan IV in the early years of the eighth century. A new monastery, as well as a nunnery, were established here by the Benedictines in 1203, and the ruins are chiefly of that date.

40 An inscription at Kirk Maughold, Isle of Man, stating in runic letters that it was 'carved by Iuan the priest'. Below this statement is the alphabet in both runic and ogham letters. The stone measures about 1 foot each way. The slab was found em-bedded in the wall during repairs to the present church, and doubtless refers to Iuan the priest mentioned in an inscription from Cornadale, also in the Isle of Man. (Ker-mode, *Manx Crosses* 213 and Macalister *Corpus Inscriptionum Insularum Celticarum,* I 483).

41 In 1892 an exact model of the Gokstad ship was made in Norway. Canadian oak had to be imported for the keel as no suitable timber could be found in Scandinavia. It seems, therefore, very unlikely that sea-going ships in the ninth and tenth centuries could have been made much larger than the Gokstad ship. The reconstructed vessel, after having a great send-off, was sailed across the Atlantic in less than a month, thus demonstrating the skilful way in which the ships of old were constructed. Several recent reconstructions of Viking ships have proved their sea-worthiness and their manoeuvrability under difficult sailing conditions.

42 The Gokstad Ship. The arts of ship-building and seamanship were very ad-vanced in Scandinavia in the days of the Vikings. Much is known of their ships, not only from the *Sagas*, but also from the re-mains of actual vessels. It was a common custom for the chieftain to be buried in his ship and several such vessels have been dis-

covered, one of the most famous being the Gokstad ship found on the shores of Oslo Fjord. The Viking ships were shallow in the beam and pointed at both ends. The Gokstad ship was an oak vessel 78 feet long and 16 feet broad amidships. It had a large, heavy square sail and there were seats for 16 pairs of rowers.

43 Silver brooches from a Viking hoard found at Jamjö in Öland, Sweden, now in the Statens Historiska Museum in Stockholm. Silver was greatly coveted in Viking Scandinavia and this hoard contained, in addition to the brooches, five spiral rings. Wherever the Vikings roamed, as pirates, traders or mercenaries, the acquiring of this precious metal was recognized as one of their objectives. Some regarded it as a means of buying other desirable things like food, wine or loyalty, while others worked it skilfully into beautiful things like the brooches shown in this plate.

44 Horse trappings from Viking burials in the Isle of Man. The bridle-mount below and the bronze strap-mount with pendant, above are both from the Balladoole site. The bridle fragment is 12.3 cms. long and consists of two strips of metal folded so as to clasp the ends of a leather strap, secured by dome-headed rivets. Portions of the original leather remain with the bridle mount. The portion of harness with pendant is 10.6 cms. long and consists of a strip of bronze folded in two to clasp the ends of a leather strap which narrows and thickens as it passes through the pendant ring. It would appear that it was customary to bury the horse harness with the dead man in such a way that it was spread over the whole length of his body (*Bibl.* 62, 20–24).

45 A sword hilt from a Viking burial mound at Ballateare, Jurby, Isle of Man. The sword itself, approximately 95.5 cms. was broken in four places (probably deliberately) and is now in bad condition. Sufficient, however, remains to indicate an original two-edged weapon sheathed in its scabbard. Swords of this type are known throughout the Viking area from Russia westwards. The associated finds in this case would suggest that the sword belongs to the late ninth or early tenth century AD. The Ballateare sword was presumably made in Norway, but it is possible that the scabbard was made separately in the British area. (*Bibl.* 62, 50–54).

46 Christian churches and sanctuaries in western Europe were obvious targets for Viking raids from the ninth to the eleventh centuries, as they contained valuable ornaments and vestments, as well as supplies of food. We hear of repeated attacks on the Welsh, Irish and Northumbrian monasteries and the killing of the monks and priests and of the great loot acquired by the raiders. Bishop Abraham of St David's met his death in such a raid in 1080. The bishop's crozier shown in this picture is almost certainly of Irish workmanship and its presence at Helgö, Ekerö in Sweden is a sure indication that it was once plundered by the Vikings from some church in the British area, possibly after the bishop had fled or had been murdered by the raiders.

47 The shrine of St Patrick's bell, Dublin. Book shrines and bell shrines are a peculiarly Irish form of piety. Frequently, the saint's little hand-bell which was rung during his lifetime to call the brethren together for work or prayer became a venerated relic and

was enclosed in an elaborate shrine. St Patrick's reputed little cow-bell presumably made of iron dipped in bronze was enclosed in the twelfth century in an elaborate shrine decorated with attractive artistic metal work of Celtic design.

The Holy Well of St Winifred, Holywell, Flintshire. Medieval society in western Europe was intimately concerned with holy wells and well-chapels. Pilgrimages to them were made at all times, but especially during wakes or festivals. Some of these chapels were elaborate, such as that of St Gwenfrewi (St Winifred) at Holywell. The well was said to mark the spot where the beheaded Virgin's head fell before it was restored by St Beuno. The well and chapel were granted in 1093 to the monastery of St Werburg. The shrine soon became one of the most famous in Britain, visited by countless pilgrims annually and by several medieval English monarchs. Its importance as a place of pilgrimage continued long after the Reformation.

The shrine of St David in St David's Cathedral, Pembrokeshire. The relics of the saint were originally placed in the usual position behind the High Altar. When the eastern end of the cathedral was built by Bishop Peter de Leia soon after 1180, an opening was provided, closed with pierced slabs, through which pilgrims standing outside the church could see the shrine within. In 1248 the cathedral was severely damaged by an earthquake and in 1275 a new shrine of St David was begun. This involved the removal of the relics of the saint from their old position behind the High Altar to the shrine which still stands, almost uninjured in its original position, in the north arcade of the choir. (*Roy. Comm. Anc. Mont. Wales.* VII (Pembrokeshire) 1925; see under *The Cathedral Church of St David's*).

50 Mont Saint-Michel, Normandy, is a famous and spectacular rocky islet 165 feet high off the coast of La Manche, united to the mainland by a narrow causeway, passable only at low water. The cult of St Michael in the west gained popularity in the sixth century and became associated with mountain sites. After the original apparition on Monte Gargano in Italy, a further alleged apparition occurred early in the eighth century on the summit of Mont Saint-Michel in Normandy. An oratory was established here by St Aubert in obedience to a command given on this occasion. It soon became an important place of medieval pilgrimage. In 996 a Benedictine monastery was established on the site in place of the original oratory. With the coming of the Normans to England there developed a close association between the Normandy site and its counterpart in Mount's Bay, Cornwall.

51 The Cathedral of St James the Apostle at Compostela in north-west Spain. Santiago de Compostela rose in importance in the Early Middle Ages, following upon the supposed discovery nearby of the remains of the body of the apostle. North-western Spain in the seventh century was an important outpost of Christianity against the Moorish invasion, and it was from these parts that the re-conquest of Spain for Christianity began. The popularity of pilgrimages to Santiago is by no means unrelated to this situation. The pronouncement by Pope Calixtus II in the twelfth century in favour of this and other pilgrimages gave it official sanction, and soon a visit to the

shrine of St James at Compostela rivalled in popularity a pilgrimage to Rome, or even to Jerusalem itself.

52 A much mutilated recumbent effigy of a Santiago pilgrim from St Mary's church, Haverfordwest, Pembrokeshire. This sepulchral effigy which can be dated to about the year 1450 shows all the appurtenances of a pilgrim, including the sclavine, or pilgrim's long robe, and a fragment of the conventional pilgrim's staff. Pilgrims who had made the journey to Santiago de Compostela carried a wallet which hung over the right shoulder onto the left-hand side. It was decorated with three scallop shells which are clearly shown in this picture. Pilgrims from Ireland to Santiago de Compostela frequently crossed over south-west Wales and western Cornwall on their journey to Spain.

53 A typical ship used by pilgrims and crusaders about the year 1300, based on a contemporary painting by Bicci de Lorenzo. Changes were introduced into the design of northern ships as shown on the Bayeux Tapestry to meet the special circumstances of the crusades, notably the *castles* constructed both forward and aft, and the fighting top added to the mast head. There were also several refinements in rigging and gear. The ship shown in this picture is of the single masted type with castles and stern-post rudder. Above, St Nicholas is shown rebuking the tempest in response to the prayers of passengers and crew.

54 The main sources of information about northern ships between the eleventh and fourteenth centuries are the Bayeux Tapestry and a number of representations of ships on coins and city seals. This illustration shows a part of the Tapestry indicating a typical northern European ship of about 1066. It shows a single-masted, double-ended, clinker-built craft with high stem and stern posts, a side rudder, and single large square sail.

55 The city and port of Bordeaux in south-western France after a wood-cut in Antoine du Pinet's *Planz* (1564). As Burdigala, Bordeaux was the chief town of the Bituriges Vivisci, and in the fourth century became the capital of Aquitania Secunda. Ausonius describes it as a square-walled city as shown here. From 1154–1453 it belonged to the English, and during this period it was one of the busiest ports in Western Europe, engaged primarily in the wine trade. The returning empty wine ships from Britain and Northern Europe brought thousands of pilgrims to Bordeaux where they met with others who had travelled overland across France. Thus united, they proceeded to the great shrine of St James at Compostela in north-west Spain.

56 The British Isles on a Portolan chart by Diego Homen, 1569. Portolan charts were for coastal navigation, appearing in the Mediterranean Lands in the fourteenth century. They began as small charts dealing with limited sections of coastline but, later, several charts were joined up for use on more extended voyages. Portolan charts were not constructed on any definite projection, but were based on measurement and the calculation of distance from one point to another. This map is obviously an improved chart, including names not found on earlier examples. It is also one of the latest specimens, being engraved on a copper plate and printed, thus forming an interesting link cartographically between the work of medieval

draughtsmen and the sixteenth-century maps which ushered in the new order.

A chart of the Bristol Channel from Lundy Island to St David's Head. This is a very good example of an English hydrographer copying the early marine charts found in Dutch atlases. This map formed part of the first English marine atlas to include portions of the western seas in the Bristol Channel area. The atlas was known as 'The English Pilot', and published by John Seller in 1672. It should be noted how the use of verbal descriptions, together with rough relief sections of the coastline for identification purposes, are included.

The Daniel Rowland Memorial at Llangeitho, Cardiganshire. The Rev. Daniel Rowland (1713–1790) was one of the leaders of the Methodist Revival in Wales in the eighteenth century. The revival was characterized by great enthusiasm as the leaders were able to appeal to the people in their native tongue. Hundreds flocked to Llangeitho to hear Daniel Rowland preach in the open fields around the church (which soon became too small to hold the large congregations). Those who came to hear him from North-west Wales made the journey partly by land and partly by sea crossing the Llŷn peninsula and then moving over Cardigan Bay, landing at various places between Aberystwyth and New Quay and completing the remainder of the journey on foot. This is a good example of the use of the sea-routes in the eighteenth century.

Polperro harbour, 6 miles east of Fowey in Cornwall is representative of the numerous small harbours around the British coasts that were so busy in the days of the sailing ships. The town itself, built on the rocky shore and ledges of a small sea inlet is intimately bound up with all that concerns 'those who go down to the sea in ships' and the tales of many an 'ancient mariner'. Although its coastal trade has declined, Polperro is still actively engaged in pilchard fishing.

60 The schooner *Alice Williams*, built in the 1890's, is a representative example of hundreds of sailing vessels that used the numerous harbours along the shores of Western Europe, following the old sea-routes, in the days before the coming of the steam-ship. The schooner was a sharp-built, swift sailing vessel, generally two-masted, as in the case of the *Alice Williams*, and rigged either with fore and aft sails on both masts, or with square-top and top-gallant sails on the foremast. Ships of this type not only traded along the coast, but regularly undertook longer voyages to Europe, North America, Africa and the Far East.

61 A Breton onion man on his rounds in Aberaeron, Cardiganshire in 1970. The sheltered coves along the western European coastland, particularly in Brittany and North-west Spain are admirably suited climatically and otherwise for the growth of temperate fruits and vegetables. These, especially onions, are brought over from places like Brest and Santander in small ships and the loads stored at various ports in western Britain. Here the onions are strung on straw ropes and taken out in second-hand motor vans to subsidiary centres. The vendors finally use their bicycles and sell the onions off a shoulder-pole from house-to-house in the countryside. The entire operation is a good illustration of local traffic still using the western sea-routes in modern times.

# Index